Prince Henry the the Hero of Port Modern Discovery, 1394-1460 A.D.

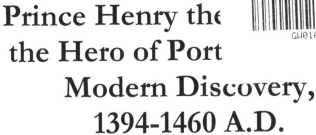
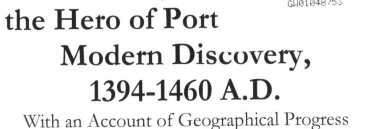

With an Account of Geographical Progress
Throughout the Middle Ages As the Preparation
for His Work.

C. Raymond Beazley

Alpha Editions

This edition published in 2024

ISBN 9789362093080

Design and Setting By

Alpha Editions

www.alphaedis.com

Email - info@alphaedis.com

Contents

PREFACE

This volume aims at giving an account, based throughout upon original sources, of the progress of geographical knowledge and enterprise in Christendom throughout the Middle Ages, down to the middle or even the end of the fifteenth century, as well as a life of Prince Henry the Navigator, who brought this movement of European Expansion within sight of its greatest successes. That is, as explained in Chapter I., it has been attempted to treat Exploration as one continuous thread in the story of Christian Europe from the time of the conversion of the Empire; and to treat the life of Prince Henry as the turning-point, the central epoch in a development of many centuries: this life, accordingly, has been linked as closely as possible with what went before and prepared for it; one third of the text, at least, has been occupied with the history of the preparation of the earlier time, and the difference between our account of the eleventh-and fifteenth-century Discovery, for instance, will be found to be chiefly one of less and greater detail. This difference depends, of course, on the prominence in the later time of a figure of extraordinary interest and force, who is the true hero in the drama of the Geographical Conquest of the Outer World that starts from Western Christendom. The interest that centres round Henry is somewhat clouded by the dearth of complete knowledge of his life; but enough remains to make something of the picture of a hero, both of science and of action.

Our subject, then, has been strictly historical, but a history in which a certain life, a certain biographical centre, becomes more and more important, till from its completed achievement we get our best outlook upon the past progress of a thousand years, on this side, and upon the future progress of those generations which realised the next great victories of geographical advance.

The series of maps which illustrate this account, give the same continuous view of the geographical development of Europe and Christendom down to the end of Prince Henry's age. These are, it is believed, the first English reproductions in any accessible form of several of the great charts of the Middle Ages, and taken together they will give, it is hoped, the best view of

Western or Christian map-making before the time of Columbus that is to be found in any English book, outside the great historical atlases.

In the same way the text of this volume, especially in the earlier chapters, tries to supply a want—which is believed to exist—of a connected account from the originals known to us, of the expansion of Europe through geographical enterprise, from the conversion of the Empire to the period of those discoveries which mark most clearly the transition from the Middle Ages to the Modern World.

The chief authorities have been:

For the Introductory chapter: (1) Reinaud's account of the Arabic geographers and their theories in connection with the Greek, in his edition of Abulfeda, Paris, 1848; (2) Sprenger's Massoudy, 1841; (3) Edrisi, translated by Amédée Jaubert; (4) Ibn-Batuta (abridgment), translated by S. Lee, London, 1829; (5) Abulfeda, edited and translated by Reinaud; (6) Abyrouny's *India*, specially chapters i., 10-14; xvii., 18-31; (7) texts of Strabo and Ptolemy; (8) Wappäus' *Heinrich der Seefahrer*, part 1.

I. For Chapter I. (Early Christian Pilgrims): (1) *Itinera et Descriptiones Terræ Sanctæ*, vols. i. and ii., published by the Société de l'Orient, Latin, Geneva, 1877 and 1885, which give the original texts of nearly all the Palestine Pilgrims' memoirs to the death of Bernard the Wise; (2) the Publications of the Palestine Pilgrims' Text Society; (3) Thomas Wright's *Early Travels in Palestine* (Bohn); (4) Avezac's *Recueil pour Servir à l'histoire de la géographie*; (5) some recent German studies on the early pilgrim records, *e.g.*, Gildemeister on Antoninus of Placentia.

II. For Chapter II. (The Vikings): (1) Snorro Sturleson's *Heimskringla* or Sagas of the Norse Kings; (2) Dozy's essays; (3) the, possibly spurious, *Voyages of the Zeni*, with the Journey of Ivan Bardsen, in the Hakluyt Society's Publications.

III. For Chapter III. (The Crusades and Land Travel): (1) Publication of the Palestine Pilgrims' Text Society; (2) Avezac's edition of the originals in his *Recueil pour Sevir à l'histoire de la géographie*; (3) Yule's *Cathay and the Way Thither*; (4) Yule's Marco Polo; (5) Benjamin of Tudela and others in Wright's *Early Travels in Palestine*; (6) Yule's *Friar Jordanus*; (7) Sir John Mandeville's *Travels*.

IV. For Chapter IV. (Maritime Exploration): (1) The Marino Sanuto Map of 1306; (2) the Laurentian Portolano of 1351; (3) The Catalan Map of 1375-6; (4) scattered notices collected in early chapters of R.H. Major's

Prince Henry the Navigator; (5) Béthencourt's *Conquest of the Canaries* (Hakluyt Society, ed., Major); (6) Wappäus' *Heinrich der Seefahrer*, part 2.

V. For Chapter V. (Geographical Science): (1) Neckam's *De Naturis Rerum*; (2) the seven chief Mappe-Mondes of the fourteenth and early fifteenth centuries; (3) the leading Portolani; (4) scattered notices, *e.g.*, from Guyot de Provins' "Bible," Brunetto Latini, Beccadelli of Palermo, collected in early chapters of Major's *Henry the Navigator*; (5) Wauwerman's *Henri le Navigateur*.

VI. For Chapter VI. (Portugal to 1400): (1) *The Chronicle of Don John I.*; (2) Oliveiro Martins' *Sons of Don John I.*; (3) A. Herculano's *History of Portugal*; (4) Osbernus de Expugnatione Lixbonensi.

VII. For Chapter VII. (Henry's position in 1415): Azurara's *Discovery and Conquest of Guinea*.

VIII. For Chapter VIII. (Ceuta): (1) Azurara's *Chronicle of the Conquest of Ceuta*; (2) Azurara's *Discovery of Guinea*.

IX. For Chapter IX. (Henry's Settlement at Sagres): (1) Azurara's *Guinea*; (2) De Barro's *Asia*; (3) Wauwerman's *Henri le Navigateur et l'École Portugaise de Sagres*.

X. For Chapter X. (Cape Bojador and the Azores): (1) Azurara's *Guinea*; (2) O. Martins' *Sons of Don John I.*

XI. For Chapter XI. (Henry's Political Life, 1433-41): (1) Pina's *Chronicle of King Edward*; (2) O. Martins' *Sons of Don John I.*; (3) Azurara's *Chronicle of John I.*; (4) Pina's *Chronicle of Affonso V.*

XII. For Chapter XII. (From Boyador to Cape Verde).—(1) Azurara's *Guinea*; (2) De Barros; (3) Pina's *Chronicle of Affonso V.*; (4) O. Martins' *Sons of Don John I.*

For Chapters XIII. to the end.—(1) Azurara's *Discovery and Conquest of Guinea*; (2) Narratives of Cadamosto and Diego Gomez; (3) Pina's *Chronicle of Affonso V.*; (4) Prince Henry's Charters.

The three modern lives of Prince Henry which I have chiefly consulted are:

R.H. Major's *Henry the Navigator*, Wappäus' *Heinrich der Seefahrer*, and De Weer's *Prinz Heinrich*, with O. Martins' *Lives of the Infants of the House of Aviz* in his *Sons of Don John I.*

The maps and illustrations have been planned in a regular series.

I. As to the former, they are meant to show in an historical succession the course of geographical advance in Christendom down to the death of Prince Henry (1460). Setting aside the Ptolemy, which represents the knowledge of the world at its height in the pre-Christian civilisation, and the Edrisi which represents the Arabic followers of Ptolemy, whose influence upon early Christian geography was very marked, all the maps reproduced belong to the science of the Christian ages and countries. The two Mappe-mondes above referred to are both placed in the introductory chapter, and are treated only as the most important examples of the science which the Græco-Roman Empire bequeathed to Christendom, but which between the seventh and thirteenth centuries was chiefly worked upon by the Arabs. Among early Christian maps, that of St. Sever, possibly of the eighth century, the Anglo-Saxon map of the tenth century, the Turin Map of the eleventh, and the Spanish map of the twelfth (1109), represent very crude and simple types of sketches of the world, in which within a square or oblong surrounded by the ocean a few prominent features only, such as the main divisions of countries, are attempted. The Anglo-Saxon example, though greatly superior to the others given here, essentially belongs to this kind of work, where some little truth is preserved by a happy ignorance of the travellers' tales that came into fashion later, but where there is only the vaguest and most general knowledge of geographical facts.

On the other hand, in the next group, to which the Psalter map is allied, and in which the Hereford map is our best example, mythical learning—drawn from books like Pliny, Solinus, St. Isidore, and Martianus Capella, which collected stories of beasts and monsters, stones and men, divine, human, and natural marvels on the principle *Credo quia impossible*—has overpowered every other consideration, and a map of the world becomes a great picture-book of curious objects, in which the very central and primary interest of geography is lost. But by the side of and almost at the same time as these specimens of geographical mythology, geographical science had taken a new start in the coast charts or portolani of Balearic and Italian seamen, some specimens of which form our next set of maps.

Dulcert's portolano of 1339 and the Laurentian of 1351 are two of the best examples of this kind of work, which gave us our first really accurate map of any part of the globe, but which for some time was entirely confined to coast drawing, and was meant to supply the practical wants of captains, pilots, and seamen. The Catalan atlas of 1375-6 shows the portolano type extended to a real Mappa Mundi; the elaborate carefulness and sumptuousness of this example prepares us for the still higher work of Andrea Bianco and of Benincasa in the fifteenth century. As the Laurentian portolano of 1351 commemorates the voyage of 1341 and marks its discoveries in the Atlantic islands, so the Catalan map of 1375-6 commemorates the Catalan voyage of 1346, and gives the best and most up-to-date picture of the N.W. African coast as it was known before Prince Henry's discoveries.

Last of these groups of maps is that of examples from Henry's own age, such as the Fra Mauro map of 1459 or the maps of Andrea Bianco and Benincasa (*e.g.*, 1436, 1448, 1468), among which the first-named is the only one we have been able to give here.

The Borgian map of 1450 is given as an extraordinary specimen of what could be done as late as 1450, not as an example of geographical progress; and the map of 1492, recording Portuguese discoveries down to the rounding of the Cape of Good Hope, is added to illustrate the advance of explorers in the years closely following Henry's death, as it was realised at the time.

The maps have in most cases been set from the modern standpoint, but, as will readily be seen by the position of the names, the normal mediæval setting was quite different, with the S. or E. at the top.

II. The illustrations aim at giving portraits or pictures of the chief persons and places connected with the life of Prince Henry. There are three of the Prince himself; one from the Paris MS. of Azurara, one from the gateway of the great convent church of Belem, one from the recumbent statue over his tomb at Batalha. Two others give: (1) The whole group of the royal tombs of Henry's house,—of his father, mother, and brothers in the aisle at Batalha, and (2) the recumbent statues of his father and mother, John and Philippa, in detail; the exterior and general effect of the same church— Portugal's Westminster, and the mausoleum of the Navigator's own family of Aviz—comes next, in a view of this greatest of Portuguese shrines.

Coimbra University, with which as rector or chancellor or patron Prince Henry was so closely connected, for which he once provided house room, and in which his benefactions earned him the title of "Protector of the studies of Portugal" is given to illustrate his life as a student and a man of science; the mother church of the order of Christ at Thomar may remind us of another side of his life—as a military monk, grand master of an order of religious chivalry which at least professed to bind its members to a single life, and which under his lead took an active part in the exploration and settlement of the African coasts and the Atlantic islands.

The portraits of Columbus, Da Gama, and Albuquerque, which conclude this set of illustrations, are given as portraits of three of Prince Henry's more or less conscious disciples and followers, of three men who did most to realise his schemes. The first of these, who owed to Portuguese advance towards the south the suggestion of corresponding success in the west, and who found America by the western route to India,—as Henry had planned nearly a century before to round Africa and reach Malabar by the eastern and southern way,—was the nearest of the Prince's successful imitators in time, the greatest in achievement; he was not a mere follower of the

Portuguese initiative, for he struck out a new line or at least a neglected one, made the greatest of all geographical additions to human knowledge, and took the most daring plunge into the unknown that has ever been taken—but Columbus, beside his independent position and interest, was certainly on one side a disciple of Henry the Navigator, and drew much of his inspiration from the impulse that the Prince had started. Da Gama, the first who sailed direct from Lisbon to India round Africa, and Albuquerque, the maker, if not the founder, of the Portuguese empire in the East, were simply the realisers of the vast ambitions that take their start from the work and life of Prince Henry, and he has a right to claim them as two leading champions of his plans and policy. In many points Albuquerque, like Columbus, is more than a follower; but in the main outline of his achievement he follows upon the work of other men, and, among these men, of none so much as the Hero of Portugal and of modern discovery.

Lastly. I have to thank many friends generally for their constant kindness and readiness to assist in any way, and in particular several for the most generous and valuable help in certain parts.

Mr. T.A. Archer, besides the benefit of his suggestions throughout, has given special aid in Chapters I., III., V., and the Introductory Chapter, especially where anything is said of the connection of geographical progress with the Crusades.[7]

Mr. F. York Powell has revised Chapter II. on the Vikings, and Professor Margoliouth has done the same for the Introductory Chapter on Greek and Arabic geography; Mr. Coote has not only given me every help in the map room of the British Museum, but has read the proofs of Chapter V. Mr. H. Yule-Oldham in Chapter XVIII. on the Voyage of Cadamosto, and Mr. Prestage in Chapters VIII. and IX. on Prince Henry's capture of Ceuta and settlement at Sagres, have been most kind in offering suggestions. For several hints useful in Chapter I.—the early Christian pilgrims—I have also to thank Professor Sanday; and for revision of a great part of the proof-sheets of the entire book, Mr. G.N. Richardson and the Rev. W.H. Hutton.

As to the illustrations, of portraits and monuments, etc., I am especially obliged to the Vice-Chancellor of Oxford University (Dr. Boyd), who has allowed his water-colour paintings of Portuguese subjects to be reproduced; and to the Rev. R. Livingstone of Pembroke, and Sir John Hawkins of Oriel, for their loan of photographs.

PRINCE HENRY THE NAVIGATOR.

The Lusitanian Prince who, heaven-inspired,
To love of useful glory roused mankind,
And in unbounded commerce mixed the world.

> THOMSON: *Seasons, Summer, 1010-2.*

INTRODUCTION.

THE GREEK AND ARABIC IDEAS OF THE WORLD, AS THE CHIEF INHERITANCE OF THE CHRISTIAN MIDDLE AGES IN GEOGRAPHICAL KNOWLEDGE.

Arabic science constitutes one of the main links between the older learned world of the Greeks and Latins and the Europe of Henry the Navigator and of the Renaissance. In geography it adopted in the main the results of Ptolemy and Strabo; and many of the Moslem travellers and writers gained some additional hints from Indian, Persian, and Chinese knowledge; but, however much of fact they added to Greek cartography, they did not venture to correct its postulates.

And what were these postulates? In part, they were the assumptions of modern draughtsmen, but in some important details they differed. And first, as to agreement. Three continents, Europe, Asia, and Africa, an encircling ocean, the Mediterranean, the Black Sea and Caspian, the Red Sea and Persian Gulf, the South Asiatic, and North and West European coasts were indicated with more or less precision in the science of the Antonines and even of Hannibal's age. Similarly, the Nile and Danube, Euphrates and Tigris, Indus and Ganges, Jaxartes and Oxus, Rhine and Ebro, Don and Volga, with the chief mountain ranges of Europe and Western Asia, find themselves pretty much in their right places in Strabo's description, and are still better placed in the great chart of Ptolemy. The countries and nations from China to Spain are arranged in the order of modern knowledge. But the differences were fundamental also. Never was there a clearer outrunning of knowledge by theory, science by conjecture, than in Ptolemy's scheme of the world (*c.* A.D. 130). His chief predecessors, Eratosthenes and Strabo, had left much blank space in their charts, and had made many mistakes in detail, but they had caught the main features of the Old World with fair accuracy. Ptolemy, in trying to fill up what he did not know from his inner consciousness, evolved a parody of those features. His map, from its intricate falsehood, backed as it was by the greatest name in geographical science, paralysed all real enlargement of knowledge till men began to question, not only his facts, but his theories. And as all modern science, in fact, followed the progress of world-knowledge, or "geography," we may see how important it was for this revolution to take place, for Ptolemy to be dethroned.

THE WORLD ACCORDING TO PTOLEMY.
(SEE LIST OF MAPS)

The Arabs, commanding most of the centres of ancient learning (Ptolemy's own Alexandria above all), riveted the pseudo-science of their predecessors on the learned world, along with the genuine knowledge which they handed down from the Greeks. In many details they corrected and amplified the Greek results. But most of their geographical theories were mere reproductions of Ptolemy's, and to his mistakes they added wilder though less important confusions or inventions of their own. The result of all this, by the tenth century A.D., was a geography, based not on knowledge, but on ideas of symmetry. It was a scheme fit for the *Arabian Nights*.

And how did Ptolemy lend himself to this?

His chief mistakes were only two;—but they were mistakes from which at any rate Strabo and most of the Greek geographers are free. He made the Indian Ocean an inland sea, and he filled up the Southern Hemisphere with Africa, or the unknown Antarctic land in which he extended Africa.[8] The Dark Continent, in his map, ran out on the one side to the south-east of China, and on the other to the indefinite west, though there was here no hint of America or an Atlantic continent. It was a triumph of learned imagination over humdrum research. Science under Hadrian was ambitious to have its world settled and known; it was not yet settled or fully known; and so a great student constructed a *mélange* of fact and fancy mainly based on a guess-work of imaginary astronomical reckonings. On the far east, Ptolemy joined China and Africa; and on this imaginary western coast, fronting Malacca and Further India, he placed various gratuitous towns and rivers. Coming to smaller matters, he cut away the whole of the Indian peninsula proper, though preserving the Further or "Golden" Chersonesus of the Malays, and he enlarged Taprobane, or Ceylon, to double the size of Asia Minor. Thus the southern coast of Asia from Arabia to the Ganges ran almost due east, with a strait of sea coming through the modern Carnatic, between the continent and the Great Spice Island, which included most of the Deccan. The Persian Gulf, much greater on this map than the Black Sea, was made equal in length and breadth; the shape of the Caspian was, so to say, turned inside out and its length given as from east to west, instead of from north to south; while the coast line, even of the familiar Euxine, Ægean, and Southern Mediterranean, was anything but true. Scandinavia was an island smaller than Ireland; Scotland represented a great eastern bend of Britain, with the Shetlands and Färoes (Thule) lying a short distance to the north, but on the left-hand side of the great island. The Sea of Azov, hardly inferior to the Euxine, stretched north half way across Russia. All Central Africa and the great Southern or Antarctic continent was described as pathless desert—"a land uninhabitable from the heat"; and the sources of the Nile were accounted for by the marshes and Mountains of the Moon.

Thus all the problems of ancient geography were explained: where Ptolemy's knowledge failed him altogether, no Western of that time had ever been, or was likely to go. The whole realised and unrealised world was described with such clearness and consistency, men thought, that what was lacking in Aristotle was now supplied.

Yet it is worth while observing how, centuries before Ptolemy, in the ages nearer to Aristotle himself, the geography of Eratosthenes and Strabo, by a more balanced use of knowledge and by a greater restraint of fancy, had composed a far more reliable chart.[9]

This earlier and discredited map avoided all the more serious perversions of Ptolemy. Africa was cut off at the limit of actual knowledge, about Cape Non on the west and Cape Guardafui on the east; and the "Cinnamon-bearing Coast," between these points, was fringed by the Mountains of Æthiopia, where the Nile rose. This was the theory which revived on the decline of the Ptolemaic, and which encouraged the Portuguese sailors with hopes of a quick approach to India round Africa, as the great eastern bend of the Guinea coast seemed to suggest. Further, on this pre-Ptolemaic map the Southern Ocean was left untouched by a supposed Southern Continent, and except for an undue shrinkage of the Old World in general as an island in the midst of the vast surrounding ocean, a reliable description of Western Asia and Central Europe and North Africa was in the hands of the learned world two hundred years before Christ.

It is true that Strabo's China is cramped and cut short; that his Ceylon (Taprobane) is even larger than Ptolemy's; that Ireland (Ierne) appears to the *north* of Britain; and that the Caspian joins the North Sea by a long and narrow channel; but the true shape of India, of the Persian Gulf and the Euxine, of the Sea of Azov and the Mediterranean, is marked rightly enough in general outline. This earlier chart has not the elaborate completeness of Ptolemy's, but it is free from his enormous errors, and it has all the advantage of science, however imperfect, over brilliant guessing.

Of course, even in Ptolemy, this guess-work pure and simple only comes in at intervals and does not so much affect the central and, for his day, far more important tracts of the Old World, but we have yet to see how, in the mediæval period and under Arabic imagination, all geography seemed likely to become an exercise of fancy.

The chief Greek descriptions of the world, we must clearly remember, were before the mediæval workers, Christian and Moslem, from the first; these men took their choice, and the point is that they, and specially the Arabs, chose with rare exceptions the last of these, the Ptolemaic system, because it was the more ambitious, symmetrical, and pretty.

Let us trace for a moment the gradual development of this geographical mythology.

Starting with the notion of the world as a disc, or a ball, the centre of the universe, round which moved six celestial circles, of the Meridian, the Equator, the Ecliptic, the two Tropics, and the Horizon, the Arab philosophers on the side of the earth's surface worked out a doctrine of a Cupola or Summit of the world, and on the side of the heavens a pseudo-science of the Anoua or Settings of the Constellations, connected with the twelve Pillars of the Zodiac and the twenty-eight Mansions of the Moon.

With Arabic astrology we are not here concerned; it is only worth noting in this connection as the possible source of early Christian knowledge of the Southern Cross and other stars famous in the story of exploration, such as Dante shows in the first canto of his *Purgatorio*. But the geographical doctrines of Islam, compounded from the Hebrew Pentateuch and the theoretical parts of Ptolemy, had a more immediate and reactionary effect on knowledge. The symmetrical Greek divisions of land into seven zones or climates; and of the world's surface,[10] into three parts water and one part *terra firma*; the Indian fourfold arrangement of "Romeland" and the East; the similar fourfold Chinese partition of China, India, Persia, and Tartary: all these reappeared confusedly in Arabic geography. From India and the Sanscrit "Lanka," they seem to have got their first start on the myth of Odjein, Aryn, or Arim, "the World's Summit"; from Ptolemy the sacred number of 360 degrees of longitude was certainly derived, beautifully corresponding to the days of the year, and neatly divided into 180 of land or habitable earth and 180 of sea, or unharvested desert. With the seven climates they made correspond the great Empires of the world—chief among which they reckoned the Caliphate (or Bagdad), China, Rome, Turkestan, and India.

The sacred city of Odjein had been the centre of most of the earlier Oriental systems; in the Arabic form of Arim ("The Cupola of the Earth"), it became the fixed point round which circled mediæval theories of the world's shape. "Somewhere in the Indian Ocean between Comorin and Madagascar," became the compromise when the mountain could not be found off any of the known coast-lines; it was mixed up with notions of the Roc, and the Moon Mountains in Africa, of the Magnet Island and of the Eastern Kingdom made out of one vast pearl; and even in Roger Bacon it serves as an algebraic sign for a mathematical centre of the world.

The enlargement of knowledge, though forcing upon Arabic science a conviction of Ptolemy's mistake in over-extending the limits of the world known to him, only led to the invention of a scholastic distinction between the real and the traditional East and West, while the confusion was made perfect by the travestied history always so popular among Orientals. The "Gades of Alexander and Hercules," the farthest points east and west, were named after the mythical conquests of the real Iskander and the mythical hero of Greeks and Phœnicians. Arim in the middle, with the pillars of Hercules and Alexander, and the north and south poles at equal distance from it—the centre and the four corners of the world as neatly fixed as geometry could define—this was the map, first of the Arabs, and then of their Christian scholars.

To form any idea of the complete spell thus cast over thought both in Islam and Christendom, we may look at the words of European scholars of the twelfth and thirteenth centuries, living far from Islam, long after its intellectual glory had begun to decay, and at a time when Christian scholastic philosophy had reached an independent position. Gerard of Cremona and Adelard of Bath (the translator of the great Arabic geographer, Mohammed Al-Kharizmy) in the twelfth century, Roger Bacon and Albertus Magnus in the later thirteenth, are all as clear about their geographical postulates as about their theological or ethical rules. And what concerns us here is that they exactly reflect the mind of the Arabic science or pseudo-science of the time just preceding, so that their words may represent to us the state of Mohammedan thought between the eighth and twelfth centuries, between the writers at the Court of Caliph Almamoun (813-833) and Edrisi at the Court of King Roger of Sicily (1150).

(1.) *Adelard*, summarising Mohammed Al-Kharizmy with the results of his Paris education, tells us of the Arabic "Examination of planets and of time, starting from the centre of the world, called *Arim*, from which place to the four ends of the earth the distance is equal, viz., ninety degrees, answering to the fourth part of the world's circumference. It is tedious and unending to attempt to place all the countries of the world and to fix all the marks of time. So the meridian is taken as the measure of the latter and *Arim* of the former, and from this starting-point it is not hard to fix other countries." "Arim," he concludes, "is under the equator, at the point where there is no latitude," and he plainly implies that there were then existing among the

Arabs tables calculating all the chief places of every country from the meridian of *Arim*.

(2.) *Gerard* of Cremona, who, though for some time a resident at Toledo, is essentially an Italian, tells us about the "Middle of the World," from which longitudes were calculated, "called Arim," and "said to be in India," whose longitude from west to east or from east to west is ninety degrees.

In his *Theory of the Planets* Gerard tells us still more wonderful things. Arim was a geographical centre known and used by Hermes Trismegistus and by Ptolemy, as well as by the great Arab geographers; Alexander of Macedon marched just as far to the east of Arim as Hercules to the west; both reached the encircling ocean, and accordingly "Arim is equidistant from both the Gades, 90 degrees; likewise from each pole, north and south, the same, 90 degrees." This all recurs in the tables of Alphonso the Wise of Castille about A.D. 1260, and two of the greatest of mediæval thinkers, Albert and Roger Bacon, reproduced the essential points of this doctrine, its false symmetry, and its balance of the true and the traditional, with variations of their own.

(3.) *Albert the Great*, Albertus Magnus, second only to Aquinas among the Continental Schoolmen, in his *View of Astronomy*, repeats Adelard upon the question of Arim, "where there is no latitude," while (4) *Roger Bacon* discusses not only the true and the traditional East and West, but even a twofold Arim, one "under the solstice, the other under the equinoctial zone." Arim he finds not to be in the centre of the real world, but only of the traditional. In another passage of the *Opus Majus*, Bacon, our first English worker in the exact sciences, allows the world-summit not to be exactly 90 degrees from the east, although so placed by mathematicians. Yet there is no contradiction, he urges, because the men of theory are "speaking of the habitable world known to them, according to the true understanding of latitude and longitude," and this "true understanding" is "not as great as has been realised in travel by Pliny and others." "The longitude of the habitable world is more than half of the whole circuit." This, reproduced in the *Imago Mundi* of Cardinal Peter Ailly (1410), fell into the hands of Columbus and helped to fix his doctrines of the shape of the world ("in the form of a pear") of the terrestrial paradise, and of the earth's circumference,—so enormously contracted as practically to abolish the Pacific.[11]

To return to the Arabs: We have seen how they not merely followed Greek theories, which their own experience as conquerors in the Further East went to discredit, but, in the great outlines of geography, added to earlier errors, put prejudice in the place of knowledge, and handed on to Christendom a half-fanciful map of the world. It only remains for us to illustrate their leading fault, of a too vivid fancy, with a few details on minor points.

(1.) Ptolemy's "Habitable Quarter" of the world, amounting to just half the longitude of the globe, was literally accepted by the Moslem world, as it accepted the Pentateuch from the moment when it began its study of science at the Court of Almamoun (813-833). But, as the conquests of the Caliphs disclosed districts in the east far beyond Ptolemy's limits, it was necessary, in case of keeping his data for the whole, to compress the part which alone was to be found fully described in his chart: "On the west, unhappily, there were no countries newly discovered to compensate for this abridgment." By Massoudy's time,—by the tenth century,—fact and theory were thus hopelessly at variance.

(2.) On the shape of Africa, the mass of Arabic opinion confirmed Ptolemy, but among the more enlightened there is traceable from Massoudy's time a tendency either to react towards Strabo's partly agnostic position, or to invent some new theory rather more in harmony with the known facts. That is, either their later map-makers cut off Africa at Cape Non or Bojador and Cape Guardafui, and gave away the rest to the "Green Sea of Darkness," or, like Massoudy, they sketched a great Southern Continent, divided from Africa by a narrow channel, which connected the Western Ocean with the Sea of Habasch—of Abyssinia or India. In either case Africa was left an island.

(3.) The words "Gog and Magog" from Jeremiah, describing the nomades of Central Asia, appear in the Koran as Yadjoudj and Madjoudj. The complete story, in the tenth century and in Edrisi's day, connects them with Alexander the Great, who is also found in the Koran as Doul-Carnain, and with the Wall of China. "When the Conqueror," said the Arabs, "reached the place near where the sun rose, he was implored to build a wall to shut off the marauders of Yadjoudj and Madjoudj from the rich countries of the South." So he built a rampart of iron across the pass by which alone Touran joined Iran, and henceforth Turks and Tartars were kept outside. Till the Arabs reached the Caucasus, they generally supposed this to answer to Alexander's wall; when facts dispelled this theory, the unknown Ural or Altai Mountains served instead; finally, as the Moslems became masters of Central Asia, the Wall of China, beyond the Gobi desert, alone satisfied the conditions of shadowy but historic grandeur, beyond all practical danger of verification.

(4.) In striking contrast with the steady advance of Arabic exploration and trade in the Eastern Sea is the Moslem horror of the Western Ocean beyond Europe and Africa, the "Green Sea of Darkness" or the Atlantic. And what we have to note is that they imparted much of this paralysing cowardice to the Christian nations. Only the Northmen of Scandinavia, living a life apart, and forced to make their way over the wild North Sea, were untouched by this southern superstition, and ventured across the ocean by the Färoes, Iceland, and Greenland, to the coast of Labrador.

The doctors of the Koran indeed thought that a man mad enough to embark for the unknown, even on a coasting voyage, should be deprived of civil rights. Ibn Said goes further, and says no one has ever done this: "whirlpools always destroy any adventurer." As late as the generation immediately before Henry the Navigator, about A.D. 1390, another light of Moslem science declared the Atlantic to be "boundless, so that ships dare not venture out of sight of land, for even if the sailors knew the direction of the winds, they would not know whither those winds would carry them, and as there is no inhabited country beyond, they would run a risk of being lost in mist, fog, and vapour. The limit of the West is the Atlantic Ocean."

This was the final judgment of the Arabic race and its subject allies upon the western limits of the world, and in two ways they helped to fix this belief, derived from the timid coasting-traders of the Roman Empire on Greek and Latin Christendom. First, the Spanish Caliphate cut off all access to the Western Sea beyond the Bay of Biscay, from the eighth to the twelfth centuries. Not till the capture of Lisbon in 1147, could Christian enterprise on this side gain any basis, or starting-point. Not till the conquest of the Algarve in the extreme south-west of the peninsula, at the end of the twelfth century, was this enterprise free to develop itself. Secondly, in the darkest ages of Christian depression, the seventh, the eighth, the ninth, the tenth centuries, when only the brief age of Charlemagne offered any chance of an independent and progressive Catholic Empire in the west, the Arabs became recognised along with the Byzantines as the main successors of Greek culture. The science, the metaphysic, the abstract ideas of these centuries came into Germany, France, and Italy from Cordova and from Bagdad, as much as from Byzantium. And on questions like the South Atlantic or Indian Ocean, or the shape of Africa,—where Islam had all the field to itself, and there was no positive and earlier discovery which might contradict a natural reluctance to test tradition by experiment— Christendom accepted the Arabic verdict with deference.

In the same way, on still more difficult points, such as the theory of a canal from the Caspian to the Black Sea, or from the Caspian to the Arctic circle, or from the Black Sea to the Baltic, Paris and Rome and Bologna and Oxford accepted the Arabic descriptions.

It has been necessary for us to attend to the defects of Arabic geography, in order to understand how in the long Saracen control of the world's trade routes and of geographical tradition, science and seamanship were so little advanced. Between Ptolemy and Henry of Portugal, between the second and the fifteenth centuries, the only great extension of men's knowledge of the world was: (1) in the extreme north, where the semi-Christian, semi-Pagan Vikings reached perhaps as far as the present site of New York and founded, on another side, the Mediæval Kingdom of Russia; (2) on the south-east coast of Africa, from Cape Guardafui to Madagascar, which was opened up by the trading interest of the Emosaid family (800-1300); (3) in the far east, in Central and Further Asia, by the discoveries of Marco Polo and the Friar preachers following on the tracks of the earlier Moslem travellers. The first of these was a Northern secret, soon forgotten, or an abortive development, cut short by the Tartars; the second was an Arabic secret, jealously guarded as a commercial right; the third alone added much direct new knowledge to the main part of the civilised world.

But throughout their period of commercial rule from the eighth to the twelfth centuries, the Arabs took a keen interest in land traffic, conquest, and exploration. They were of small account at sea; it took them some time to turn to their own purposes Hippalus' discovery (in the second century A.D.) of the monsoon in the Indian Ocean; but, on land, Moslem travellers and writers—generally following in the wake of their armies, but sometimes pressing on ahead of them—did not a little to enlarge the horizon of the Mohammedan world, though it was not till Marco Polo and the Franciscan missionaries of the thirteenth and fourteenth centuries, that Christian Europe shared in this gain.

As the early Caliphs conquered, they made surveys of their new dominions. Thus after Tarik and Mousa had overrun Spain, Walid at Damascus required from them an account of the land and its resources. The universal obligation of the Mecca pilgrimage compelled every Moslem to travel once in his life; and many an Arab, after the Caliphate was settled in power from the Oxus to the Pyrenees, journeyed to and fro with the joy of a master going over vast estates, shewing his dreaded turban to subjects of every nation.

This, however, was not geographical science, or even pseudo-science. Before Mohammed the Arabs had possessed some knowledge of the stars and used it for astrology; but it was at the Court of Almamoun (813-833) that their inquiring spirits first set themselves to answer the great question of geography—Where? Through the ninth and tenth centuries there arose a succession of travellers and thinkers who, with all their wild dreamings, preserved the best results of Greek maps and would have made much greater advances but for their helplessness in original work. As they could not recast Aristotle in philosophy, so they could not with all their new knowledge of the Further East recast the geography of Ptolemy and Strabo.

A few great ages, the age for instance of Almamoun in Bagdad (A.D. 830), of Mahmoud in Ghazneh (A.D. 1000), of Abderrahman III. in Cordova (A.D. 950), give us the history of Arabic geography.

Beginning in the latter years of the eighth century, Moslem science was reformed and organised, in the New Empire, by the patronage of the Caliphs of the ninth. Itineraries of victorious generals, plans and tables prepared by governors of provinces, and a freshly acquired knowledge of Greek and Indian and Persian thought, made up the subject-matter of study. The barbarism of the first believers was passing away, and Mohammed's words were recalled: "Seek knowledge, even in China." By the end of the eighth century Ptolemy's Geography and the now lost work of Marinus of Tyre had already been translated. Almamoun drew to his Court all the chief "mathematicians" or philosophers of Islam, such as Mohammed Al-Kharizmy, Alfergany, and Solyman the merchant. Further he built two observatories, one at Bagdad, one at Damascus, and procured a chart fixing the latitude and longitude of every place known to him or his savants. Al-Kharizmy interpolated the new Arabic Ptolemy with additions from the Sanscrit, and made some use of Indian trigonometry. Alfergany wrote the first Arab treatise on the Astrolabe and adopted the Greek division of the seven Climates to the new learning. Solyman, at the time of closest intercourse between China, India, and the Caliphate, travelled in every country of the Further East, sailed in the "Sea of Pitchy Darkness" on the east coast of Asia, and by his voyages became the prototype of Sinbad the Sailor.

The impulse given by Almamoun did not die with him. About 850 Alkendy made a fresh version of Ptolemy; as early as 840 the Caliph Vatek-Billah sent to explore the countries of Central Asia, and his results have been preserved by Edrisi. A few years later (*c.* 890) Ibn-Khordadbeh, "Son of the Magi," described the principal trade-routes, the Indian by the Red Sea from Djeddah to Scinde, the Russian by the Volga and North Caspian, the Persian by way of Balkh to China. It was by this last that some have thought the envoys of the English King Alfred went in 883, till they turned south to seek India and the Christians of San Thomé.

The early scientific movement in Islam reached its height in Albateny and Massoudy at the beginning of the tenth century. The former determined, more exactly than before, various problems of astronomical geography.[12] The latter visited every country from Further India to Spain;—even China and Madagascar seem to have been within the compass of his later travels; and his voyages in the Indian Ocean bring us to the real Sinbad Saga of the tenth century.

Sinbad, as his story appears in the *Arabian Nights*, has been traced to an original in the Indian tales of *The Seven Sages*, in the voyages of the age of Chosroes Nushirvan or of Haroun-Al-Rashid, but the tale appears to be an Arabic original, the real account, with a little more of mystery and exaggeration than usual, of the ninth-and tenth-century travellers, from Solyman to Massoudy, reproduced in form of a series of novels.[13]

With Massoudy begins also the formal discussion of geographical problems affecting Islam. Was the Caspian a land-locked sea? Did it connect with the Euxine? Did either or both of these join the Arctic Ocean? Was Africa an island? If so, was there also an unknown Southern Continent? What was the shape of South-Eastern Asia? Was Ptolemy's longitude to be wholly accepted, and if not, how was it to be bettered? By a use of Strabo and of Albateny rather than of Ptolemy, Massoudy arrived at fairly accurate and very plausible results. His chief novelties were the long river channel from the Sea of Azov to the North Sea, and the strait between South Africa and the shadowy Southern Continent. On his scheme the Indian Ocean, or Sea of Habasch, contains most of the water surface of the world, and the Sea of Aral appears for the first time in Moslem geography. Lastly his account of the Arab coasting voyages from the Persian Gulf to Socotra and Madagascar proves, implicitly, that as yet there was no use of the compass.

Massoudy cut down the girth of the world even more than Ptolemy. The latter had left an ocean to the west of Africa: the former made the Canaries or Fortunate Islands, the limit of the known Western world, abut upon India, the limit of the Eastern.

The first age of Arabic geography ends with Massoudy, its greatest name, in the middle of the tenth century. The second age is summed up in the work of the Eastern sage Albyrouny and of Edrisi, the Arabic Ptolemy (A.D. 1099-1154), who found a home at the Christian Court of Roger of Sicily. In the far East and West alike, in Spain and Morocco, in Khorassan and India, Moslem science was now driven to take refuge among strangers on the decay of the Caliphates of Bagdad and Cordova. The Ghaznevides Mahmoud and Massoud in the first half of the eleventh century, attracted to their Court not only Firdusi and Avicenna, but Albyrouny, whose "Canon" became a text-book of Mohammedan science, and who, for the range of his knowledge and the trained subtlety of his mind, stands without a rival for his time.[14] The Spanish school, as resulting directly in Edrisi, half Moslem, half Christian, like his teachers, is of still more interest. One of its first traces may be found in the Latin translation of the Arab *Almanack* made by Bishop Harib of Cordova in 961. It was dedicated and presented to Caliph Hakem—one of our clearest proofs of the conscious interworking of Catholic and Mahometan philosophy in the age of Pope Sylvester II. and of our own St. Dunstan. A century later, on the recapture of Toledo by Alfonso VI. (1084), an observatory was built, served by Jews and Moslems, who had been steadily producing, through the whole of the eleventh century, astronomical and geographical tables and dictionaries. A whole tribe of commentators on place-names, on the climates and constellations, and on geographical instruments was at work in this last age of the Spanish Caliphate, and their results are brought together by Abou Hamid of Granada and by Edrisi.

Born at Ceuta in 1099, this great geographer travelled through Spain, France, the Western Mediterranean, and North Africa before settling at the Norman Court of Palermo. Roger, the most civilised prince in Christendom, the final product of the great race of Robert Guiscard and William the Conqueror, valued Edrisi at his proper worth, refused to part with him, and employed men in every part of the world to collect materials for his study. Thus the Moor gained, not only for the Moslem world but for Southern Europe as well, an approximate knowledge even of Norway, Sweden, Finland, and the coasts of the White Sea. His work, dedicated to Roger and called after him, *Al-Rojary*, was rewarded with a peerage, and it was as a Sicilian Count that he finished his Celestial Sphere and Terrestrial Disc of silver, on which "was inscribed all the circuit of the known world and all the rivers thereof."

Each of his great Arabic predecessors, along with Eratosthenes, Ptolemy, and Strabo, was welded into his system—the result of fifteen years of abstract study, following some thirty of practical activity in travel.[15]

A special note may be made on Edrisi's account of the voyage of the Lisbon "Wanderers" ("Maghrurins") some time before 1147, the date of the final Christian capture of the Portuguese capital. For this is the earliest recorded voyage, since the rise of Islam, definitely undertaken on the Western Ocean to learn what was on it and what were its limits. The Wanderers, Edrisi tells us, were eight in number, all related to one another. They built a transport boat, took on board water and provisions for many months, and started with the first east wind. After eleven days, they reached a sea whose thick waters exhaled a fetid odour, concealed numerous reefs, and were but faintly lighted. Fearing for their lives, they changed their course, steered southwards twelve days, and so reached an island, possibly Madeira,—which they called El Ghanam from the sheep found there, without shepherd or anyone to tend them. On landing, they found a spring of running water and some wild figs. They killed some sheep, but found the flesh so bitter that they could not eat it, and only took the skins. Sailing south twelve more days, they found an island with houses and cultivated fields, but as they neared it they were surrounded, made prisoners, and carried in their own boats to a city on the sea-shore, to a house where were men of tall stature and women of great beauty. Here they stayed three days, and on the fourth came a man, the King's interpreter, who spoke Arabic, and asked them who they were and what they wanted. They replied they were seeking out the wonders of the ocean and its limits. At this the King laughed heartily, and said to the interpreter: "Tell them my father once ordered some of his slaves to venture out on that sea and after sailing across the breadth of it for a month, they found themselves deprived of the light of the sun and returned without having learnt anything." Then the Wanderers were sent back to their prison till a west wind arose, when they were blindfolded and put on board a boat, and after three days reached the mainland of Africa. Here they were put ashore, with their hands tied, and so left. They were released by the Berbers, and after their reappearance in Spain, a "street at the foot of the hot bath in Lisbon," concludes Edrisi, "took the name of Street of the Wanderers."

On the other extremity of the Moslem world, on the south-east coast of Africa, there was more real progress. By Edrisi's day that important addition of Arabic travellers and merchants to the geographical knowledge of the world, by the remarkable trade-ventures of the Emosaids, had been already made.

It had taken long in the making.

THE WORLD ACCORDING TO EDRISI.
(SEE LIST OF MAPS)

About A.D. 742, ten years after the battle of Tours, the Emosaid family, descended from Ali, cousin and son-in-law of Mahomet, tried to make Said, their clan-chieftain, Ali's great-grandson, Caliph at Damascus. The attempt was foiled, and the whole tribe fled, sailed down the Red Sea and African coast, and established themselves as traders in the Sea of India. First of all, Socotra seems to have been their mart and capital, but before the end of the tenth century they had founded merchant colonies at Melinda, Mombasa, and Mozambique, which, in their turn, led to settlements on the opposite coasts of Asia. Thus the trade of the Indian Ocean was secured for Islam, the first Moslem settlements arose in Malabar, and when the Portuguese broke into this *mare clausum*, in 1497-8, they found a belt of "Moorish" coast towns, from Magadoxo to Quiloa, controlling both the Indian and the inland African trades, as Ibn Batuta had found in 1330.

By Edrisi's day, moreover, the steady persistence and self-evident results of Arabic overland exploration had become recognised by a sort of "Traveller's Doctorate." It was not enough for the highest knowledge to study the Koran, and the Sunna, and the Greek philosophers at home; for a perfect education, a man must have travelled at least through the length and breadth of Islam. All the successors of Edrisi, in the twelfth and thirteenth centuries, shew this mingling of science and religion, of practical and speculative energy.

Tradition still governed Moslem thought, but there had come into being a sort of half-acknowledged appendix to tradition, made up of real observations on men and things. And in these observations, geographical interest was the main factor.

The Life of Al Heravy of Herat (1173-1215), the "Doctor Ubiquitus" of Islam in the age of the Crusades, gives us a picture of another Massoudy. The friend of the Emperor Manuel Comnenus, the "first man among Christians," Heravy seems able in his own person to break down the partition wall of religious feud by the common interest of science. In 1192 he was offered the patronage of the Crusading princes, and Richard Cœur de Lion begged for the favour of an interview, and begged in vain. Heravy, who had been on one of his exploring journeys, angrily refused to see the King whose men had broken his quiet and wasted his time. Before his death, he had run over the world (men said) from China to the Pyrenees and from Abyssinia to the Danube, "scribbling his name on every wall," and his survey of the Eastern Empire was the single matter in which Turks and "Romans" made common cause,—for Greeks and Latins at Byzantium alike read Heravy, like a Christian doctor. Another example of the same catholic spirit is "Yacout the Roman,"[16] whose *Dictionary*, finished in the earlier half of the thirteenth century, was a summary of geographical advance since Edrisi, like the similar work of Ibn Said, of the same period.

But as a matter of fact, the balance both of knowledge and power was now shifting from Islam to Christendom. The most daring and successful travellers after the rise of the Mongols were the Venetian Marco Polo and the Friar Preachers who revived Chinese Christianity (1270-1350); Madeira and the Canaries (off Moslem Africa) were finally rediscovered not by Arabic enterprise, but by the Italian Malocello in 1270, by the English Macham in the reign of our Edward III., and by Portuguese ships under Genoese captains in 1341; in 1291 the Vivaldi ventured beyond Cape Bojador, where no Moor had ever been, except by force of storm, as in the doubtful story of Ibn Fatimah, who "first saw the White Headland," Cape Blanco, between Cape Bojador and Cape Verde.

In the fourteenth century the map of Edrisi was superseded by the new Italian plans and coast-charts, or Portolani. As the Moslem world fell into political disorder, its science declined. "Judicial astrology" seemed gaining a stronger and stronger hold over Islam, and the irruption of the Turks gradually resulted in the ruin of all the higher Moslem culture. Superstition and barbarism shared the honour and the spoils of this victory.

But two great names close the five hundred years of Arab learning.

1. Ibn Batuta (*c.* 1330), who made himself as much at home in China as in his native Morocco, is the last of Mohammedan travellers of real importance. Though we have only abridgments of his work left to us, Colonel Yule is well within his rights in his deliberate judgment, "that it must rank at least as one of the four chief guide books of the Middle Ages," along with the *Book of Ser Marco Polo* and the journals of the two Friar-travellers, Friar Odoric and Friar William de Rubruquis.

2. With *Abulfeda* the Eastern school of Moslem geography comes to an end, as the Western does with Ibn Batuta. In the early years of the fourteenth century he rewrote the "story and description of the Land of Islam," with a completeness quite encyclopædic. But his work has all the failings of a compilation, however careful, in that, or any, age. It is based upon information, not upon inspection; it is in no sense original. As it began in imitation, so it ended. If it rejects Ptolemy, it is only to follow Strabo or someone else; on all the mathematical and astronomical data its doctrine is according to the Alexandrians of twelve hundred years before, and this last *précis* of the science of a great race and a great religion can only be understood in the light of its model—in Greek geography.

CHAPTER I.

EARLY CHRISTIAN PILGRIMS.

CIRCA 333-867.

The special interest of the life and work of Henry the Navigator (1394-1460) lies in the relation it bears to the general expansion of Europe and Christendom—an expansion that had been slowly gathering strength since the eleventh century. But even before the tide had turned in the age of Hildebrand and the First Crusade, even from the time that Constantine founded the Christian Empire of Rome, the Christian Capital on the Bosphorus, and the State Church of the Western World,—pilgrimage, trade, conquest, and colonisation had been successively calling out the energies of the moving races, "the motor muscles" of Europe. It is through the "generous Henry, Prince of Portugal," that this activity is brought to its third and triumphant stage—to the time of Columbus and Da Gama and Magellan,—but it is only by tracing the earlier progress of that outward movement, which has made Europe the ruling civilisation of the world, that we can fairly grasp the import of that transition in which Henry is the hero.

More than any other single man he is the author of the discovering movement of the fifteenth, sixteenth, and seventeenth centuries,—and by this movement India has been conquered, America repeopled, the world made clear, and the civilisation which the Roman Empire left behind has conquered or utterly overshadowed every one of its old rivals and superiors—Islam, India, China, Tartary.

But before the fifteenth century, before the birth of Prince Henry, Christendom, Greek and Latin, was at best only one of the greater civilising and conquering forces struggling for mastery; before the age of the Crusades, before the eleventh century, it was plainly weaker than the Moslem powers; it seemed unable to fight against Slav or Scandinavian Heathendom; it was only saved by distance from becoming a province of China; India, the world's great prize, was cut off from it by the Arabs. Even before the rise of Islam, under Constantine or Theodosius or Justinian, the Church-State of the Byzantine Cæsars, though then ruling in almost every province of Trajan's empire, was in a splendid but sure decline from the exhaustion of the southern races. Our story then begins naturally with the worst time and climbs up for a thousand years, from the Heathen and Mohammedan conquests of the fifth and seventh centuries, to the reversal of that judgment, of those conquests, in the fifteenth. The expansion of Europe is going on all this time, but at our beginning, in the years before and after Pope Gregory the Great, even the legacy of Greece and Rome, in wide knowledge of the world and practical exploring energy, seemed to have passed from sight.

And in the decline of the old Empire, while Constantine and Justinian are said to receive and exchange embassies with the Court of China, there is no real extension of geographical knowledge or outlook. Christian enterprise in this field is mainly one of pilgrimage, and the pilgrims only cease to be important when the Northmen, first Heathen, then Christian, begin to lead, in a very different manner, the expansion of Europe. Into this folk-wandering of the Vikings, the first great outward movement of our Europe in the Middle Ages, is absorbed the reviving energy of trade, as well as the ever-growing impulse of pilgrimage. The Vikings are the highest type of explorers; they do not merely find out new lands and trade with them, but conquer and colonise them. They extend not merely the knowledge, but the whole state and being of Europe, to a New World.

Lastly, the partial activity of commerce and religion made universal and "political" by the leading western race—for itself only—is taken up by all Christendom in the Crusades, borrowed in idea from Spain, but borrowed with the spirit of the Norse rovers, and made universal for the Latin world, for the whole federation of Rome. In the eleventh, twelfth, and thirteenth centuries we have the preparation for the discovery and colonisation of the outside world by Europeans in the fifteenth, sixteenth, and seventeenth centuries of the Christian era.

From the conversion of Constantine to the Reformation the story of Christendom is unbroken; the later Roman Empire is the Church-State of a Christian Prince, as modern Europe is the Church-State of a nominally Christian society. Mediæval Europe thought of itself as nothing but the old world-state under religion; from Spain to Russia men were living under a Holy Roman Empire of an Italian, or Teutonic, or Byzantine, or independent type. England and Russia were not parts of the Germanic revival of Charlemagne, but they had just the same two elements dominant in their life: the classical tradition and the Christian Church.

And so throughout this time, the expansion of this society—by whatever name we may call it, discovery, exploration, geographical knowledge—has a continuous history. But before the rise of Islam, in the seventh century, throws Christendom into its proper mediæval life, before the new religion begins the really new age, at the end of which lived Henry himself, we are too far from our subject to feel, for instance in the fourth and fifth-century pilgrims and in Cosmas Indicopleustes, anything but a remote preparation for Henry's work. It is only with the seventh century, and with the time of our own Bede and Wilfrid, that the necessary introduction to our subject really begins.

Yet as an illustration of the general idea, that discovery is an early and natural outlet of any vigorous society and is in proportion to the universal activity of the State, it is not without interest to note that Christian Pilgrimage begins with Constantine. This, the first department of exploring energy, at once evidences the new settlement of religion and politics. Helena, the Emperor's mother, helped, by her visit to Palestine, her church at Bethlehem, and her discoveries of relics in Jerusalem, to make a ruling fashion out of the custom of a few devotees; and eight years after the council of Nicæa, in 333, appeared the first Christian geography, as a guide-book or itinerary, from Bordeaux to the Holy Places of Syria, modelled upon the imperial survey of the Antonines. The route followed in this runs by North Italy, Aquileia, Sirmium, Constantinople, and Asia Minor, and upon the same course thousands of nameless pilgrims journeyed in the next three hundred years, besides some eight or nine who have left an account mainly religious in form, but containing in substance the widest view of the globe then possible among Westerns.

Most of the pilgrims, like Jerome's friend Paula, Bishop Eucherius, and Melania, tread the same path and stop at the same points, but three or four of them distinctly add some fresh knowledge to the ordinary results.

St. Silvia, of Aquitaine (c. 385), not only travels through Syria, she visits Lower Egypt and Stony or Sinaitic Arabia, and even Edessa in Northern Mesopotamia, on the very borders of hostile and heathen Persia. "To see the monks" she wanders through Osrhöene, comes to Haran, near which was "the home of Abraham and the farm of Laban and the well of Rachel," to the environs of Nisibis and Ur of the Chaldees, lost to the Roman Empire since Julian's defeat; thence by "Padan-aram" back to Antioch. When crossing the Euphrates the pilgrims saw the river "rush down in a torrent like the Rhone, but greater," and on the way home by the great military road, then untravelled by Saracens, between Tarsus and the Bosphorus, Silvia makes a passing note on the strength and brigand habits of the Isaurian mountaineers, who in the end saved Christendom from the very Arabs with whom our pilgrim couples them.

Again, Cosmas Indicopleustes, in the time of Justinian, is at the end, as Silvia is at the beginning, of a definite period, the period of the Christian empire of Rome, while still "Cæsarean" and not merely Byzantine, "patrician" and not papal, "consular" and not Carolingian.

And contemporary with Cosmas are two of the chief among the earlier or primitive pilgrims, Theodosius and Antoninus the Martyr. The first-named indulges in a few excursions—in fancy—beyond his known ground of

Palestine, going as far east as Susa and Babylon, "where no one can live for the serpents and hippo-centaurs," and south to the Red Sea and its two arms, "of which the eastern is called the Persian Gulf," and the western or Arabian runs up to the "thirteen cities of Arabia destroyed by Joshua,"— but, for the rest, his knowledge is not extensive or peculiar. Antoninus of Placentia, on the other hand, is very interesting, a sort of older Mandeville, who mixes truth and its opposite in fairly even proportions and with a sort of resolute partiality to favourite legends.

He tells us how Tripolis has been ruined by the late earthquake (July 9, 551); how silk and various woven stuffs are sold at Tyre; how the pilgrims scratched their names on the relics shewn in Cana of Galilee—"and here I, sinner that I am, did inscribe the names of my parents"; how Bethshan, the metropolis of Galilee, "is placed on a hill," though really in the plain; how the Samaritans hate Christians and will hardly speak to them; "and beware of spitting in their country, for they will never forgive it"; how "the dew comes down upon Hermon the Little, as David says, 'The dew of Hermon that fell upon the hill of Zion'"; how nothing can live or even float in the Dead Sea, "but is instantly swallowed up"—as exact an untruth as was ever told by traveller; how the Jordan opens a way for pilgrims "and stands up in a heap every year at the Epiphany during the baptism of Catechumens, as David told, 'The sea saw that and fled, Jordan was driven back'"; how at Jericho there is a Holy Field "sown by the Lord with his own hand." A report had been spread that the salt pillar of Lot's wife had been "lessened by licking"; "it was false," said Antoninus, the statue was just the same as it had always been.

In Jerusalem the pilgrims first went up the Tower of David, "where he sang the Psalter," and into the Basilica of Sion, where among other marvels they saw the "Corner-stone that the builders rejected," which gave out a "sound like the murmuring of a crowd."

We come back again to fact with rather a start when told in the next section of the Hospitals for 3000 sick folk near the Church of St. Mary, close to Sion; then with the footprints and relics of Christ, and the miraculous flight of the Column of Scourging—"carried away by a cloud to Cæsarea," we are taken through a fresh set of "impressions."

The same wild notions of place and time and nature follow the Martyr through Galilee to Gilboa, "where David slew Goliath and Saul died, where no dew or rain ever falls, and where devils appear nightly, whirled about like fleeces of wool or the waves of the sea"—to Nazareth, where was the "Beam of Christ the Carpenter"—to Elua, where fifteen consecrated virgins had tamed a lion and trained it to live with them in a cell—to Egypt, where the Pyramids become for him the "*twelve* Barns of Joseph," for the legend had not yet insisted that the actual number should be made to fit the text of the seven years of plenty.

But with all this Antoninus now and then gives us glimpses of a larger world. In Jerusalem he meets Æthiopians "with nostrils slit and rings about their fingers and their feet." They were so marked, they told him, by the Emperor Trajan "for a sign."

In the Sinai desert he tells us of "Saracen" beggars and idolaters; in the Red Sea ports he sees "ships from India" laden with aromatics; he travels up the Nile to the Cataracts and describes the Nilometer at Assouan, and the crocodiles in the river; Alexandria he finds "splendid but frivolous, a lover of pilgrims but swarming with heresies."

But far more wonderful than the practical jumble of Antoninus Martyr is the systematic nonsense of Cosmas, who invented or worked out a theory and scheme of the world, a "Christian topography," which required nothing more than a complete disuse of human reason. His assurance was equal to his science.

It may have been his voyage to India, or his monastic profession, or his study of Scripture, or something unknown that made him take up the part of a Christian Aristotle; in any case he felt himself called into the field to support the cause of St. Augustine against infidelity, and to refute the "anile fable" of the Antipodes. Cosmas referred men back to Revelation on such matters, and his system was "demonstrated from Scripture, concerning which a Christian is not allowed to doubt." Man by himself could not understand the world, but in the Bible it was all clear enough. And from the Bible this much was beyond dispute.

The universe is a flat parallelogram; and its length is exactly double of its breadth. In the centre of the universe is our world surrounded by the ocean, and by an outer world or ring where men lived before the Flood. Noah and his Ark came over sea from this to the present earth.

To the north of our world is a great hill, like the later Moslem and older Hindu "Cupola of the Earth," which perhaps was Cosmas' own original. Round this the sun and moon revolve, making day and night as they appear or disappear behind it.

The sky consists of four walls meeting in the "dome of heaven" over the floor on which we live, and this sky is "glued" to the edges of the outer world, the world of the Patriarchs.

But this heaven is also cut in two by the firmament, lying between our atmosphere and that "New Heaven and New Earth wherein dwelleth Righteousness"; and the floor of this upper world is covered by the "waters that be above the firmament"; above this is Paradise, and below the firmament live the angels, as "ministers" and "flaming fires" and "servants of God to men."

The proofs of this are simple, mainly resting on some five texts from the Old Testament and two passages of St. Paul.

First the Book of Genesis declared itself to be the "Book of the Generation of the Heaven and the Earth"—that is, of everything in the heavens, and the earth. But the "old wives' fable of the Antipodes" would make the heaven surround and contain the earth, and God's word would have to be changed "These are the generations of the sky." For the same truth—the twofold and independent being of heaven and earth—Cosmas quotes the additional testimony of Abraham, David, Hosea, Isaiah, Zachariah, and Melchisedek, who clenched the case against the Antipodes. "For how indeed could even rain be said to 'fall' or to 'descend,' as in the Psalms and the Gospels, in those regions where it could only be said to 'come up'?"

Again, the world cannot be a globe, or sphere, or be suspended in mid-air, or in any sort of motion, for what say the Scriptures? "Earth is fixed on its foundations"; "Thou hast laid the foundations of the earth and it abideth"; "Thou hast made the round world so sure, that it cannot be moved"; "Thou hast made all men to dwell upon the face of the whole earth"—not "upon every face," or upon any more than one face—"upon *the* face," not the back or the side, but the broad flat face we know. "Who then with these passages before him, ought even to speak of Antipodes?"

So much against false doctrine; to establish the truth is simpler still. For the same St. Paul, who disposes of science falsely so called, does not he speak, like David, like St. Peter and St. John, of our world as a tabernacle? "If our earthly house of this tabernacle be dissolved," "We that are in this tabernacle do groan, being burdened," which points to the natural conclusion of enlightened faith, that Moses' tabernacle was an exact copy of the universe. "See thou make all things according to the pattern shewn thee in the Mount." So the four walls, the covered roof, the floor, the proportions of the Tent of the Wilderness, shewed us in small compass all that was in nature.

If any further guidance were needed, it was ready to hand in the Prophet Isaiah and the Patriarch Job. "That stretcheth out the heavens as a curtain and spreadeth them out as a tent to dwell in"; "Also can any understand the spreadings of the clouds or the noise of his tabernacle?"

The whole reasoning is like the theological arguments on the effects of man's fall upon the stars and the vegetable world, or the atmospheric changes due to angels.

But though Cosmas states his system with the claims of an article of faith, there were not wanting men, and even saints, who stood out on the side of reason in geography in the most traditional of times. Isidore of Seville, and Vergil, the Irish missionary of the eighth century, both maintained the old belief of Basil and Ambrose, that the question of the Antipodes was not closed by the Church, and that error in this point was venial and not mortal. For the positive tabernacle-system of "the man who sailed to India" there was never much support; his work was soon forgotten, though it has been called by some paradox-makers "the great authority of the Middle Ages"—in the face of the known facts, that this was the real position of Ptolemy and Strabo, that no one can speak of the "Middle Ages" in this unqualified way any more than of the Modern or Ancient worlds; and that Cosmas is almost unnoticed in the great age of mediæval science, from the twelfth century.

And whatever we may think of Cosmas and his *Christian System of the Whole World, Evolved out of Holy Scripture*, he is of interest to us as the last of the old Christian geographers, closing one age which, however senile, had once been in the truest sense civilised, and preparing us to enter one that in comparison is literally dark. From the age of Justinian, and from the rise of Islam in the early years of the seventh century, the geographical knowledge of Christendom is on a par with its practical contraction and apparent decline. There are travellers; but for the next five hundred years there are no more theorists, cosmographers, or map-makers of the Universe or Habitable Globe.

From the time that Islam, after a century of world-conquest, began to form itself into an organised state, or federation of states, in the later eighth and earlier ninth centuries A.D.,—thus making itself until the thirteenth century the principal heir of the older Eastern culture,—Christendom was content to take its geography, its ideas of the world in general, from the Arabs, who in their turn depended upon the pre-Christian Greeks.

The relation of Ptolemy and Strabo to modern knowledge is best seen through the work of the Arabic geographers, but the Saracens did much to destroy before they began to build up once more. As the northern barbarians of the fifth century interrupted the hope of a Christian revival of Pagan literature and science, so the Moslems of the seventh and eighth cut short the Catholic and Roman revival of Justinian and Heraclius, in which the new faith and the old state had found a working agreement.

Between Cosmas and the Viking-Age, "Christian," "Roman," "Western" exploration falls within very narrow limits: the few pilgrims whose recollections represent to us the whole literature of travel in the seventh, eighth, and ninth centuries, add nothing fresh even of practical discovery;

theory and theoretical work has ceased altogether, and the first stirrings of the new life in the commerce and voyages of Amalphi, and in the sudden and splendid outburst of Norse life in its age of piracy, are not yet, are not really before the world until the time of Alfred of England, of Charles the Bald, of Pope Nicholas I. "the Great." Yet such as it is, this pilgrim stage of European development stands for something. Religion, as it is the first agent in forming our modern nations, is the first impulse towards their expansion. And to us there is a special interest.

For the best known of western travellers in this darkest of the Christian ages (600-870 A.D.), Arculf and Willibald, are both connected with England and the beginnings of English science in the age of Bede.

Arculf, a Frank or Gallican Bishop, who about 690 visited, first of "Latin" writers since the Mohammedan conquest, Jerusalem, the Jordan valley, Nazareth, and the other holy places of Syria, was driven by storms on his return to the great Irish monastery of Iona. There he described his wonders to the Abbot Adamnan, who then sat in the seat of the Irish Apostles Patrick and Columba, and by Adamnan this narrative was presented and dedicated to Aldfrith the Wise, last of the great Northumbrian Kings, in his Court at York (c. A.D. 701). Not only does the original remain to us, but we have also two summaries of it, one longer, another shorter, made by Baeda, the Venerable Bede, as a useful manual for Englishmen, *Concerning the Holy Sites*. We are again reminded by this how constantly fresh life is growing up under an appearance of death. The conversion of England, which Gregory the Great, Theodore, and the Irish monks had carried through in the seventh, that darkest of Christian centuries, was now bearing its fruit in the work of Bede, who was really the sign of a far more permanent intellectual movement than his own, and in that of Boniface, Wilbrord, and Willibald, who began to win for Christendom in Germany more than a counterpoise for her losses in the South and East, from Armenia to Spain.

Arculf is full of the mystical unscientific spirit of the time. He notes in Jerusalem "a lofty column, which at mid-day casts no shadow, thus proving itself to be the centre of the earth for as David says, 'God is my king of old, working salvation *in the midst of the* earth.'"

"At the roots of Lebanon" he comes to the place "where the Jordan has its rise from two fountains Jor and Dan, whose waters unite in the single river Jordan." In the Dead Sea a lighted lamp would float safely, and no man could sink if he tried; the bitumen of this place was almost indissoluble; the only fruit here about were the apples of Sodom, which crumbled to dust in the mouth.

The three churches on the top of Tabor were "according to the three tabernacles described by Peter."

From Damascus Arculf made for the port of Tyre, and so came by Jaffa to Egypt. Alexandria he found so great that he was one entire day in merely passing through. Its port he thought "difficult of access and something like the human body in shape, with a narrow mouth and neck, then stretching out far and wide."

The great Pharos tower was still lit up every night with torches. Here was the "Emporium of the whole world"; "countless merchants from all parts": the "country rainless and very fertile."

The Nile was navigable to the Town of Elephants; beyond this, at the Cataracts, the river "runs in a wild ruin down a cliff." Its embankments, its canals, and even its crocodiles, "not so large as ravenous," are all described, and Arculf, returning home by Constantinople, concludes with an account of the capital of Christendom, "beyond doubt the metropolis of the Roman Empire, and by far the greatest city therein"; lastly, as the pilgrim sails by Sicily he sees the "isle of Vulcan vomiting smoke by day and flame by night, with a noise like thunder, which is always fiercer on Fridays and Saturdays."

Willibald, a nephew of St. Boniface and related through his mother to King Ina of Wessex, started for the East about 721, passed ten years in travel, and on his return followed his countrymen to mission work and to death among the heathen of Upper Germany. He went out by Southampton and Rouen, by Lucca and the Alps, to Naples and Catania, "where is Mount Etna; and when this volcano casts itself out they take St. Agatha's veil and hold it towards the fire, which ceases at once." Thence by Samos and Cyprus to Antaradus and Emesda, "in the region of the Saracens," where the whole party, who had escaped the Moslem brigands of Southern Gaul, were thrown into prison on suspicion of being spies. A Spaniard made intercession for them and got their release; but Willibald went up country one hundred miles, and cleared himself of all suspicion before the Caliph at Damascus. "We have come from the West, where the sun has his setting, and we know of no land beyond—nothing but water." This was too far for spies, he pleaded, and the Caliph agreed, and gave him a pass for all the sites of Palestine, with which he traversed the length and breadth of the Holy Land four times, finding the same trouble in leaving as he had found in entering. Like Arculf, he saw the fountains of Jor-Dan, the "glorious church" of Helena at Bethlehem, the tombs of the Patriarchs at Hebron, the wonders of Jerusalem. Especially was he moved at the sight of the columns in the Church of the Ascension on Olivet, "for that man who can creep between those columns and the wall is freed from all his sins." Tyre and Sidon he passed again and again "on the coast of the Adriatic Sea (as he calls the Levant), *six* miles from one another"; at last he got away to Constantinople, with some safely smuggled trophies of pilgrimage, and some "balsam in a calabash, covered with petroleum," but the customs officers would have killed all of them if the fraud had been found out—so Willibald believed. After two years of close intercourse with the Greek Christians of New Rome, living in a "cell hollowed out of the side of a church" (possibly Saint Sophia), the first of English-born travellers returned to Old Rome, as Arculf had done, by sea, noticing, like him, "Theodoric's Hell" in the Liparis. He could not get up the mountain, though curious to see "what sort of a hell it was" where the Gothic "Tyrant" was damned for the murder of Böethius and Symmachus, and for his own impenitent Arianism. But though he could not be seen or heard, all the pilgrims remarked how the "pumice that writers use was thrown up by the flame from the hell, and fell into the sea, and so was cast upon the shore and gathered up."

Such was the philosophy of Catholicism about the countries of the known world in the eighth century, for Willibald's account was published with the imprimatur of Gregory III., and, with Arculf's, took rank as a satisfactory comment on the old Bordeaux Itinerary of four hundred years ago.

Again, the impression given by our two chief Guide-Books, Arculf and Willibald, is confirmed by the monk Fidelis, who travelled in Egypt about 750, and by Bernard the Wise of Mont St. Michel, who went over all the pilgrim ground a century later (867). Fidelis, sailing up the Nile, was astonished at the sight of the "Seven Barns of Joseph, (the Pyramids) looking like mountains, but all of stone, square at the base, rounded in the upper part and twisted at the summit like a spire. On measuring a side of one of them, it was found to be four hundred feet." From the Nile Fidelis sailed by the freshwater canal of Necho, Hadrian, and Amrou, not finally blocked up till 767, direct to the Red Sea, "near where Moses crossed with the Israelites." The pilgrim wanted to go and look for Pharaoh's chariot-wheels, but the sailors were obstinate, and took him round the Peninsula of Sinai, down one arm of the sea and up another, to Eziongeber and Edom.

Bernard, "the French Monk" of Mont St. Michel, took the straight route overland by Rome to Bari, then a Saracen city, whose Emir forwarded the pilgrims in a fleet of transports carrying some nine thousand Christian slaves to Alexandria. Here, like Willibald, Bernard found himself "suspect"—thrown into prison till Backsheesh had been paid, then only allowed to move stage by stage as fees were prompt and sufficient, for a traveller must pay, as an infidel, not only the ordinary tribute of the subject Christians of Egypt, but the "money of the road" as well. Islam has always made of strangers a fair mark for extortion.

Safe at last in Jerusalem, the party (Bernard himself and two friends, one a Spaniard, the other a monk of Beneventum) were lodged "in the Hostel of the glorious Emperor Charles, founded for all the pilgrims who speak the

Roman tongue," and after making the ordinary visits of devotion, and giving us their account of the Easter Miracle of the Holy Fire at the Church of the Sepulchre, they took ship for Italy, and landed at Rome after sixty days of misery at sea.

Bernard's account closes with the Roman churches—the Lateran, where the "keys of the whole city are given every night into the hands of the Apostolic Pope," and St. Peter's on the "West side of Rome, that for size has no rival in the world."

At the same time, or a little earlier than the Breton traveller (c. 808-850), another Latin had written a short tract *On the Houses of God in Jerusalem*, which, with Bernard's note-book, is our last geographical record before the age of the Northmen.

A new time was coming—a time not of timid creeping pilgrims only, but of sea-kings and seamen, who made the ocean their home, and, for the North of Europe at least, broke the tradition of land journeys and coasting voyages.

But the early pilgrims after all have their place. It is of no use insisting that the mental outlook of these men is infantile;—that is best proved by their own words, their own scale of things; but it is necessary to insist that in these travellers we have comparatively enlarged experience and knowledge; and as comparison is the only test of any age, or of any man therein, the very blunders and limitations of the past, as we see them to be, have a constant, as well as an historical, value to us. That is, we are always being reminded, first, how we have come to the present mastery over nature, over ourselves, over all being; and, secondly, how imperfect, how futile, our work is still, and seems always doomed to be, if judged from a really final standpoint, or rather from our own dreams of the ultimately possible.

So if in the case of our mediæval travellers their interests are the very reverse of ours; if they take delight in brooding over thoughts which to us do not seem worth the thinking; if their minds seem to rest as much on fable implicitly accepted as on the little amount of experienced fact necessary for a working life, it will not be for us to judge, or to pity, or to despise the men who were making our world for us, and through whose work we live.

THE MAPPE-MONDE OF ST. SEVER.
(SEE LIST OF MAPS)

Especially we cannot afford to forget this as we reach the lowest point of the fortunes, the mental and material work and position and outlook, of Europe and Christendom. A half-barbarised world had entered upon the inheritance of a splendid past, but it took centuries before that inheritance was realised by the so altered present. In this time of change we have men writing in the language of Cæsar and Augustine, of Alexander and Plato and Aristotle, who had been themselves, or whose fathers had been, pirates, brigands, nomades,—"wolves of the land or of the sea"—to Greeks or Romans of the South; who had been even to the Romanised provincials of the North, as in Britain, mere "dogs," "whelps from the kennel of barbarism," the destroyers of the order of the world. The boundless credulity and servile terror, the superstition and feudal tyranny of the earlier Middle Ages, mark the first stage of the reconstruction of society, when savage strong men who had conquered were set down beside the overworked and outworn masters of the Western world, to learn of them, and to make of them a more enduring race.

CHAPTER II.

VIKINGS OR NORTHMEN.

CIRCA 787-1066.

The discoveries and conquests and colonies of the Norse Vikings, from the White Sea to North America, are the first glimpses of light on the sea of darkness round the little island of the known world that made up Christendom. And from the needs of the time these were the natural, the only natural beginnings of European expansion. From the rise of Islam, Saracens controlled the great trade-routes of the South and East. It was only on the West and North that the coast was clear—of all but natural dangers.

In the Moslem Caliphate men were now busy in following up the old lines of trade, the immemorial traditions of the East, or as in southern Africa, extending the sphere of commercial activity and so of civilisation; men of science were commenting on the ancient texts of Greeks and Latins, or adapting them to enlarged knowledge.

But in Christendom, in the atrophy both of mental and physical activity, broken for short periods and in certain lands by the revivals of Charles the Great, of the Isaurian Emperors, of Otto I., of Alfred and his House, the practical energy of Heathen enemies,—for the Northmen were not seriously touched by Christianity till about the end of the first millennium,—was the first sign of lasting resurrection. After the material came the spiritual revival; the whole life of the Middle Ages awoke on the conversion of the Northern nations and of Hungary; but in the abundant and brilliant energy of the eleventh, the twelfth, the thirteenth centuries, we must recognise the offspring of the irrepressible Norsemen as well as of the Irish and Frank and English missionaries, who in the Dark Ages of Christendom were working out the empire of Innocent III.

In exploration, especially, it was true that theory followed achievement. Flavio Gioja, of Amalphi, did not apply the magnet to navigation—did not "give sailors the use of the magnet"—till navigation itself had begun to venture into the unknown Atlantic. The history of geographical advance in the earlier Middle Ages is thus rather a chronicle of adventure than of science.

But the Norse discoveries are not only the first, they are the leading achievements of Western travel and enterprise in the true Unknown, between the time of Constantine and the Crusades. The central fact of

European expansion in the Dark Ages (from the seventh to the eleventh century) is the advance of the Vikings to the Arctic Continent and to America about the year 1000. All that precedes this on the same line is doubtful and unimportant. For, of the other voyages to the West in the sixth, the eighth, the tenth centuries, which, on Columbus' success, turned into prior claims to the finding of the New World, there is not one that deserves notice.

St. Brandon in 565, the Seven Spanish Bishops in 734, the Basques in 990 may or may not have sighted their islands of "Antillia," of "Atlantis," of the "Seven Cities." They cannot be verified or valued, any more than the journeys of the Enchanted Horse or the Third Calendar. We only know for certain a few unimportant, half-accidental facts, such as the visits of Irish hermits to Iceland and the Färoes during the eighth century, and the traces of their cells and chapels—in bells and ruins and crosses—found by the Northmen in the ninth.

It was in 787 that the Vikings first landed in England; by the opening of the next century they were threatening the whole coast line of Christendom, from Gallicia to the Elbe; in 874 they began to colonise Iceland; in 877 they sighted Greenland; in 922 Rolf the Ganger won his "Normandy" from Charles the Simple, by the Treaty of Clair-sur-Epte; as early as 840 was founded the first Norse or Ostman kingdom in Ireland, and in 878 the Norse earldom of the Orkneys, while about the same time the first Vikings seem to have reached the White Sea and the extreme North of Europe.

This advance is almost as rapid as that of the early Saracens; within a hundred years from the first disturbance of Danes and Northmen by the growing, all-including power of the new national kingdoms,—within three generations from Halfdan the Black,—first the flying rebels, and then the royalists in pursuit of them, had reached the farthest western and northern limits of the known world, from Finisterre in "Spanland" to Cape Farewell in Greenland, from the North Cape in Finland to the Northwest Capes of "Irland," from Novgorod or "Holmgard" in Russia to "Valland," between the Garonne and the Loire.

The chief lines of Northern advance were three—by the north-west, south-west, and north-east, but each of these divided, after a time, with important results.

The first sea-path, running by Caithness, Orkneys, Shetlands, and Färoes, reached Iceland, Greenland, and at last Vinland on the North American Continent; but from the settlements on the coasts and islands of northern Scotland, a fresh wave of pirate colonists swept down south-west into the narrow seas of St. George's Channel and beat upon the east and north and south of Ireland and the western coasts of England and of "Bretland."

The second invasion ran along the North German coast, and on reaching the Straits of Dover, fell upon both sides of the English Channel, according as the resistance was stronger or weaker in Wessex or in Frankland. The advanced guard reunited with Ostmen and Orkneyers in the Scilly Isles, and in Cornwall, and pressed on to the plunder of the Bay of Biscay and its coasts. The most restless of all were not long in finding out the wealth of the Moslem Caliphate of Cordova, and trying to force their way up the Douro and the Tagus.

The expansion on this side was not to stop till it had founded, from the Norman colony on the Seine, a Norman kingdom of England, and a dominion in the Two Sicilies, but this was the work of the eleventh century, the time of organisation and settled empire.

On the third side of northern expansion, to east and north-east, there were two separate roads from the first; one taking the Baltic for its track, and dividing northwards to Finland, up the Gulf of Bothnia, eastwards to Russia and Novgorod ("Gardariki" and "Holmgard"), the other coasting along "Halogaland" to Biarmaland, along Lapland to Perm and the Archangel of later time.

Of these three lines of movement by far the most vital to our subject is the first, which is also the earliest; the second, to south and south-west, hardly gives any direct results for our story; and the third, to east and north, is mainly concerned with Russian history. While King Alfred was yet unborn, Norse settlements had been permanently founded in the outlying points, coasts, and islands of Scotland and Ireland, and in the years of his boyhood, about 860, Nadodd the Fäeroe Jarl sighted Iceland, which had been touched at by the Irish monks in 795 but was now to be first added as a lasting gain to Europe, as a new country, "Snowland"—something more than a hermitage for religious exiles from the world. Four years later (in 864) Gardar the Swede reached this new Ultima Thule, and re-named it from himself "Gardar's Holm." Yet another Viking, Raven Floke, followed the track of the first explorer in 867, before Iceland got its final name and earliest colonisation from the Norsemen Ingolf and Leif and the sheep-farmers of the Färoes in 874, the third year of Alfred's reign in Wessex.

THE ANGLO-SAXON MAP.
(SEE LIST OF MAPS)

Three years later, 877-8, at the very time of the farthest Danish advance in England, when Guthrum had driven the English King into the Isle of Athelney, the Norsemen reached their farthest point of northern advance in Europe; Gunnbiorn sighted a new land to the north-west, which he called "White Shirt," from its snow-fields, and which Red Eric a century later re-named Greenland—"for there is nothing like a good name to attract settlers." By this the Old World had come nearer than ever before to the discovery of a new one.

Geographically, this side of the Arctic Continent falls to the share of North America, and once its fiords had been made in their turn centres of colonisation and of further progress, the actual reaching of Newfoundland and Cape Cod was natural enough. The real voyage lay between Cape Farewell and the European mainland; it was a stormy and dangerous passage from the Greenland Bays to Labrador, but not a long one, and, as far as can be judged from scanty records, neither so cold nor so icebound as at present.

But exploration had outrun settlement. It was not till 986, more than one hundred years after Gunnbiorn's discovery, that Eric the Red, one of the chiefs of the Iceland colonists, led a band of followers and friends into a permanent exile in the unknown land. The beginnings of several villages were made in the next few years, and the first American discoveries followed at once. About 989 one Bjarni Herjulfson, following his father from Iceland to Eric's Fiord in Greenland, was driven west by storms first to a flat, well-wooded country, then to a mountainous island, covered with glaciers. He bore away with a fresh breeze and reached his home in Eric's Fiord in four days.

But his report aroused great interest; the time had come, and the men, and Norse rovers, who after so much in the past were ready to dare anything in the future, eagerly volunteered to follow up the new route; Bjarni himself visiting Norway and telling his story, was blamed for his slackness, and when he went back to Greenland there was "much talk of finding unknown lands." In the year 1000 Leif, a son of Red Eric, started with a definite purpose of discovery. He bought Bjarni's ship, manned it with five and twenty men and put out. First they came to the land Bjarni had sighted last, and went on shore. There was no grass to be seen, but great snowy ridges far inland, "and all the way from the coast to these mountains was one field of snow, and it seemed to them a land of no profit,"—so they left, calling it Helluland, or Slate-land, perhaps the Labrador of the sixteenth century.

They put to sea again and found another land, flat and wooded, with a white sand shore, low-lying towards the sea. This, said Leif, we will call after its nature, Markland (Woodland). Thence driving for two days before a north-east wind, they came to an island, where they landed to wait for good weather. They tasted the dew on the grass and thought they had never known anything so sweet. Sailing on again into a sound between the island and a ness, they reached a place where a river came out of a lake; into this they towed the ship and anchored, carrying their beds out on the shore and setting up their tents, with a large hut in the middle, and made all ready for wintering there.

There was no want of fish food—"the largest salmon in the lake they had ever seen"—and the country seemed to them so good that they would need no fodder for cattle in the winter. There was no frost; the grass seemed fresh enough all the year round, and day and night were more equal than in Iceland or in Greenland. The crew were divided in two parts: one worked at the huts and the other explored the country, returning every night to the camp. From the wild vines found by the foragers, the whole district was called Vinland, and samples of these, enough to fill the stern boat, and of the trees and "self-sown wheat" found in the fields were taken back to Eric's Fiord. Thereafter Leif was called the Lucky, and got much wealth and fame, but Thorwald Ericson, his brother, thought he had not explored enough, and "determined to be talked about" even more than the first settler of Vinland.

He put to sea with thirty men and came straight to Leif's Booths in Vinland, where he stayed the winter. On the first signs of spring Thorwald ordered his vessel to be rigged, and sent his longboat on ahead to explore.

All alike thought the land beautiful and well-wooded; they noticed that the distance was small between the forest and the sea, that the beach was all of white sand, and that there were many islands off the shore and very shallow water; but they saw no trace of man or beast, except a wooden corn-barn on an island far to the west. After coasting all the summer they came back in the autumn to the booths.

The next spring Thorwald went eastwards, and "towards the north along the land they drove upon a cape and broke their keel and stayed long to repair, and called the place Keel-Ness (Kjalarness) from this." Then they sailed away eastwards along the country, everywhere thickly wooded, till at one place Thorwald drew up his ships to the land and laid out gangways to the shore, saying, "I would gladly set up my farm here."

But now they came upon the first traces of other men; far off upon the white sandy beach three specks were sighted—three skin boats of the Skrælings or Esquimaux, with three men hiding under each. Thorwald's men captured and killed eight of them, but one escaped "to where within the fiord were several dwellings like little lumps on the ground." A heavy drowsiness now fell upon the Norsemen, in the Saga, till a "sudden scream came to them, and a countless host from up the fiord came in skin boats and laid themselves alongside."

The Vikings put up their shield-wall along the gunwale and kept off the arrows of the Esquimaux till they had shot them all away, and "fled off as fast as they could," leaving Thorwald with a mortal wound under the arm. He had time just to bid his men "carry him to the point he had wished to dwell at, for it was true that he would stay there awhile, but with a cross at head and feet; and so died and was buried as he had said." The place was called Crossness from the dead chief, but the crew stayed all the winter and loaded the ship with vines and grapes, and in the spring came back to Eric in Greenland.

And now, after the first mishap, discovery became more serious—not to be undertaken but by strong and well-armed fleets. It was this that checked the expansion of these Arctic colonies; at their best they were too small to do more than hold their own against nature and the Skræling savages in their tiny settlements along the coast, where the ice-fields have long since pushed man slowly but surely into the sea, with his painfully won patches of hay and corn and pasturage.

But the colonists would never say die till they were utterly worn out; now they only roused themselves to conquer the new lands they had found, and found disputed.

First a third son of Red Eric, Thorstein, bethought him to go to Vinland for his brother Thorwald's body. He put to sea and lost all sight of land, beating about in the ocean the whole summer, till he came back to Greenland in the first week of winter. (1004-6.)

He was followed by the greatest of the Vinland sailors, Thorfinn Karlsefne, who really took in hand the founding of a new settlement over the Western Sea. He came from Norway to Iceland soon after Thorwald's death in 1004, passed on to Greenland about 1005, "when, as before, much was talked about a Vinland voyage," and in 1006 made ready to start with one hundred and sixty men and five women, in three ships. They had with them all kinds of cattle, meaning to settle in the land if they could, and they made an agreement, Karlsefne and his people, that each should have an equal share in the gain. Leif lent them his houses in Vinland, "for he would not give them outright," and they sailed first to Helluland (Labrador), where they found a quantity of foxes, then to Markland, well-stocked with forest animals, then to an island at the mouth of a fiord, unknown before, covered with eyder ducks. They called the new discoveries Stream Island and Stream Fiord, from the current that here ran out into the sea, and sent off a party of eight men, in search of Vinland, in a stern boat. This was driven by westerly gales back to Iceland, but Thorfinn, with the rest, sailed south till he came to Leif Ericson's "river that fell into the sea from a lake, with islands lying off the mouth of the stream, low grounds covered with wheat growing wild, and rising grounds clad with vines."

Here they settled, re-named the country "Hope, from the good hope they had of it," and began to fell the wood, to pasture their cattle in the upland, and to gather the grapes.

After the first winter the Skrælings came upon them, at first to traffic with furs and sables against milk and dairy produce, and then to fight; for as neither understood the other, and the natives tried to force their way into Thorfinn's houses, and to get hold of his men's weapons, a quarrel was bound to come.

Fearing this, Karlsefne put a fence round the settlement and made all ready for battle, "and at this very time was a child born to him in the village, called Snorre, of Gudrid his wife, the widow of Thorstein Eric-son, whom he had brought with him." Then the Esquimaux came down upon them, "many more than before, and there was a battle, and Thorfinn's men won the day and saved the cattle," and their enemies fled into the forest.

Thorfinn stayed all the winter, but towards spring he grew tired of his enterprise, and returned to Greenland, "taking much goods," vines, wood for timber, and skin-wares, and so came back to Eric's Fiord in the summer of 1008.

Thus ends the story of the last serious effort to colonise Vinland, and the Saga, while giving no definite cause for this failure upon failure, seems to show that even the trifling annoyance of the Skrælings was enough to turn the scale. Natural difficulties were so immense, men were so few, that a pigmy enemy had all the power of the last straw in a load, the odd man in a council. The actual resistance of American natives to European colonists was never very serious in any part of the continent, but the distance from the starting-point and the difficulties of life in the new country were able, even in the time of Raleigh and De Soto, to keep in check men who far more readily founded and kept up European empires in the Indian seas.

So now, though on Thorfinn's return the "talk began to turn again upon a Vinland voyage, as both gainful and honourable," and a daughter of Red Eric, named Freydis, talked men over—especially two brothers, Helge and Finnboge—to a fresh attempt in the country where all the House of Eric had tried and failed; though Leif lent his booths as before, and sixty able-bodied men, besides women, were found willing to go, the colony could never be firmly planted. Freydis and her allies sailed in 1011, reached the settlement, which was now for the third time recolonised, and wintered there;—but jealousies soon broke up the camp, Helge and Finnboge were murdered with all their followers, and the rest came back in 1013 to Greenland, "where Thorfinn Karlsefne was just ready for sailing back to Norway, and it was common talk that never did a richer ship leave Eric's Fiord than that which he steered." It was that same Karlsefne who gave the fullest account of all his travels, concludes the Saga, but whether Thorfinn ever returned to Vinland, whether there were any more attempts to settle at Leif's Booths or elsewhere, whether the account we have of these voyages is really an Eric Saga, only telling the deeds of Red Eric and his House—for after Bjarni, almost every Vinland leader is of this family—we cannot tell. We can only fancy that all these suggestions are probable, by the side of the few additional facts known to the Norse Skalds or Bards. The first of these is, that in 983-4, Are Marson of Reykianes in Iceland was driven by storms far West to White Man's Land, where he was followed by Bjarni

Asbrandson in 999, and by Gudleif Gudlangson in 1029. This was the tale of his friend Rafn, "the Limerick trader," and of Are Frode, his great-great-grandson, who called the unknown land Great Ireland.[17] True or untrue, in whatever way, this would be a later discovery than those of Eric and his sons, if the news of it did not come into Iceland or Norway till after Thorfinn Karlsefne's voyage, as is generally supposed. Again, the length of the voyage is a difficulty, and the whole matter has a doubtful look—an attempt to start a rival to the Eric Saga, by a far more brilliant success a few years earlier.

We seem to be on more certain ground in our next and last chapter of Viking exploration in the north-west, in the fragmentary notices of Greenland and Vinland voyages to the middle of the fourteenth century, and in the fairly clear and continuous account of the two Greenland settlements of the western and the eastern Bays.

We hear, for instance, of Bishop Eric going over from Eric's Fiord to Vinland in 1121; of clergy from the Eastern Bay diocese of Gardar sailing to lands in the West, far north of Vinland, in 1266; of the two Helgasons discovering a country west of Iceland in 1285; of a voyage from Greenland to Markland in 1347 by a crew of seventeen men, recorded in 1354.

Unless these are pure fabrications, they would seem to prove something of constant intercourse between the mother and daughter colonies of north-west Europe and north-east America, and something of a permanent Christian settlement of Northmen in the New Continent is made probable by assuming such intercourse. Between 981-1000, both Iceland and Greenland had become "Catholic in name and Christian in surname"; in 1126 the line of Bishops of Gardar begins with Arnold, and the clergy would hardly have ventured on the Vinland voyage to convert Skrælings in an almost deserted country.

The later story of the Greenland colonies, interesting as it is, and traceable to the year 1418, is not part of the expansion but of the contraction of Europe and Christendom. And the voyages of the Zeni in 1380-95 to Greenland and the Western islands Estotiland and Drogeo, belong to another part; they are the last achievements of mediæval discovery before Henry of Portugal begins his work, and form the natural end of an introduction to that work.

But it is curious to notice that just as the ice and the Esquimaux between them were bringing to an end the last traces of Norse settlement in the Arctic Continent, and just as all intercourse between Vinland, Greenland, Iceland, and Norway entirely ceases—at any rate to record itself—the Portuguese sailors, taking up the work of Eric and Leif and Thorfinn, on another side, were rounding Cape Verde and nearing the southern point of

Africa, and so providing for the mind of Columbus suggestions which resulted in the lasting discovery of the world that the Vikings had sighted and colonised, but were not able to hold.

The Venetian, Welsh, and Arabic claims to have followed the Norsemen in visits to America earlier than the voyage of 1492, belong rather to the minute history of geographical controversy. It is a fairly certain fact that the north-west line of Scandinavian migration reached about A.D. 1000 to Cape Cod and the coasts of Labrador. It is equally certain that on this side the Norsemen never made any further advance, lasting or recorded. Against all other mediæval discoveries of a Western Continent, one only verdict can stand:—Not Proven.

The other lines of Northern advance, though marked by equal daring and far greater military exploits, have less of original discovery. There was fighting in plenty, the giving and taking of hard knocks with every nation from Archangel to Cordova and from Limerick to Constantinople; and the Vikings, as they reached fresh ground, re-named most of the capes and coasts, the rivers and islands and countries of Europe, of North Africa, of Western Asia. Iberia became "Spanland"; Gallicia, "Jacobsland"[18]; Gallia, "Frankland"; Britannia, "England," "Scotland," "Bretland"; Hibernia, "Irland"; Islam, outside "Spanland," passed into "Serkland" or Saracenland. Greece was "Grikland"; Russia, "Gardariki"; the Pillars of Hercules, the Straits of Gibraltar, were "Norva's Sound," which later days derived from the first Northman who passed through them. The city of Constantine was the Great Town—"Miklagard"; Novgorod was "Holmgard," the town of all others that most touched and influenced the earlier, the Viking age, of Northern expansion. For was it not their own proudest and strongest city-state, and "Who can stand before God, or the Great Novgorod?" except the men who had built it, and would rush to sack it if it turned against them?

But all this was only the passing of a more active race over ground which had once been well known to Rome and to Christendom, even if much of this was now being forgotten. It was only in upland Russia and in the farthest North that the Norsemen sensibly enlarged the Western world to east or north-east, as they did through their Iceland settlements on the north-west.

On the south and south-west no Vikings or Royalist followers of Vikings, like Sigurd the Crusader, sailed the seas beyond Norva's Sound and Serkland,[19] and as pilgrims, traders, travellers, and conquerors in the Mediterranean, their work was of course not one of exploration. They bore a foremost share in breaking down the Moslem incubus on southern Europe; they visited the Holy sites

"When sacred Hierosolyma they'd relievèdAnd fed their eyes on Jordan's holy floodWhich the dear body of Lord God had lavèd";[20]

they fought as Varangian body-guards in the armies of the great Byzantines, Nikephoros Phokas, John Tzimiskes, Basil II. or Maniakes; but in all this they discovered for themselves rather than for Europe.

But Russia, that is, Old Russia round Novgorod and Kiev, the White Sea, the North Cape and Finland coasts, as well as the more outlying parts of Scotland and Ireland, were first clearly known to Europe through the Northmen. The same race did much to open up the modern Lithuania and Prussia, and the conversion of the whole of Scandinavia, mother country and colonies alike, in the tenth and eleventh centuries added our Norway, Sweden, and Denmark, with all the Viking settlements, to the civilised world and church of Rome.

First, on the eastern side, it was in 862 that the Russians invited help from their less dreaded neighbours around Upsala against their more vexatious neighbours around Kiev, and in September of the same year Ruric arrived at Novgorod and founded the Mediæval Kingdom of Russia, which in the tenth century under Oleg, Igor, and Vladimir was first the plunderer, then the open enemy, and finally the ally in faith and in arms of the Byzantine Empire.

All through this time and afterwards, till the time of the Tartar deluge, the intercourse of Swedes, Danes, and Northmen with Gardariki was constant and close, and not least in the time of the Vinland voyages, when Vladimir and Jaroslav reigned at Novgorod, and the two Olafs, the son of Trygve and the Saint, found refuge at their court before and after their hard rule in Norway.

Olaf Trygveson's uncle had grown old in exile at Novgorod when young Olaf and his mother fled from Norway to join him there and were captured by Vikings in the Baltic and kept six years in the Gulf of Riga before they got to Holmgard (972).

In 1019 Ingigerd of Sweden was married to Jaroslav; ten years later St. Olaf was driven from Norway by revolt, and flying into Russia, was offered a Kingdom called Volgaria—the modern Casan, whose old metropolis of Vulghar was known to the Arab travellers of the ninth century, and whose ruins can still be seen. Olaf hesitated between this and a pilgrim's death in Jerusalem and at last preferred to fight his way back to Norway.

The next King of the Norsemen, Magnus the Good, came from Novgorod by Ladoga to Trondhjem, when Olaf's son Harold Hardrada fled back to his father's refuge, to the court of Jaroslav; while Magnus had been in exile, men had asked news of him from all the merchants that traded to Novgorod.

Last of these earlier kings, Harold Hardrada, during all the time of his wild romance in East and South, before he went to Miklagard, and after his flight, and all the time of his service in the Varangian Guard of the Empress Zoe, made Novgorod his home. His pilgrim relics from Holy Land and his war spoils from Serkland—Africa and Sicily—were all sent back to Jaroslav's care till their master could come and claim them, and when he came at last, flying from Byzantine vengeance across the Black Sea into the Sea of Azov and "all round the Eastern Realm" of Kiev, he found his wealth untouched and Princess Elizabeth ready to be his wife and to help him with Russian men and money to win back Norway and to die at Stamford Bridge for the Crown of England (1066).

Harold is the type of all Vikings, of the Norse race in its greatest, most restless energy. William the Conqueror, or Cnut the Great, or Robert Guiscard, or Roger of Sicily, are all greater and stronger men, but there is no "ganger," no rover, like the man who in fifty years, after fighting in well-nigh every land of Christians or of the neighbours and enemies of Christendom, yet hoped for time to sail off to the new-found countries and so fulfil his oath and promise to perfect a life of unmatched adventure by unmatched discovery. He had fought with wild beasts in the Arena of Constantinople; he had bathed in the Jordan and cleared the Syrian roads of robbers; he had stormed eighty castles in Africa; he had succoured the Icelanders in famine and lived as a prince in Russia and Northumberland; by his own songs he boasts that he had sailed all round Europe; but he fell, the prototype of sea-kings like Drake or Magellan, without one discovery. Men of his own nation and time had been before him everywhere, but he united in himself the work and adventures, the conquests and discoveries of many. He was the incarnation of Northern spirit, and it was through the lives and records of such as he that Europe became filled with that new energy of thought and action, that new life and knowledge, which was the ground and impulse of the movement led by Henry the Navigator, by Columbus, and the Cabots.

Harold's wars kept him from becoming a great explorer, but Norse captains who took service under peaceful kings did something of what he aimed at doing.

We must retrace our steps to the voyages of Ohthere and Wulfstan under King Alfred about the year 890, about the time when a Norse King, Harold Fair-hair, was first seen in the Scotch and Irish seas. Their discovery of the White Sea, the North Cape, and the gulfs of Bothnia and Finland was followed up by many Norsemen, such as Thorer Hund under St. Olaf, in the next one hundred and fifty years,[21] but Ohthere's voyage was the first and chief of these adventures both in motive and result.

"He told his lord King Alfred that he dwelt northmost of all Northmen on the land by the Western Sea and he wished to find how far the land lay right north, or whether any man dwelt north of the waste. So he went right north near the land;—for three days he left the waste land on the right and the wide sea on the left, as far as the whale hunters ever go"; and still he kept north three days more (to the North Cape of Europe).

"Then the land bent right east, and with a west wind he sailed four days till the land bent south, and he sailed by it five days more to a great river—the Dwina—that lay up into the land, and where beyond the river it was all inhabited"—the modern country of Perm and Archangel.

Here he trafficked with the people, the first he had met, except the Finn hunters, since leaving his fiord. Besides his wish to see the country, he was looking for walrus-ivory and hides.

The Finns and Biarma-men (men of Archangel), it seemed to him, spoke nearly the same language, but between his home and this Biarmaland no human being lived in any fixed dwelling, and all the Northman's land was long and narrow and thinly peopled, decreasing in breadth as it stretched northward, from sixty to three days' journey.

Again Alfred told how Ohthere, sailing south for a month from his house, having *Ireland* on his right and coasting Norway all the time on his left, came to Jutland, "where a great sea runs up into the land, so vast that no man can see across it," whence in five days more he reached the coast, "from which the English came to Britain."

Wulfstan, in the service of the same king, told him how he sailed in seven days from Sleswick to Truso and the Vistula, having Wendland (or Pomerania and Prussia) on his right all the way. He described "Witland near the Vistula and Estland and Wendland and Estmere and the Ilfing running from the Truso lake into Eastmere," but neither the king nor his captains knew enough to contradict the old idea, found in Ptolemy and Strabo, of Scandinavia as one vast island.

Thus it was for the satisfaction of their Saxon Lord that Wulfstan and Ohthere, by their voyages along the coasts of Norway and Lapland, of Pomerania and Prussia, round the White Sea and the Gulf of Riga and southern Finland, added a more coherent view of north-east Europe, and specially of the Baltic Gulf, to Western geography; but these Norse discoveries, though in the service of an English king, were scarcely used save by Norsemen, and they must partly go to the credit of Vikings, as well as of Alfred the Great. Thus in 965 King Harold Grayskin of Norway "went and fought with the folk on the banks of the Dwina," and plundered them, and in 1026 Thorer Hund joined himself to a fleet sent by St. Olaf to the White Sea, pillaged the temple of the idol Jomala, and destroyed his countrymen by treachery on their way home. Where two expeditions are recorded they may well stand for twenty unknown and uneventful ones, and the same must be equally granted as to the gradual advance of knowledge through the unceasing attacks of the Norse kings and pirates on the lands to the south of the Baltic, where lived the Wends.

Thus on the west and east, north-west and north-east, the Northmen could and did make a definite advance into the unknown; even the south-west lines of Northern invasion and settlement, though they hardly yield any general results to discovery, certainly led to a more thorough inclusion of every part of the British isles in the civilised West, through the Viking earldoms in Caithness, in the Orkneys and the Shetlands, in Man and the Hebrides, and on the coast of Ireland, where the Ostman colonies grew into kingdoms. From about 840, when the first of these settlements was fairly and permanently started, to the eleventh century, when a series of great defeats,—by Brian Boru at Clontarf in 1014, by Godwine and Harold in England from 1042 to 1066, and by the Norman and Scottish kings in the next generation,—practically destroyed the Norse dominion outside the Orkneys,—for those two hundred years, Danes and Northmen not only pillaged and colonised, but ruled and reorganised a good half of the British isles.

By the time of Alfred the Viking principalities were scattered up and down the northern and western coasts of the greater of our two islands, and were fringing three sides of the lesser. About A.D. 900 the pioneer of the Norse kings, Harold Fair-hair, pursued his traitors, first to Shetlands and Orkneys, then to Caithness, the Hebrides, and Man. His son Eric, who followed him, ranged the Northern seas from Archangel to Bordeaux, and so Hakon the Good in 936 and other Norse princes in 946, 961, 965, above all, the two great Kings Olaf in 985-9 and 1009-14, fought and triumphed through most of the world as known to the Northmen. Thus, Frankland, England, Ireland, Scotland were brought into a closer unity through the common danger, while as the sea-kings founded settled states, and these grew by alliance, first with one another and then with their older Christian victims, as the Norse kingdoms themselves became parts of Latin Christendom, after Latin Christendom had itself been revived and re-awakened by their attacks, the full value of the time of trial came out on both sides, to conquered and to conquerors.

For the effects—formative, invigorative, provocative,—of the Northern invasions had a most direct bearing on the expansion that was to come in the next age even for those staid and sober Western countries, England and

France and Italy, which had long passed through their time of migration, and where the Vikings could not, as in the far north-east and north-west, extend the area of civilisation or geographical knowledge.

Lastly, the new start made by England in exploration, and trade, and even in pilgrimage, is plainly the result—in action and reaction—of the Norse and Danish attacks, waking up the old spirit of a kindred race, of elder cousins that had sunk into lethargy and forgotten their seamanship.

But from the Peace of Wedmore (878) Alfred first of all began to build an English navy able to meet and chase and run down the Viking keels; then established a yearly pilgrimage and alms-giving at the Threshold of the Apostles in Rome; then sent out various captains in his service to explore as much of the world as was practicable for his new description of Europe. His crowning effort in religious extension was in 883, when Sigehelm and Athelstan bore Alfred's gifts and letters to Jerusalem and to India, to the Christians of San Thomé; the corresponding triumph of the King's scientific exploration, the discoveries in the White Sea and the Baltic, seem to have happened nearer the end of the reign, somewhere before 895.

CHAPTER III.

THE CRUSADES AND LAND TRAVEL.
CIRCA 1100-1300.

The pilgrims were the pioneers of the growth of Europe and of Christendom until Charlemagne, in one sense, in another and a broader sense until the Crusades.

Their original work, as far as it can be called original at all, was entirely overshadowed by the Vikings, who made real discoveries of the first importance in hunting for new worlds to conquer; but when first the Viking rovers themselves, and then the Northmen, settled in the colonies and the old home, took up Christianity as the Arabs had taken up Islam, the pilgrim spirit was translated, as it were, into new and more powerful forms. Through the conversion of Hungary and of Scandinavia,[22]— Europe, Christian Europe, was compacted together in a stronger Empire than that of Constantine or of Charlemagne—a spiritual federation, not a political unity—one and undivided not in visible subordination, but in a common zeal for a common faith. This was the state of the Latin world, and in a measure of the Greek and Russian world as well, by the middle of the eleventh century, when the Byzantine Emperors had broken the strength of the Eastern Caliphate, and recovered most of the realm of Heraclius; when the Roman Papacy under Leo IX., Hildebrand, and Urban began its political stage, aiming, and in great part successfully aiming, at an Imperial Federation of Europe under religion; when on every side, in Spain, in France, in England, in Germany, and in Italy, the nations that had been slowly built into that *Domus Dei* were filled with fresh life and purpose from the Norsemen, who, as pirates, or conquerors, or brothers, had settled among them. The long crusade that had gone on for four hundred years in Spain and in southern Italy and in the Levant, which had raged round the islands of the Mediterranean, or the passes of the Alps and Pyrenees, or the banks of the Loire and the Tiber,—was now, on the eve of the first Syrian Crusade of 1096, rapidly tending to decisive victory. Toledo was won back in 1084; the Norman dominion in the Two Sicilies had already taken the place of a weak and halting Christian defence against Arab emirs; pilgrims were going in thousands where there had been tens or units by the reopened land route through Hungary; only in the far East the first appearance of the Turks as Moslem champions,[23] threatened an ebb of the tide. Christendom had seen a wonderful expansion of the Heathen North; now that it had won the Northmen to itself, it was ready to imitate their example. The deliberate purpose of the Popes only gave direction to the universal feeling of restless and abundant energy longing for wider action. But it was not the crusading movement itself which brought so much new light, so much new knowledge of the world, to Europe, as the *results* of that impulse in trade, in travel, and in colonisation.

THE TURIN MAP OF THE ELEVENTH CENTURY.
(SEE LIST OF MAPS)

(1) From the eleventh century, from the beginning of this period, all the greater pilgrims, Sæwulf the English-merchant, King Sigurd of Norway, Abbot Daniel of Kiev, and their followers, have something more in view than piety; they have a general interest in travel; some of them a special interest in trade; most of them go to fight as well as to pray.

(2) But as the warlike spirit of the Church Militant seems to grow tired, and its efforts at founding new kingdoms—in Antioch, in Jerusalem, in Cyprus, in Byzantium—more and more fruitless, the direct expansion of European knowledge, begins in scientific travel. Vinland and Greenland and the White Sea and the other Norse discoveries were discoveries made by a great race for itself; unconnected as they were with the main lines of trade or with religious sentiment, they were unrealised by the general consciousness of the West. A full account of the Norse voyages to America was lying at the Vatican when Columbus was searching for proofs of land within reach,—of India, as he expected, in the place where he found an unknown continent and a new world. But no one knew of these; even the Greenland colony had been lost and forgotten in the fifteenth century; in 1553 the English sailors reached the land of Archangel without a suspicion that Ohthere or Thorer Hund had been there six hundred years before; Russia from the thirteenth to the sixteenth centuries was almost out of sight and mind under the Tartar and Moslem rule; but the missionaries and merchants and travellers who followed the crusading armies to the Euphrates, and crept along the caravan routes to Ceylon and the China Sea, added Further and Central Asia—"Thesauri Arabum et divitis Indiæ"—to the knowledge of Christendom.

And as this knowledge was bound up with gain; as the Polos and their companions had really opened to the knowledge of the West those great prizes of material wealth which even the Rome of Trajan had never fully grasped, and which had been shared between Arabs and natives without a rival for so long; it was not likely to be easily forgotten. From that time, at the end of the thirteenth century, to the success of the Portuguese on another road, at the end of the fifteenth, European interest was fairly engaged in pressing in upon the old land-routes and getting an ever larger share of their profits.

(3) There was another side of the same problem, a still brighter hope for men who could dare to try it. By finding a sea-path to the Indian store-house, mariners like the Venetians and Genoese, or their Spanish pupils, might cut into the treasuries of the world at their very source, found a trade-empire for their country, and gain the sole command of heaven on earth, of the true terrestrial paradise.

Then masters of the wealth of the East and of the fighting power of the West, the Christian nations might crush their old enemy, Islam, between two weights, hammer and anvil; might fairly strike for the rule of the entire habitable globe.

It was with thoughts of this kind, vaguely inspired by the Crusades and their legacy of discovery from Bagdad to Cathay, that the Vivaldi left Genoa to find an ocean way round Africa in 1281-91, "with the hope of going to the parts of the Indies"; that Malocello reached the Canary Islands about 1270; and that volunteers went on the same quest nearly twenty times in the next four generations before their spasmodic efforts were organised and pressed on to achievement by Henry and his Portuguese (1412-1497).

(4) Lastly, the renaissance of Europe in the crusading age was not only practical but spiritual. Science was at last touched and changed by the new life scarcely less than the art of war, or the social state of the towns, or the trade of the commercial republics. And geography and its kindred were not long in feeling some change, though it was very slowly realised and made useful. The first notice of the magnet in the West is of about 1180; the use of this by sailors is perhaps rightly dated from the thirteenth century and the discoveries of Amalphi.

But to return. We must trace more definitely the preparation which has been generally described for the work of Prince Henry first in the pilgrim-warriors, and the travellers of the New Age, merchants or preachers or sight-seers, who follow out the Eastern land-routes; next in the seamen who begin to break the spell of the Western Ocean and to open up the high seas, the true high-roads of the world; lastly in the students who most of all, in their maps and globes and instruments and theories, are the trainers and masters and spiritual ancestors of the Hero of Discovery.

The first of these classes supplied the matter, the attractions and rewards of the exploring movement; the others may be said to provide the form by which success was reached, genius in seamanship.

And the one was as much needed as the other.

Human reason did its work so well because of a reasonable hope; men crept round Africa in face of the Atlantic storms because of the golden East beyond.

It was as we have seen the land travellers of the twelfth and thirteenth and fourteenth centuries who laid open that golden East to Europe, and added inspiring knowledge to a dream and a tradition. And of these land travellers the first worth notice are Sæwulf of Worcester, Adelard of Bath, and Daniel of Kiev, three of that host of peaceful pilgrims who followed the conquerors of the First Crusade (1096-9). All of these left their recollections and all of them are of the new time, in sharp contrast with the hordes of earlier pilgrims, even the most recent, like Bishop Ealdred of Worcester and York, who crowned William the Conqueror, or Sweyn Godwineson or Thorer Hund, whose visits are all mere visits of penitence. Every fresh conversion of the Northern nations brought a fresh stream of devotees to Italy and to Syria, a fresh revival of the fourth century habit of pilgrimage; but when mediæval Christendom had been formed, and religious passion was more steady and less unworldly, the discoverer and observer blends with the pilgrim in all the records left to us.

Sæwulf was a layman and a trader, who went on a pilgrimage (1102), and became a monk at the instance of his confessor, Wulfstan, Bishop of Worcester. But though his narrative has been called an immense advance on all earlier guide-books, it ends with the Holy Land and does not touch even the outlying pilgrim sites, in Mesopotamia or Egypt, visited and described by Silvia or Fidelis.

Starting some three years after the Latin capture of Jerusalem in 1099, the English traveller takes us up six different routes from Italy to Syria, evidence of the vast development of Mediterranean intercourse and of practical security against pirates, gained very largely since the second millennium began.

His own way, by Monopoli, Corfu, Corinth, and Athens, took him to Rhodes "which once had the Idol called Colossus, one of the Seven Wonders of the World, but destroyed by the Persians, with nearly all the land of Roumania, on their way to Spain. These were the Colossians to whom St. Paul wrote."

Thence to Myra in Lycia, "the port of the Adriatic as Constantinople is of the Ægean."

Landing at Jaffa, after a sail of thirteen weeks, Sæwulf was soon among the wonders of Jerusalem, that had not grown less since Arculf's day. At the head of the Sepulchre Church was the famous Navel of the Earth, "now called Compas, which Christ measured with his own hands, working salvation in the midst, as say the Psalms." For the same legends were backed by the same texts as in the sixth or seventh century.

Going down to the Jordan, "four leagues east of Jericho," Arabia was seen beyond "hateful to all who worship God, but having the Mount whence Elias was carried into Heaven in a chariot of fire."

Eighteen days journey from the Jordan is Mount Sinai, by way of Hebron, where "Abraham's Holm Oak" was still standing, and where, as pilgrims said, he "sat and ate with God," but Sæwulf himself did not go outside Palestine, on this side. After travelling through Galilee and noting the House of Saint Archi-Triclin (Saint "Ruler-of-the-Feast"), at Cana, he made his way to Byzantium by sea, escaping the Saracen cruisers and weathering the storms that wrecked in the roads of Jaffa before his eyes some twenty of the pilgrim and merchant fleet then lying at anchor. But not only can we see from this how the religious and commercial traffic of the Mediterranean had been increased by the Crusades; the main lines of that traffic had been changed. Since the Moslem conquest, visitors had mostly come to Palestine through Egypt; the Christian conquest of Syria re-opened the direct sea route as the conversion of Hungary and north-east Europe had re-opened the direct land route one hundred years before (c. 1000-1100). The lines of the Danube valley and of the "Roman Sea" were both cleared, and the West again poured itself into the East as it had not done since Alexander's conquest, since the Oriental reaction had set in about the time of the Christian era, rising higher and higher into the full tide of the Persian and Arabian revivals of Asiatic Empire.

Among the varied classes of pilgrim-crusaders in Sæwulf's day were student-devotees like Adelard and Daniel from the two extremes of Christendom, England and Russia, Bath and Kiev; northern sea-kings like Sigurd, or Robert of Normandy; even Jewish travellers, rabbis, or merchants like Benjamin of Tudela. All these, as following in the wake of the First Crusade, and for the most part stopping at the high-water mark of its advance, belong to the same group and time and impulse as Sæwulf himself, and are clearly marked off from the great thirteenth century travellers, who acted as pioneers of the Western Faith and Empire rather than as camp-followers of its armies.

But except Abbot Daniel (c. 1106) and Rabbi Benjamin (c. 1160-73) who stand apart, none of our other pilgrim examples of twelfth century exploration have anything original or remarkable about them.

Adelard or Athelard, the countryman of Sæwulf and Willibald, is still more the herald of Roger Bacon and of Neckam. He is a theorist far more than a traveller, and his journey through Egypt and Arabia (*c.* 1110-14) appears mainly as one of scientific interest. "He sought the causes of all things and the mysteries of Nature," and it was with "a rich spoil of letters," especially of Greek and Arab manuscripts, that he returned to England to translate into Latin one of the chief works of Saracen astronomy, the Kharizmian tables. We have already met with him in trying to follow the transmission of Greek and Indian geography or world-science through the Arabs to Europe and to Christendom.

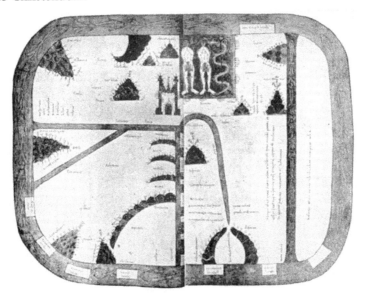

THE SPANISH-ARABIC MAP OF 1109.
(SEE LIST OF MAPS)

Abbot Daniel of Kiev in himself is a very ordinary and rather mendacious traveller, a harmless, devout pilgrim, as careless in all matters of fact as Antonine the Martyr. But, as representing the beginnings of Russian expansion, he is of almost unique interest and value. His tract upon the Holy Road is one of the first proofs of his people's interest in the world beyond their steppes, and of that nation's readiness and purpose to expand Christian civilisation in the East as the Franks, after breaking through the Western Moslems, were now doing. Mediæval Russia, Russia before the Tartars, after the Northmen, was now a very different thing from the "people fouler than dogs" of the Arab explorers. The House of Ruric had guided and organised a nation second to none in Europe, till it had fallen into the general lines of Christian development. Jury trial and justices in assize it had taken from the West; its church and faith and architecture, its manners and morals came to it from the court of the Roman Empire on the Bosphorus. Daniel and the other Russians, who passed through that Empire in the age of Nestor for trade or for religion, were the vanguard of a great national and race expansion that is now just beginning to "bestride the world."

In 1022 and 1062 two monks of Kiev are recorded, out of a crowd of the unknown, as visitors to Syria, and about 1106, probably through the news of the Frankish conquest, Daniel left his native river, the Snow, in Little Russia, and passed through Byzantium and by way of the Archipelago and Cyprus to Jaffa and Jerusalem, describing roughly in versts or half-miles the whole distance and that of every stage.

His tone is much like Sæwulf's and his mistakes are quite as bad, though he tells of "nothing but what was seen with these self-same eyes." The "Sea of Sodom exhales a burning and fetid breath that lays waste all the country, as with burning sulphur, for the torments of Hell lie under it." This, however, he did not see; Saracen brigands prevented him, and he learnt that "the very smell of the place would make one ill."

His measurements of distance are all his own. Capernaum is "in the desert, not far from the Great Sea (Levant) and eight versts (four miles) from Cæsarea," half the distance given in the next chapter as between Acre and Haifa, and less than half the breadth of the Sea of Tiberias. The Jordan reminds Daniel of his own river, the Snow, especially in its sheets of stagnant water.

Samaria, or "Sebastopol," he confuses with Nablous; Bethshan with Bashan; Lydda with Ramleh; Cæsarea Philippi with the greater Cæsarea on the coast. Not far from Capernaum and the Jordan is "another large river that comes out of the Lake of Gennesaret, and falls into the Sea of Tiberias, passing by a large *town* called Decapolis." From Mt. Lebanon "six rivers flow east into the Lake of Gennesaret and six west towards great Antioch, so that this is called Mesopotamia, or the land between the rivers, and Abraham's Haran is between these rivers that feed the Lake of Gennesaret."

Daniel has left us also an account of his visits to Mar Saba Convent in the Kedron gorge near the Dead Sea, to Damascus in the train of Prince Baldwin, and to the Church of the Holy Sepulchre in Jerusalem, to witness the miracle of the Holy Fire, noticed by Bernard the Wise, as a sort of counterpart to the wonder of Beth-Horon, also retold by Daniel "when the sun stood still while Joshua conquered King Og of Bashan."

It is not in outlook nor in knowledge nor even in the actual ground traversed that these later pilgrims shew any advance on the chief of the earlier travellers; it is in the new life and movement, in the new hope they give us of greater things than these. This is the interest—to us—in King Sigurd of Norway (1107-11), a Crusader-Norseman in the new age that owed so much of its very life to the Northmen, but who is only to be noticed here as a possible type of the explorer-chief—possible, not actual—for his voyage added nothing definite to the knowledge or expansion of Christendom. His campaign in Jacob's Land or Gallicia, and his attack on Moslem Lisbon, some forty years before it became the head and heart of Portugal, like his exploits in the Balearics, shew us a point in the steady decline of western Islam, and so far may be called a preparation for Prince Henry's work, but properly as a chapter of Portuguese, not of general European, growth.

There were many others like Sigurd,—Robert of Normandy, Godric the English pirate, who fought his way through the Saracen fleets with a spear-shaft for his banner, Edgar the Ætheling, grandson of Edmund Ironside, the Dartmouth fleet of 1147 which retook Lisbon,—but the Latin conquest of Syria has now brought us past the Crusades, in the narrower sense, to their results, in the exploration of the Further East.

The first great name of this time, of our next main chapter of Preparation, is Benjamin of Tudela, but standing as he does well within the earlier age, when the primary interest was the Holy War itself, he is also the last of the Palestine travellers—of those Westerns whose real horizon was the sacred East of Syria. He is a little before the awakening of universal interest in the unknown world, for the Christian Northmen lost with the new definiteness of the new faith much of their old infinite unrest and fierce inquisitive love of wandering, and their spirit, though related to the whole Catholic West by the crusading movement, was not fully realised till the world had been explored and made known, till the men of Europe were at home in every country and on every sea.

Benjamin, as a Jew and a rabbi, has the interest of a sectary, and his work was not of a kind that would readily win the attention of the Christian world. So the value of his travels was hidden till religious divisions had ceased to govern the direction of progress. He visited the Jewish communities from Navarre to Bagdad, and described those beyond from Bagdad to China, but he wrote for his own people and none but they seem to have cared about him. What he discovered (*c.* 1160-73) was for himself and for Judaism, and only his actual place in the twelfth century makes him a fore-runner of the Polos or of Prince Henry. We may see this from his hopeless strangeness and confusion in Rome, like a Frank in Pekin or Delhi. "The Church of St. Peter is on the site of the great palace of Julius Cæsar, near which are eighty Halls of the eighty Kings called Emperors from Tarquin to Pepin the father of Charles, who first took Spain from the

Saracens.... In the outskirts of the city is the palace of Titus, who was deposed by three hundred senators for wasting three years over the siege of Jerusalem which he should have finished in two."

And so on—with the "Hall of Galba, three miles round and having a window for each day in the year," with St. John Lateran and its Hebrew trophies, "two copper pillars from the temple of Solomon, that sweat at the anniversary of the burning of the Temple," and the "statues of Samson and of Absalom" in the same place. So with Sorrento, "built by Hadarezer when he fled before King David," with the old Roman tunnel between Naples and Pozzuoli, "built by Romulus who feared David and Joab," with Apulia, "which is from King Pul of Assyria"—in all this we have as it were Catholic mythology turned inside out, David put into Italy when the West put Trajan at the sources of the Nile. It was not likely that writing of this sort would be read in the society of the Popes and the Schoolmen, the friars and the crusaders, any more than the Buddhist records of missionary travel from China one thousand years before. The religious passion which had set the crusaders in motion, would keep Catholics as long as it might from the Jews, Turks, infidels, and heretics they conquered and among whom they settled.

But with the final loss of Jerusalem by the Latins, and the overthrow of the Bagdad Caliphate by the Mongol Tartars (1258), the barrier of fanatic hatred was weakened, and Central Asia became an attraction to Christendom instead of a dim horror, without form and void, except for Huns and Turks and demons. The Papal court sent mission after mission to convert the Tartars, who were wavering, as men supposed, between Islam and the Church, and with the first missionaries to the House of Ghenghiz went the first Italian merchants who opened the court of the Great Khan to Venice and to Genoa.

As early as 1243 an Englishman is noticed as living among the Western Horde, the conquerors of Russia; but official intercourse begins in 1246 with John de Plano Carpini. This man, a Franciscan of Naples, started in 1245 as the Legate of Pope Innocent IV. to the Tartars, took the northern overland route through Germany and Poland, reached Kiev, "the metropolis of Russia," through help of the Duke of Cracow, and at last appeared in the camp of Batou, on the Volga. Hence by the Sea of Aral, "of moderate size with many islands," to the court of Batou's brother, the Great Khan "Cuyuc" himself, where the Christian stranger found himself one of a crowd of four thousand envoys from every part of Asia (1246).

After sixteen months Carpini made his way back by the same route, "over the plains" and through Kiev, to give at Rome the first genuine account of Tartary, in its widest sense, from the Dnieper to China (1247).

The great rivers and lakes and mountains of Russia and Turkestan, the position and distribution of the land and its peoples, "even from the Caspian to the Northern Ocean, where men are said to have dogs' faces," are now first described by an honest and clear-headed and keen-eyed observer, neither timid nor credulous.

Carpini really begins the reliable western map of Further Asia. His personal knowledge did not reach China or India, but in his *Book of the Tartars*, Europe was told nearly the whole truth, and almost nothing but the truth, about the vast tract and the great races between the Carpathians and the Gobi Desert. In the same was included the first fair account of the manners and history of the "Mongols whom we call Tartars," and the simple truthfulness of the Friar stands out in all the allusions that make his work so human;—his interviews with the Tartar Chiefs and with brother-travellers, his dangers and difficulties from Lettish robbers and abandoned or guarded ferries, his passage of the Dnieper on the ice, his last three weeks on "trotting"[24] hacks over the steppes.

We have gone a good way from Abbot Daniel, for in John de Plano Carpini Christian Europe has at last a real explorer, a real historian, a genuine man of science, in the service of the Church and of discovery.

Carpini was followed after six years by William de Rubruquis, a Fleming sent by St. Louis of France on the same errand of conversion and discovery (1253), but by a different route, through the Black Sea, and Cherson, over the Don "at the Head of Azov, that divides Europe and Asia, as the Nile divides Asia and Africa," to the great camp on the Volga, "the greatest river I had ever seen, which comes from Great Bulgaria in the north and falls into a lake (the Caspian Sea), that would take four months to journey round." Higher in their course the Don and the Volga "are not more than ten days' journey apart, but diverge as they run south." The Caspian is "made out of the Volga and the rivers that flow into it from Persia." Thence through the Iron Gates of Derbend, between the Caspian and the Caucasus, "which Alexander made to shut the barbarians out of Persia." Helped by a Nestorian, who possessed influence at the Tartar Court, like so many of his Church, Rubruquis reached the "Alps" of the Altai country, where he found a small Nestorian lordship, governed like the Papal States, by a priest, who was at least one original of the great mediæval phantom— Prester John.

Crossing the great steppes of eastern "Tartary," "like the rolling sea to look at," Rubruquis at last reached the Mongol headquarters at Caracorum, satisfied on the way that the Caspian had no northern outlet, as Strabo and

Isidore had imagined. Thence he made his way home without much fresh result.

THE PSALTER MAP OF THE THIRTEENTH CENTURY.
(SEE LIST OF MAPS)

Though Rubruquis is well called the most brilliant and literary of the mediæval travellers, his mission was fruitless, and the interest of his work lay rather in recording custom and myth—in sociology—than in adding anything definite to the geographical knowledge of the West. John de Plano had already been over the ground to Caracorum, and recorded all the main characteristics of the lands west of the Gobi Desert. The further advance, east to China, south to India, was yet to come.

But while Rubruquis was still among the Tartars, Nicolo and Matteo Polo, the uncles of the more famous Marco, were trading (1255-65) to the Crimea and the districts of southern Russia that were now under the Western Horde,—and soon after, following the caravans to Bokhara, they were drawn on to the court of Kublai Khan, then somewhere near the wall of China. After a most friendly reception they were sent back to Europe with presents and a letter to Pope Clement IV., offering a welcome and maintenance to Christian teachers. Kublai "had often questioned the Polos of the Western lands," and now he asked for one hundred "Latins, to shew him the Christian faith, for Christ he held to be the only God." Furnished with the imperial passport of the Golden Tablet, our merchants made their way back to Acre in April, 1269.

They found the old pope dead, Gregory X. in his place, and he shewed a coolness in answering the Khan's requests, but in 1271 they set out on their second journey to the furthest East, taking with them two friar preachers and their nephew Marco, now nineteen years of age.

In Armenia the friars took alarm at the troubled state of the nearer East and turned back, just as Augustine of Canterbury tried to find a way out of the mission to the English that Pope Gregory I. laid upon him in 597. For the Church it was perhaps as momentous a time now as then; the thirteenth century, if it had ended in the Christianising of the Mongol Empire, would have turned the Catholic victory of the fourth and sixth centuries in the West, the victory that had been worked out in the next seven hundred years to fuller and fuller realisation, into a world empire,—which did come at last for European civilisation, but not for Christendom.

The Polos however kept on their way north-east for more than "one thousand days," three years and a half, till they stood in the presence of Kublai Khan; beyond Gobi and the Great Wall and the mountain barriers of China, in Cambaluc or Pekin, "princess encrowned of cities capital."

Their journey was first through Armenia Lesser and Greater, then through Mosul (Nineveh) to Bagdad, where the last "Caliph and Pope of the Saracens" had been butchered by Holgalu and his Tartars, sewn in a sack and thrown into the Tigris by one account, walled up alive by another, in 1258. But though the stories in Marco's journal are a main interest of his work, as a summary and reflection of the science and history and general culture of the Christian world of his time, we must not here look outside his geography. And his first place-note of value is on the Caspian, "which containeth in circuit twenty-eight hundred miles and is like a lake, having no union with other seas and in which are many islands, cities, and castles." The extent of the Nestorian missions, "through all parts of India and to Cairo and Bagdad, and wherever Christians dwell," strikes him even now at the beginning of his travels—much more when he finds their churches on the Hoang Ho and the Yang-Tse-Kiang—declining indeed, but still living to witness to the part which that great heresy had played as an intermediary between the further and the nearer East—a part which history has never yet worked out. Entering Persia as traders, the Polos went naturally to Ormuz, already the great mart of Islam for the Indian trade, where

Europeans really entered the third, and, to them, unknown belt of the world, after passing from a zone of known home-land through one of enemies' country, known and only known as such. Failing to take the sea route at Ormuz for China, as they had hoped, our Italians were obliged to strike back north-east, through Persia and the Pamir, the Kashgar district and the Gobi steppes, to Cathay and the pleasure domes of Kublai, visiting Caracorum and the Altai country on the way, by a turn due north. In 1275 they were in Shang-tu, the Xanadu[25] of Coleridge—the summer capital of Kublai Khan—and not till 1292 did they get leave to turn their faces to the West once more.

Here the Polos became what may be called consulting engineers to the Mongol Court; Marco was even made in 1277 a commissioner of the Imperial Council, and soon after sent upon government missions to Yunnan in extreme south-west China and to Yangchow city.

The greater part of Marco's own memoirs is taken up with his account of the thirty-four provinces of the Tartar Empire that centred round the "six parts of Cathay and the nine parts of Mangi," the districts of northern and southern China as we know them,—an account of the roads, rivers, and towns, the trade, the Court and the Imperial Ports, the customs and manner of life among the subject peoples in that Empire, perhaps the largest ever known. Especially do the travellers dwell on the public roads from Pekin or Cambaluc through all the provinces, the ten thousand Royal inns upon the highways, the two hundred thousand horses kept for the public service, the wonderful speed of transit in the Great Khan's embassages, "so that they could go from Pekin to the wall of China in two days."

But scarcely less is said about the great rivers—the arteries of Chinese commerce, even more than the caravan routes,—above all, the Yang-Tse-Kiang, "the greatest stream in the world, like an arm of the sea, flowing above one hundred days' journey from its source into the ocean, and into which flow countless others, making it so great that incredible quantities of merchandise are brought by this river. It flows," exclaims Marco, "through sixteen provinces, past the quays of two hundred cities, at one of which I saw at one time five thousand vessels, and there are other marts that have more."

The breadth and depth and length and merchandise of the Pulisangan and the Caramaran are only less than the Kiang's; from the point where Marco crossed the second of these, there was not another bridge till it reached the ocean, hundreds of miles away, "by reason of its exceeding greatness."

Lastly Pekin, the capital of the Empire, with Quinsai and the other provincial capitals of Mangi and Cathay, call out the unbounded admiration of the Polos as of every other Western traveller, from the Moslem Ibn Batuta to the Christian friars of the fourteenth century.

Pekin, two days' journey from the ocean, the residence of the Court in December, January, and February, in the extreme north-east of Cathay, had been lately rebuilt in a "central square of twenty-four miles in compass, and twelve suburbs, three or four miles long, adjoining each of the twelve gates," where merchants and strangers lived, each nation with separate "burses" or store-houses, where they lodged. From this centre to the land of Gog and Magog and the champaign-land of Bargu, the Great Khan travelled every year in midsummer for the fresh air of the plateau country of central Asia, as well as for a better view of the great Russian and Bactrian sub-kingdoms of his House. The six months of spring and autumn were spent in slow progresses through central and southern China to Thibet on one side, and to Tonquin on the other. But greater even than Pekin, Quinsai, or Kansay, the City of Heaven, in southern China, though no longer the capital even of a separate Kingdom of Mangi, was the crowning work of Chinese civilisation. It surpassed the other cities of Kublai, as much as these overshadowed the Rome or Venice of the thirteenth century.

"In the world there is not its like, for by common report it is one hundred miles in circuit, with a lake on one side and a river on the other, divided in many channels and upon these and the canals adjoining twelve thousand bridges of stone; there are ten market places, each half a mile square; great store-houses of stone, where the Indian merchants lay by their goods; palaces and gardens on both sides of the main street, which, like all the highways in Mangi, is paved with stone on each side, and in the midst full of gravel, with passages for the water, which keeps it always clean." Salt, silk, fruit, precious stones, and cloth of gold are the chief commodities; the paper money of the Great Khan is used everywhere; all the people, except a few Nestorians and Moslems, are "idolaters, so luxurious and so happy that a man would think himself in Paradise."

It was only in recent years that Kublai, or his general, Baian, had captured Quinsai and driven out the King of Mangi with his seraglio and his friends. The exile till then had only thought of pleasure, of wine, women, and song, the "sweet meat which cost him the sour sauce ye have heard," on the approach of danger, had fled on board the ships he had prepared to "certain impregnable isles in the ocean," and if these impregnable islands may be identified with Zipangu or Japan, the conquerors pursued him even here. There is nothing more interesting in Polo's book than his story of the Mongol failure in the Eastern islands, fifteen hundred miles from the coast of Mangi, now first discovered to Christian knowledge.

This country of Japan, "very great, the people white, of gentle manners, idolaters in religion, under a King of their own," was attacked by Kublai's fleet in 1264 for the gold they had, and had in such plenty that "the King's house, windows, and floors were covered with it, as churches here with lead, as was reported by merchants—but these were few and the King allowed no exportation of the gold."

The expedition was as disastrous a failure as the old Athenian attack upon Sicily, and was not repeated, although fleets were sent by the Great Khan after this into the Southern Seas, which were supposed to have made a discovery of Papua, if not of the Australian Continent. "In this Sea of China, over against Mangi," Marco reported, from hearsay "of mariners and expert pilots, are 7440 islands, most of them inhabited, whereon grows no tree that yields not a pleasant smell—spices, lignum-aloes, and pepper, black and white." The ships of Zaitum (the great Chinese mart for Indian trade) knew this sea and its islands, "for they go every winter and return every summer, taking a year on the voyage, and all this though it is far from India and not subject to the Great Khan."

But not only did Polo in these sections of his Guide Book or Memories of Travel, record the main features of a coast and ocean scarcely guessed at by Europeans, and flatly denied by Ptolemy and the main traditional school of Western geography. In his service under Kublai, and in his return by sea to Aden and Suez, he opened up the eight provinces of Thibet, the whole of south-east Asia from Canton to Bengal, and the great archipelago of further India.

Four days' journey beyond the Yang-Tse-Kiang, Marco entered "the wide country of Thibet, vanquished and wasted by the Khan for the space of twenty days' journey, and become a wilderness wanting inhabitants, where wild beasts are excessively increased." Here he tells us of the Yak-oxen and great Thibetan dogs as great as asses, of the musk deer, and spices, "and salt lakes having beds of pearls," and of the cruel and bestial idolatry and social customs of the people.

Still farther to the south-west, Commissioner Polo came to the Cinnamon river, called Brius, on the borders of the province of Caindu, to the porcelain-making districts of Carazan, governed by Kublai's son, and so to Bengal, "which borders upon India," and where Marco laughs at the tattoo customs of "flesh embroidery for the dyeing of fools' skins."

Thence back to China, the richest and most famous country of all the East, where was "peace so absolute that shops could be left open full of wares all night and travellers and strangers could walk day and night through every part, untouched and fearing none."

But the Polos wearied even of the Court favours and their celestial home; they longed to come back to earth, to Frankland and Christendom, where life was so rough, and poor, and struggling, but for whose sake they had come so far and braved so much. But the Khan was hurt at the least hint of their wishes, and it was only a fortunate chance that restored them to Europe. Twenty years after their outward start, they were dismissed for a time and under solemn promise of return, as the guides of an embassy in charge of a Mongol bride for a Persian Khan, living at Tabrez and related to Kublai himself. So, in 1292, they embarked for India at Zaitum, "one of the fairest ports in the world, where is so much pepper that what comes by Alexandria to the West is little to it, and, as it were, one of a hundred." Then striking across the Gulf of Cheinan, for fifteen hundred miles, and passing "infinite islands, with gold and much trade,"—a gulf "seeming in all like another world"—they reached Ziambar and, after another run of the same distance, Java, then supposed by mariners to be the greatest island in the world, "above three thousand miles round and under a king who pays tribute to none, the Khan himself not offering to subject it, because of the length and danger of the voyage."

One hundred miles south-east the fleet touched at Java the Less "in compass about two thousand miles, with abundance of treasure and spices, ebony, and brazil, and so far to the south that the North Star cannot be seen, and none of the stars of the Great Bear." Here they were in great fear of "those brutish man eaters," with whom they traded for victuals and camphire and spices and precious stones, being forced to stay for five months by stress of weather—till they got away into the Bay of Bengal, the extreme point of European knowledge until this time, "where there are savages living in the deep sea islands with dogs' heads and teeth, as I was told, all naked, both men and women, and living the life of beasts (Andamans)."[26]

Sailing hence a thousand miles to the west, adds Marco, is Ceylon, "the finest island in the world, 2400 miles in circuit, and once 3600, as is seen in old maps, but the north winds have made great part of it sea."

Again west for sixty miles, to Malabar, "which is firm continent in India the Greater," and where the Polos re-entered as it were the horizon of Western knowledge, at the shrine of St. Thomas, the Apostle of India.

Here we must leave the Venetians, with only a bare mention of their homeward route from Malabar by Murfili and the Valley of Diamonds, by Camari, where they had a glimpse of the Pole-Star once more, and by Guzerat and Cambay to Socotra, where Marco, in his stay, heard and wrote down the first news ever brought to Europe of the "great isle Magaster," or Madagascar, and of Zensibar or Zanzibar.[27]

Of Polo's account of Hindu customs,—self-immolation and especially Suttee, of Caste, of the Brahminical "thread with one hundred and four beads by which to pray"; of their etiquette in eating, drinking, birth, marriage, and death—only the simple fact can be noticed here, that the first serious and direct Christian account of India, as of China, is also among the most accurate and well judged, and that both in what he says and what he leaves unsaid, Messer Marco is a true Herodotus of the Middle Ages.

But not only does his account discover for Europe the extreme east and south of Asia; in his last chapter he returns to the Tartars, and after adding a few words on the nomades of the central plains, gives us our first "Latin" account of Siberia, "where are found great white bears, black foxes, and sables; and where are great lakes, frozen except for a few months in the year, and crossed in sledges by the fur-traders."

Beyond this the Obscure Land reaches to the furthest North, "near which is Russia, where for the most of winter the sun appears not, and the air is thick and dark as betimes in the morning with us, where the men are pale and squat and live like the beasts, and where on the East men come again to the Ocean Sea and the islands of the Falcons."

The work of Marco Polo is the high-water mark of mediæval land travel; the extension of Christendom after him was mainly by the paths of the sea; the Roman missions to the Tartars and to Malabar, vigorously and stubbornly pressed as they were, ended in unrelieved collapse; only by the revolt and resurrection of the Russian kingdom did the European world permanently and markedly expand on the side of Asia. But a crowd of missionaries followed the first traders to Cathay and to Mangi—Friar Odoric, John de Monte Corvino, John de Cora; statesmen like Marignolli the Papal Legate, sight-seers like Mandeville followed these; Bishop Jordanus of Capua worked for years in Coulam near Cape Comorin (c. 1325-35); the martyrdom of four friars on April 1, 1322, at Tana, in India, became one of the great commemorations of the Latin Church; there seemed no cause why Christian missions which had won north and north-east Europe should not win central and eastern Asia, whose peoples seemed as indifferent, as agnostic, as our own Norse or English pagans.

"The fame of the Latins," says Jordanus, about 1330—and he is borne out by Marino Sanuto—"is greater in India than among ourselves. Here our arrival is always looked for, and said to be predicted in their books. Once gain Egypt and launch a fleet even of two galleys on this sea and the battle is won." As Egypt could not be gained by arms, it was turned by seamanship. Before Polo returned from China, the coasting of Africa had begun, and Italian mariners were already in search of the longer way to the East.

But there is no work of land travel after that of Messer Marco which really adds anything decisive to European knowledge before the fifteenth century; the advance of trade intercourse between India and the Italian Republics, the gradual liberation of Russia the use made of the caravan routes by some of the most active of the Western clergy, are the chief notes of the time between the Polos and Prince Henry; and the flimsy fabrications of Mandeville—"of all liars that type of the first magnitude"—would be fairly left without a word even in a minute history of discovery, if he had not, like Ktesias with Herodotus, won a hearing for himself and drawn men's minds away from the truth-telling original that he travestied, by the sheer force of impudence.

The Indian travels of the Italian Nicolo Conti and the Russian merchant Athanasius Nikitin belong to a later time, to the age of the Portuguese voyages; they are not part of the preparation for our central subject, they are only a somewhat obscure parallel to that subject.

For in the later Middle Ages the chief interest lies elsewhere. The expansion of Christendom in the fourteenth century, and still more in the fifteenth (Prince Henry's own), is the story of the ventures and the successes, not so much of landsmen, as of mariners.

CHAPTER IV.

MARITIME EXPLORATION.

CIRCA 1250-1410.

Italian, Catalan, French, and English sailors were the forerunners of the Portuguese in the fourteenth century, and the latter years of the thirteenth. And as in land travel, so in maritime, the republics of Italy, Amalphi, Pisa, Venice, and Genoa, were the leaders and examples of Europe. Just as the Italian Dante is the first great name in the new literatures of the West, so the Italian Dorias and Vivaldi and Malocelli are the first to take up again the old Greek and Phœnician enterprise in the ocean. Since Hanno of Carthage and Pharaoh Necho's Tyrians, there had been nothing in the nature of a serious trial to find a way round Africa, and even the knowledge of the Western or Fortunate Islands, so clear to Ptolemy and Strabo, had become dim. The Vikings and their crusader-followers had done nothing south of Gibraltar Straits.

THE S.W., OR AFRICAN SECTION OF THE HEREFORD MAP. C. 1275-1300.
(SEE LIST OF MAPS)

But while the Crusades were still dragging along a weary and hopeless warfare under St. Louis of France and Prince Edward of England, discovery began again in the Atlantic. In 1270 Lancelot Malocello found the Canaries; in 1281 or 1291 the Genoese galleys of Tedisio Doria and the Vivaldi, trying to "go by sea to the ports of India to trade there," reached Gozora or Cape Non in Barbary, the southern Ultima Thule, and according to a later story "sailed the Sea of Ghinoia (Guinea) to a city of Æthiopia," where even legend lost sight of them, for in 1312 nothing more had been heard. From the frequent and emphatic references to this attempt in the literature of the later Middle Ages, it is clear that the daring Genoese drew upon themselves the attention of the learned and mercantile worlds, as much as one would naturally expect. For these men are the pioneers of

Christian explorations in the southern world—the precursors of all the ocean voyages that led to the discoveries of Prince Henry, Da Gama, Columbus, and Magellan,—the first who directly challenged the disheartening theories of geographers, such as Ptolemy, the inaction and traditionalism of the Arabs, and the elaborate falsities of story tellers, who, in the absence of real knowledge, had a grand opening for terrible fairy tales.

The first age, if so it may be called, of South Atlantic and African voyages was purely Italian; the second was chiefly marked by the efforts of the Spanish States to equip fleets and send out explorers under Genoese captains. In 1317 the Genoese Emmanuel Pessanha became Admiral of Portugal; in 1341 three ships manned by Portuguese and "other Spaniards" with some Italians put out from Lisbon in search of Malocello's "Rediscovered" islands, granted by the Pope to Don Luis of Spain in a Bull of November 15, 1334, and now described, from the original letters of Florentine merchants and partners in the venture of 1341, by Boccaccio. "Land was found on the fifth day after leaving the Tagus" (July 1); the fleet stayed till November, and then brought back four natives and products of the islands. The chief pilot thought these were near nine hundred miles from Seville, and we may fully suppose that the archipelago of thirteen, now first explored and described, represents the Fortunate Islands of Greek geography, the Canaries of modern maps, and that the five chief islands with their naked but not quite savage people, with excellent wood houses, and flocks of goats, palms, and figs, gardens and corn patches, rocky mountains and pine forests, were our Ferro, Palma, Gomera, Grand Canary, and Teneriffe. The last they took to be thirty thousand feet high, with its white scarped sides looking like a fortress, but terrified at signs of enchantment they did not dare to land, and returned to Spain, leaving the Islands of the Rediscovered to be visited as a convenient slave depot by merchants and pirates from the Peninsula till the Norman Conquest of Béthencourt in 1402.

The voyage of 1341 gained much by attempting little; the Catalan voyage of 1346, which followed close upon it, was something of a return to the wilder and larger schemes of the first Genoese. On August 10, 1346, Jayme Ferrer left Majorca "to go to the River of Gold," but of the said galley, says the Catalan map of 1375, no news has since been heard. On the same map, however, the explorers' boat is sketched off the "Cape Finisterre of west Africa," and there is, after all, some ground for supposing this to be nothing more than a mercantile venture to the Gold Coast of Guinea, which was becoming known to the traders of Nismes, Marseilles, and the Christian Mediterranean by the caravan traffic across the Sahara. Even

Prince Henry began in the same way; Guinea was his half-way house for India.

About the same date (c. 1350) as the Catalan voyage is the Book of the Spanish Friar, "of the voyage south to the River of Gold," which gives a more than half fabulous story of travel, first by sea beyond Capes Non and Bojador, then by land across the heart of Africa to the Mountains of the Moon, the city of Melli, where dwelt Prester John, and "the Euphrates, which comes from the terrestrial Paradise," where behind some real notes of Barbary coasting, perhaps gained from the Catalans of 1346, there is little but a confused transcript of Edrisi's geography. Yet this was one of the books which helped to fix the notion of a double Nile, Northern and Western, a Nile of Egypt and a Nile of the Blacks, with a common source in the Mountains of the Moon, upon the Christian science of the time, as the Arab geographers had fixed it upon Islam.

The next piece of Atlantic exploration was a romantic accident. In the reign of Edward III., an Englishman named Robert Machin eloped with Anne d'Arfet from Bristol (c. 1370), was driven from the coast of France by a north-east wind, and after thirteen days sighted an island, Madeira, where he landed. His ship was swept away by the storm, his mistress died of terror and exhaustion, and five days after Machin was laid beside her by his men, who had saved the ship's boat and now ran her upon the African coast. They were enslaved, like other Christian captives of the Barbary corsairs, but in 1416 a fellow-prisoner, one Morales of Seville, an old pilot, was ransomed with others and sent back to Spain. On his way Morales was captured by a Portuguese captain, Zarco, the servant of Prince Henry, the rediscoverer of Madeira, and through this the full story of Machin and his island, came to be known in the court of the Navigator Prince, who promptly made his gain of the new knowledge a lasting one, by the voyage of Zarco in 1420.

Last among the immediate predecessors of Prince Henry's seamen come the French. In the seventeenth century it was claimed, on newly found evidence, that between 1364 and 1410 the men of Dieppe and Rouen opened a regular trade in gold, ivory, and malaguette pepper with the coast of Guinea, and built stations at Petit Paris, Petit Dieppe, and La Mine, which they named from the precious metal found there. But all this is more than doubtful, and the genuine Norman voyage of De Béthencourt in 1402 shows us nothing but the Canaries and the north-west coast of Morocco. Cape Non, or Cape Bojador, was still the European Furthest on the African coast.

The French Seigneur was stirred up to attack the Fortunate Islands by two events. First in 1382 one Lopez, a captain of Seville sailing to Gallicia, was driven by a tempest to Grand Canary, and lived among the natives seven years till he and his men were denounced for writing home and inviting rescue. To stop this intrigue they, the "thirteen Christian brothers" whose testament reached Béthencourt twelve years later, were all massacred. News of this and of the voyage of a Spaniard named Becarra to the same islands at the same time, reached Rochelle about 1400, and found several French adventurers ready for a trial. The chief of these, Jean de Béthencourt, Lord of Grainville, and Gadifer de la Salle, a needy knight, started in July, 1402, to conquer in the sea a new kingdom for themselves. Though the leaders quarrelled and Grand Canary beat off all attacks, the enterprise was successful in the main, and several of the islands became Christian colonies,—a first step towards the colonial empires of the great European expansion, as the record of Béthencourt's chaplains is the first chapter of modern colonial history.

But nothing is clearer in this tract than its limitations. The French colonists as late as 1425 seem to know nothing of the African coast beyond Cape Bojador; they look upon the Canaries rather as an extension of Spain and of Europe than as the beginning of a new world. They are anxious to get to the River of Gold and traffic there, but they do not know the way, save by report. De Béthencourt had been to Bojador himself, and "if things in that country are such as they are described in the Book of the Spanish Friar," he meant to open a way to the River of Gold, for, the Friar says, "it is only one hundred and fifty leagues from Cape Bojador, and the map proves the same—which is only a three days' voyage for sailing boats—whereby access would be gained to the land of Prester John, whence come so many riches." But as yet our Normans are only "eager to know the state of the neighbouring countries, both islands and *terra firma*:" they do not know the coast beyond the "Utmost Cape" of Bojador, which had taken the place of the first Arab Finisterre, Cape Non,[28] Nun, or Nam, as the limit of navigation.

We are now at the very time of Prince Henry himself; his first voyage was in 1412. De Béthencourt died in 1425, and it is quite needless to follow out at length the stories, however interesting, of sporadic navigation in other parts of the European Seas. Between 1380-95 the Venetian Zeni sailed in the service of Henry Sinclair, Earl of the Orkneys, to Greenland, and brought back fisher stories, which read like those of Central America, of its man-eating Caribs and splendid barbarism. Somewhat earlier, about 1349, Ivar Bardsen of Norway paid one of the last of Christian visits to the Arctic colonies of Greenland, the legacy of the eleventh century, now sinking into ruin; but neither of these voyages gives us any new knowledge of the Unknown which was now being pierced, not from the North and East, but from the South and West.

Both in land travel and sea voyages we have traced the progress of Western exploration and discovery up to its Hero, the real central figure both in the history of Portugal and of the European expansion. A little remains to be said on the other lines of preparation for his work in scientific theory and national development from the Age of the Crusades.

CHAPTER V.

GEOGRAPHICAL SCIENCE IN CHRISTENDOM FROM THE FIRST CRUSADES.

CIRCA 1100-1460.

Before the Crusades of the eleventh and twelfth centuries, the scientific geography of Christendom, as we have seen, was mainly a borrowed thing. From the ninth century to the time of the Mediæval and Christian Renaissance, in the eleventh, twelfth, and thirteenth centuries, the Arabs were the recognised heirs of Greek science, and what Franks or Latins knew of Ptolemy or Strabo was either learnt or corrected in the schools of Cordova and Bagdad.

But when the Northmen and the Holy War with Islam had once thoroughly aroused the practical energies of Christendom, it began to expand in mind as well as in empire, and in the time of Prince Henry, in the fifteenth century, a Portuguese could say: "Our discoveries of coasts and islands and mainland were not made without foresight and knowledge. For our sailors went out very well taught, and furnished with instruments and rules of *astrology* and geometry, things which all mariners and map-makers must know."

THE WORLD ACCORDING TO MARINO SANUTO. C. 1306.
(SEE LIST OF MAPS)

In fact, compass, astrolabe, timepiece, and charts, were all in use on the Mediterranean about 1400, just as they were to be found among the Arab traders of the Indian Ocean.

In this section it will be enough to glance hastily at the later and growingly independent science of Christendom, from the time that it ceased merely to follow the lead of Islam, and thought and even invented for itself. In another chapter we have seen something of the lasting and penetrating influence of Greek and Moslem and Hindu tradition upon the Western thought, which has conquered by absorbing all its rivals; we must not forget that some original self-reliant work in geographical theory not less than in practical exploration is absolutely needed to explain the very fact of Prince Henry and his life—a student's life, far more even than a statesman's. And after all, the invention of instruments, the drawing of maps and globes, the reckoning of distances, is not less practical than the most daring and successful travel. For navigation, the first and prime demand is a means of safety, some power of knowing where you stand and where to go, such as was given to sailors by the use of the magnet.

"Prima dedit nautis usum magnetis Amalphis," says Beccadelli of Palermo, but the earliest mention of the "Black ugly stone" in the West is traced to an Englishman. Alexander Neckam, a monk of St. Albans, writing about 1180 on "The Natures Of Things," tells us of it as commonly used by sailors, not merely as the secret of the learned. "When they cannot see the sun clearly in cloudy weather, or at night, and cannot tell which way their prow is tending, they put a Needle above a Magnet which revolves till its point looks North and then stops." So the satirist, Guyot de Provins, in his *Bible* of about 1210, wishes the Pope were as safe a point to steer by in Faith as the North Star in sailing, "which mariners can keep ahead of them, without sight of it, only by the pointing of a needle floating on a straw in water, once touched by the Magnet."

It might be supposed from this not merely that the magnet was in use at the end of the twelfth century, but that it had been known to a few *savants* much earlier; yet when Dante's tutor, Brunetto Latini, visits Roger Bacon at Oxford about 1258, and is shown the black stone, he speaks of it as new and wonderful, but certain, if used, to awake suspicion of magic. "It has the power of drawing iron to it, and if a needle be rubbed upon it and fastened to a straw so as to swim upon water, the needle will instantly turn towards the Pole-Star. But no master mariner could use this, nor would the sailors venture themselves to sea under his command if he took an instrument so like one of infernal make."

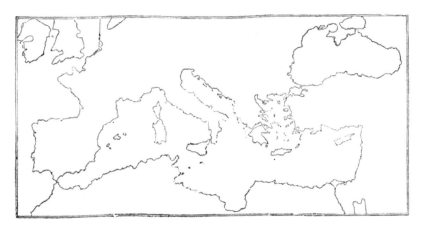

SKETCH-MAP OF DULCERT'S PORTOLANO OF 1339.
(SEE LIST OF MAPS)

It was possibly after this that the share of Amalphi came in; it may have been Flavio Gioja, or some other citizen of that earliest commercial republic of the Middle Ages, which filled up so large a part of the gap between two great ages of progress, who fitted the magnet into a box, and by connecting it with the compass-card, made it generally and easily available. This it certainly was before Prince Henry's earliest voyages, where he takes its use for granted even by merchant coasters, "who, beyond hugging the shore, know nothing of chart or needle." In any case it would seem that prejudice was broken down, and the mariner's compass taken into favour, at least by Italian seamen and their Spanish apprentices, in the early years of the fourteenth century, or the last years of the thirteenth, and that when the Dorias set out for India by the ocean way in 1291, and the Lisbon fleet sailed for the western islands in 1341, they had some sort of natural guide with them, besides the stories of travellers and their own imaginings. About the same time (c. 1350) mathematics and astronomy began to be studied in Portugal, and two of Henry's brothers, King Edward and the Great Regent Pedro, left a name for observations and scientific research. Thus Pedro, in his travels through most of Christendom, collected invaluable materials for discovery, especially an original of Marco Polo and a map given him at Venice, "which had all the parts of the earth described, whereby Prince Henry was much furthered."

Good maps indeed were almost as valuable to him as good instruments, and they are far clearer landmarks of geographical knowledge. There are at least seven famous charts (either left to us or described for us) of the fourteenth and early fifteenth centuries, which give a pretty clear idea of what Henry's own age and his father's thought and knew of the world—

some of which we believe to have been used by the Prince himself, and each of which follows some advance in actual exploration.

First of all comes the Venetian map of Marino Sanuto, drawn about 1306, and putting into map-form the ideas that inspired the first Italian voyages in the Atlantic. On this the south of Africa is washed by the sea as the Vivaldi had hoped to find it, but the old story of a central zone "uninhabitable from the heat" still finds a place, helping to keep up the notion of the Tropical Seas, "always kept boiling by the sun," that held its own so long. Besides this, in Sanuto's map there is no evidence that anyone had really been coasting Africa; Henry is not anticipated and can hardly have been much helped by this very hypothetical leap in the dark.

But the Florentine map of 1351, called the Laurentian Portolano, is to all appearance a record of the actual discoveries of 1341 and 1346, and a wonderful triumph of guess-work if it is nothing better. For Africa is not only made an island, but the main outline of its coast is fairly drawn; in its western corner the headlands, bays, and rivers are laid down as far as Bojador, and the three groups of Atlantic islands, Azores, Canaries, and Madeira, appear together for the first time. Beyond this names grow scarce, and on the great indent of the Gulf of Guinea, enormously exaggerated as it is, there is nothing to show for certain any past discovery, which suggests that this map was made for two purposes. First, to record the results of recent travel; secondly, and chiefly, to put forward geographical theories based upon tradition and inference, what men of old had told and what men of the present could fancy.

Long after the Italian leadership in exploration had passed westward, Italian science kept control of geographical theory; the Venetian maps of the brothers Pizzigani in 1367, and of the Camaldolese convent at Murano in 1380 and 1459, and the work of Andrea Bianco in 1436 and 1448, are the most important of mediæval charts, after the Laurentian, and along with these must be reckoned that mentioned above as given in 1425-8 to Henry's brother, Don Pedro, on his visit to Venice. This treasure has disappeared, but it was said by men of Henry's day and aftertime, who saw it in the monastery of Alçobaça, to show "as much or more discovered in time past than now." If their account is even an approach to the truth, it was in itself proof sufficient of the supremacy and almost monopoly of Italians in geographical theory.

With 1375 and the Catalan map of that year, which specially refers to the Catalan voyage of 1346 and may be taken as one result of the same, we come to Spanish parallels; but until the death of Henry in 1460, Italian draughtsmen were in possession, and Fra Mauro's great map of 1459, the evidence and result, in great measure, of the Navigator's work, could only be drawn by Venetians for the men whose discoveries it recorded.

But there is one other point in Italian map-science which is worth remembering. At a time when most schemes of the world were covered with monsters and legends, when cartography was half mythical and half miscalculated, the coasting voyagers of the Mediterranean had brought their *Portolani* or sea charts to a very different result. And how was this? Did they get right, as it were, by chance? "They never had for their object," says the great Swedish explorer and draughtsman, Baron Nordenskjold, "to illustrate the ideas of some classical author, of some learned prelate, or the legends and dreams of feats of Chivalry within the Court circle of some more or less lettered feudal lord." They were simply guides to mariners and merchants in the Mediterranean seaports; they were seldom drawn by learned men, and small enough, in return, was the attention given them by the learned geographers, the men of theory, in the fifteenth and sixteenth centuries.

But these plans of practical seamen are a wonderful contrast in their almost present-day accuracy to the results of theory let loose, as we see them in Ptolemy and the Arabian geographers, and in such fantastics as the Hereford Mappa Mundi, so well known in England. Map-sketches of this sort, were unknown to Greeks and Romans, as far as we can tell. The old Peripli were sailing directions, not drawn but written, and the only Arabian coast-chart known to us was copied from an Italian one. But from the opening of the twelfth century, if not before, the western Mediterranean was known to Christian seamen—to those at least concerned in the trade and intercourse of the great inland sea,—by the help of these practical guides.

THE LAURENTIAN PORTOLANO OF 1351.
(SEE LIST OF MAPS)

From the middle of the thirteenth century, when the use of the compass began on the coasts of southern Europe, the Portolani began to be drawn with its aid, and by the end of the same century, by the time of our Hereford map (*c.* 1300), these charts had reached the finish that we see and admire in those left to us from the fourteenth century. For, of the 498 specimens of this kind of practical map now left to us, there is not one of earlier date than the year 1311. Among these specimens not merely the mass of materials, but the most important examples, not merely 413 out of 498, but all the more famous and perfect of the 498 are Italian. The course begins with Vesconte's chart, of the year 1311, and with Dulcert's of 1339, and the outlines of these two are faithfully reproduced, for instance, in the great Dutch map of the Barentszoons (*c.* 1594), for the type once fixed in the fourteenth century, recurs steadily throughout the fifteenth, and sixteenth. The type was so permanent because it was so reliable; every part of the Mediterranean coast was sketched without serious mistake or disproportion, even from a modern point of view, while the fulness and detail of the work gave everything that was wanted by practical seamen. Of course this detail was in the coast lines, river mouths, and promontories; it only touched the land features as they touched the seas. For the Portolani were never meant to be more than mariners' charts, and became less and less trustworthy if they tried to fill up the inland spaces usually left blank. For this, we must look to the highest class of mediæval theoretical maps, those founded on Portolani, but taking into their view land as well as water and coast line. And such were the celebrated examples[29] we have noticed already.

NOTE.—It was a man of theory, Raymond Lulli (1235-1315), of Majorca, the famous Alchemist, who is credited with the first suggestion of the idea of seeking a way to India by rounding Africa on the West and South.

CHAPTER VI.

PORTUGAL TO 1400.

1095-1400.

Henry the Navigator is the Hero of Portugal, as well as of discovery, the chief figure in his country's history, as well as the first leader of the great European expansion; and the national growth of three hundred years is quite as much a part of his life, quite as much a cause of his forward movement, as the growth of Christendom towards a living interest in the unknown or half-known world around.

The chief points of interest in the story of Portugal are first the stubborn restless independence of the people, always rising into fresh vigour after a seeming overthrow, and secondly their instinct for seamanship, which Henry was able to train into exploring and colonising genius. There was no physical justice in the separate nationality of the Western Kingdom of Lisbon any more than of the Eastern Kingdom of Barcelona. Portugal[30] was essentially part of Spain, as the United Provinces of William of Orange were essentially part of the Netherlands; in both cases it was only the spirit and endurance of the race that gave to some provincials the right to become a people, while that right was denied to others.

And Portugal gained that right by a struggle of three hundred years, which was first a crusade against Islam; then a war of independence against brother Christians of Castille; last of all a civil strife against rebels and anarchists within.

In the twelfth century the five kingdoms of Spain were clearly marked off from the Moslem States and from one another; by the end of the fifteenth there is only the great central Realm of Ferdinand and Isabella, and the little western coast-kingdom of Emanuel the Fortunate, the heir of Prince Henry. Nations are among our best examples of the survival of the fittest, and by the side of Poland and Aragon we may well see a meaning in the bare and tiresome story of the mediæval kingdom of Portugal. The very fact of separate existence means something for a people which has kept on ruling itself for ten generations. Though its territory was never more than one fourth of the peninsula, nor its numbers more than one third of the Spanish race—from the middle of the twelfth century, Portugal has stood alone, with less right to such independence from any distinction of place or blood, than Ireland or Navarre, fighting incessantly against foes without, from north, east, and south, and keeping down the still worse foes of its own household.

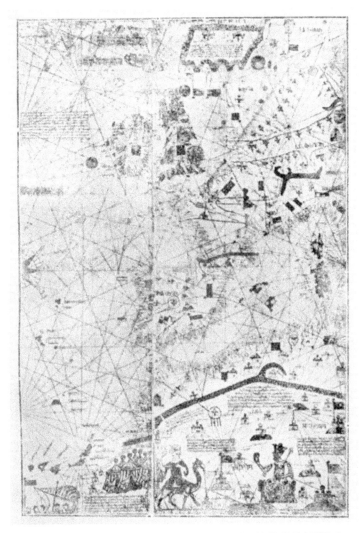

N.W. SECTION OF THE CATALAN MAP OF 1375-6.
(SEE LIST OF MAPS)

But the meaning of the growth of the Portuguese power is not in its isolation, its stubbornly defended national distinction from all other powers, but in its central and as it were unifying position in modern history—as the guide of Europe and Christendom into that larger world which marks the real difference between the Middle Ages and our own day.

For Henry the Navigator breathed into his countrymen the spirit of the old Norse rovers, that boundless appetite for new knowledge, new pleasures, new sights and sounds, which underlay the exploration of the fifteenth and sixteenth centuries—the exploration of one half of the world's surface, the finding of a new continent in the south and in the west, and the opening of the great sea-routes round the globe. The scientific effects of this, starting from the new proof of a round world won by a Portuguese seaman, Magellan; and the political effects, also beginning with the first of modern colonial empires, founded by Da Gama, Cabral, and Albuquerque, are too widespread for more than a passing reference in this place, but this reference must be connected with the true author of the movement. For if the industrial element rules modern development; if the philosophy of utility, as expressing this element, is now our guide in war and peace; and if the substitution of this for the military spirit[31] is to be dated from that dominion in the Indian seas which realised the designs of Henry—if this be so, the Portuguese become to us, through him, something like the founders of our commercial civilisation, and of the European empire in Asia.

By the opening years of the fifteenth century, Portugal—in a Catholic rather than a Classical Renaissance—had already entered upon its modern life, some three generations before the rest of Christendom. But its mediæval history is very much like that of any other of the Five Spanish Kingdoms. Like the rest, Portugal had joined in driving the Moors from the Asturias to Andalusia, in the two hundred years of successful Western Crusade (1001-1212). In the same time, between the death of the great vizier Almanzor, the last support of the old Western Caliphate (1001), and the overthrow of the African Moors, who had supplanted that Western Caliphate,—between those two points of Moslem triumph and Christian reaction, the Portuguese kingdom had been formed out of the County granted in 1095 by Alfonso VI. of Leon to the free-lance Henry of Burgundy.

For the next three hundred years (1095-1383), under his descendants who reigned as kings in Guimaraëns or Lisbon, we may trace a gradual but chequered national rise, to the Revolution of 1383 with two prominent movements of expansion and two relapses of contraction and decline.

First comes the formation of a national spirit by Count Henry's widow Donna Theresa and her son Affonso Henriquez, who from a Lord of Coimbra and Oporto, dependent on the Kingdom of Gallicia or of Leon, becomes the first free King of Portugal. His victories over the Moors in taking Lisbon (1147) and winning the day of Ourique (1139), are followed by the first wars with Castille and by the time of quiet organisation in his last years under the regency of his son Sancho, the City Builder. The building and planting of Sancho is again followed by the first relapse, into the weakness of Affonso II., and the turbulent minority of Sancho II. Constitutional troubles begin with the First Sancho's quarrel with Innocent III. and with the appearance of the first national Cortés under Chancellor Julian.

The second forward movement starts with Affonso III., "of Boulogne," who saves the kingdom from anarchy and conquers the Algarves, on the south coast, from Islam; who first organises the alliance of Crown and people against nobles and clergy, and, in the strength of this, defies the interdict of Urban IV.

Diniz, his bastard son, for whose legitimation he had made this same struggle with Rome, follows Affonso III., in 1279, and with him begins the wider life of Portugal, her navy and her literature, her agriculture, justice, and commerce.

The second relapse may be dated from the Black Death (1348), which threatened the very life of the nation, and left behind a sort of chronic weakness. National spirit seemed worn out; Court intrigue and political disaster the order of the day; the Church and Cortés alike effete and useful only against themselves.

But in the revival under a new leader, John, the father of Prince Henry, and a new dynasty—the House of Aviz—and its "Royal Race of Famous Infants," in the years that follow the Revolution of 1383, the older religious and crusading fervour is joined with the new spirit of enterprise, of fierce activity, and the Portugal thus called into being is a great State because the whole nation shares in the life and energy of a more than recovered liberty.

Before the age of King Diniz, before the fourteenth century, there is little enough in the national story to suggest the first state-profession of discovery and exploration in Christian history. But we must bring together a few of the suggestive and prophetic incidents of the earlier time, if we are to be fully prepared for the later.

(1.) Oporto, the "port" of Gallicia, from the formation of the county or "march" of Henry of Burgundy, seems to have given the district its name of "Portugallia," at one time as a military frontier against Islam, then as an independent State, lastly as an imperial Kingdom. Also, as the earliest centre of Portugal was a harbour, and its earliest border a river, there was a sort of natural, though slumbering, fitness for seamanship in the people.

(2.) Again, in the alliance of the Crown with the towns, first formed by Count Henry's wife Theresa in her regency after his death, 1114-28, and renewed by her grandson Sancho, the City Builder, and by Affonso III., the "Saviour of the Kingdom," we have an early example of the power of that class, which was the backbone of the great movement of expansion, when the meaning of this was fairly brought home to them.

(3.) In the capture of Lisbon, in 1147, by Affonso Henriquez, Theresa's son, at the head of the allied forces of native militia and northern Crusaders—Flemish, French, German, and English—we have brought clearly before us, not merely the facts of the gain of a really great city by a rising Christian State, not merely the result of this in the formation of a kingdom out of a county, but the more general connection of the crusading spirit with the new nations of Europe. Portugal is the most lasting monument of crusading energy; it was this that strengthened the "Lusitanians" to make good their stand both against the Moors and against Castille; and it was this which brought out the maritime bent of the little western kingdom, and drew out its interest on the one and only side where that could be of great and general usefulness. The Crusades without and the policy of statesmen within, we may fairly say, made the Portuguese ready to lead the expansion of Christendom, made possible the work of Henry the Navigator. The foreign help given at Lisbon in 1147 was only a repetition on a grand scale of what had long been done on a smaller, and it was offered again and again till the final conquest of the southern districts, between Cape St. Vincent and the Guadiana (c. 1250), left the European kingdom fully formed, and the recovery of Western Spain from the Moslem had been achieved.

Chart of the Mediterranean Sea by WILLEM BARENTSZOON. Engraved in copper 1595.
Almost unaltered copy of a Portolano from the 14th century. (Orig. size 418 x 855 m.m.).
(SEE LIST OF MAPS)

(4.) And when the Crusading Age passed away, it left behind an intercourse of Portugal with England, Flanders, and the North Sea coasts, which was taken up and developed by Diniz and the kings of the fourteenth century, till under the new Royal House of Aviz, in the boyhood of Henry the Navigator, this maritime and commercial element had clearly become the most important in the State, the main interest even of Government.

So, from the first mercantile treaty of 1294, between the traders of Lisbon and London, we feel ourselves beyond the mere fighting period, and before the death of Diniz (1325), there is a good deal more progress in the same direction. The English treaty of exchange is followed by similar ones with France and with Flanders, while for the protection of this commerce, as well as to prove his fellowship or his rivalry with the maritime republics of Italy, Diniz,[32] the "Labourer King," built the first Portuguese navy, founded a new office of state for its command, and gave the post to a great Genoese sailor, Emanuel Pessanha, 1317. With the new Lord High Admiral begins the Spanish-Italian age of ocean voyages, and the rediscovery of the Canaries in 1341 is the first result of the alliance. In 1353 the old treaty of 1294 is enlarged and safeguarded by fresh clauses signed in London, as if to guard against future trouble in the dark days then hanging over Portugal.

For the next generation (1350-1380), the national politics are bound up with Spanish intrigues and lose nearly all reference to that larger world, to which the kingdom was recalled by the Revolution of 1383, the overthrow of Castille on the battle-field of Aljubarrota, and the accession of John of Aviz. Once more intensely, narrowly national, one might almost say provincial, in peninsular matters, Portugal then returned to its older ambition of being, not a make weight in Spanish politics, but a part of the greater whole of commercial and maritime Europe. Almost ceasing to be Spanish, she was, by that very transfer of interest from land to sea, fitted for her special part,—

"to open up those wastes of tideNo generation openèd before."

It was through a love affair that the crisis came about. Ferdinand the Handsome, the last of the House of Burgundy to reign in Lisbon, became the slave of the worst of his subjects, the evil genius of himself and his kingdom, Leonora Telles. For her sake he broke his marriage treaty with Castille (1372), and brought down the vengeance of Henry of Trastamara, whom the Black Prince of England had fought and seemed to conquer at Navarette, but who in the end had foiled all his enemies—Pedro the Cruel, Ferdinand of Portugal, and Prince Edward of Creçy and Poictiers.

For Leonor's sake Ferdinand braved the great riot of the Lisbon mob, when Fernan Vasquez the Tailor led his followers to the palace, burst in the gates, and forced from the King an oath to stand by the Castilian marriage he had contracted. For her sake he broke his word to his artisans, as he had broken it to his nobles and his brother monarch.

Leonor herself the people hunted for in vain through the rooms and corridors of the palace; she escaped from their lynch law to Santarem. The same night Ferdinand joined her. Safe in his strongest fortress, he gathered an army and forced his way back into the capital. The mob was scattered; Vasquez and the other leaders beheaded on the spot. Then at Oporto, without more delay, the King of Portugal married his paramour, in the face of her husband, of Castille, and of his own people.

"Laws are nil," said the rhyme, "when kings will," but though nobles and people submitted in the lifetime of Ferdinand, the storm broke out again on his death in October, 1383. During the last ten years the Queen had practically governed, and the kingdom seemed to be sinking back into a province of Spain. Ferdinand's bastard brother, John, Master of the Knights of Aviz, and father of Henry the Navigator, was the leader of the national party, and Leonor had in vain tried to get rid of him, silent and dangerous as he was. She forged some treasonable letters in his name, and procured his arrest; then as the King would not order him to execution without trial, she forged the warrant, too, and sent it promptly to the Governor of Evora Castle, where the Master lay in prison. But he refused to obey without further proof, and John escaped to lead the national restoration.

On the death of Ferdinand his widow took the regency in the name of her daughter Beatrice, just married to the King of Castille. It was only a question of time, this coming subjection of Portugal, unless the whole people rose and made monarchy and government national once more. And in December, 1383, they did so. Under John of Aviz the patriots cut to pieces the Queen's friends, and made ready to meet her allies from Castille. On the battle field of Aljubarrota (August 14, 1385), the struggle was decided. Castille was finally driven back, and the new age, of the new dynasty, was fairly started. The Portuguese people under King John I. and his sons Edward, Pedro, Henry, and Ferdinand, passed out of the darkness of their slavery into the light and life of their heroic age.

WEST FRONT OF THE MONASTERY CHURCH OF BATALHA
WHERE PRINCE HENRY LIES BURIED.

The founder of the House of Aviz, John, the King of Good Memory, is the great transition figure in his country's history, for in his reign the age of the merely European kingdom is over, and that of discovery and empire begins. That is, the limits of territory and of population, as well as the type of government and of policy, both home and foreign, secured by his victory and his reign, are permanent in themselves, and as the conditions of success they lie at the root of the development of the next hundred years.

Even the drift of Portuguese interests, seawards and southwards, is decided by his action, his alliance with England, his encouragement of trade, his wars against the Moors. For, by the middle of his reign, by the time of the Ceuta conquest (1415), his third son, Prince Henry, had grown to manhood.

Yet, King John's personal work (1383-1433) is rather one of settlement and the providing of resources for future action than the taking of any great share in that action. His mind was practical rather than prophetic, common-sense rather than creative; but in his regeneration of the Court and trade and society and public service of the kingdom, he fitted his people to play their part, to be for a time the "very foremost men of all this world."

First of all, he founded a strong centralised monarchy, like those which marked the fifteenth century in France and England and Russia. The spirit, the aim of Louis XI., of the Tudors, of Ivan III., was the same as that of John I. of Portugal—to rule as well as govern in every department, "over all persons, in all causes, as well ecclesiastical as civil, within their dominions supreme." The Master of Aviz had been the people's choice; the Lisbon populace and their leaders had been among the first who dared to fight for him; but he would not be a simple King of Parliaments. He preferred to reign with the help of his nobles. For though he distrusted feudalism, he dreaded Cortés still more. So, while in most of the new monarchies of Europe the subjection or humiliation of the baronage was a primary article of policy, John tried to win his way by lavish gifts of land, while resolutely checking feudalism in government, curtailing local immunities, and guarding the liberties of the towns against noble usurpers.

We shall see the results of this in the life of Prince Henry; at present there is only space to notice the general fact. The other lines of John's home government—his reform of criminal procedure, his sanction of the vernacular in legal and official business in place of Latin, his attempt to publish the first collection of Portuguese laws, his settlement of the Court in the true national capital of Lisbon—are only to be linked with the life of his son, as helping one and all of them towards that conscious political unity on which Henry's work was grounded.

The same was the result of his foreign policy, which was nothing more than the old state-rules of Diniz. Systematic neutrality in Spain and a commercial alliance with England and the northern nations, were but the common-sense securities of the restored kingdom; but they played another part than one of mere defence, in drawing out the seamanship and worldly knowledge, and even the greed of Portuguese traders. In the marts of Bruges and London, "the Schoolmasters of Husbandry to Europe," Henry's countrymen met the travellers and merchants of Italy and Flanders and England and the Hanse Towns, and gained some inkling of the course and profits of the overland trade from India and the further East, first as in Nismes and Montpellier they saw the Malaguette pepper and other merchandise of the Sahara and Guinea caravans.

The Windsor and Paris treaties of 1386 and 1389; the marriage of John himself with Philippa, daughter of old "John of Gaunt, time-honoured" and time-serving "Lancaster," and the consequent alliance between the House of Aviz and the House of our own Henry IV., are proofs of an unwritten but well understood Triple Alliance of England, Flanders, and Portugal, which had been fostered by the Crusades and by trade and family politics. And through this friendship had come into being what was now the chief outward activity of Portuguese life, an interest in commerce, which was the beginning of a career of discovery and colonisation. Lastly, besides good government, besides saving the kingdom and keeping it safely in the most prosperous path, Portugal owed to King John and his English wife the training of their five sons, Edward the Eloquent, Pedro the Great Regent, Henry the Navigator, John the Constable, Ferdinand the Saint—the cousins of our own Henry V., Henry of Azincourt.

Edward, the heir of John the Great and his unfortunate successor (1433-8), unlucky as most literary princes, but deserving whatever courage and honesty and the best gifts can deserve, was a good ruler, a good son, a good brother, a good lawyer, and one of the earliest writers in his own Portuguese. As a pupil of his father's great Chancellor, John of the Rules, he has left a tract on the *Ordering of Justice*; as a king, two others, on *Pity* and *A Loyal Councillor*; as a cavalier, *A Book of Good Riding*. Still more to our purpose, he was always at the side of his brother Henry, helped him in his schemes and brought his movement into fashion at a critical time, when enterprise seemed likely to slacken in the face of unending difficulties.

But the Navigator's right-hand man was his next brother Pedro the Traveller, who, after visiting all the countries of Western Europe and fighting with the Teutonic knights against the heathen Prussians, brought back to Portugal for the use of discovery that great mass of suggestive material, oral and written, in maps and plans and books, which was used for the first ocean voyages of Henry's sailors.

On his judgment and advice, more than of any other man, Henry relied, and after Edward's death it was due to him as Regent that the generous support of the past was more than kept up, that so many ships and men were found for the rounding of Cape Verde, and that Edward's son and heir Affonso V., was trained in the mind of his father and his uncle, to be their successor in leading the expansion of Portugal and of Christendom.

AISLE IN BATALHA CHURCH CONTAINING THE TOMBS OF
HENRY AND HIS BROTHERS.

John and Ferdinand, Henry's two younger brothers, are not of much importance in his work, though they were both of the same rare quality as the elder Infantes, and the worst disaster of Henry's life, the Tangier campaign, is closely bound up with the fate of "Fernand the Constant Prince," but as we pass from the earlier story of Portugal to the age of its great achievements, it would be hard to doubt or to forget that the mother of the Navigator was also of some account in the shaping of the heroes of her house. Through her at least the Lusitanian Prince of Thomson's line is half an Englishman:

"The Lusitanian prince, who, Heaven-inspired,To love of useful glory
roused mankind,And in unbounded commerce mixed the world."

[NOTE 1.—The Old Roman Lusitania, but with a wider stretch on the North, and a narrower stretch on the East. So the Portuguese are "Lusians," "Lusitanians," etc., in poetry. *Cf.* Camoëns, *Lusiads.*]

[NOTE 2.—

What Diniz willèdHe ever fulfillèd

—said the popular rhyme.]

CHAPTER VII.

HENRY'S POSITION AND DESIGNS AT THE TIME OF THE FIRST VOYAGES, 1410-15.

Then from ancient gloom emerged
The rising world of trade: the genius then,
Of Navigation, held in hopeless sloth,
Had slumbered on the vast Atlantic deep
For idle ages, starting, heard at last
The Lusitanian Prince, who, Heaven-inspired,
To love of useful glory roused mankind,
And in unbounded commerce mixed the world.

THOMSON, *Seasons, Summer, 1005-1012.*

The third son of John the Great and of Philippa was the Infant Henry, Duke of Viseu, Master of the Order of Christ, Governor of the Algarves, born March 4, 1394, who might have travelled from Court to Court like his brother Pedro, but who refused all offers from England, Italy, and Germany, and chose the life of a student and a seaman,—retiring more and more from the known world that he might open up the unknown.

After the capture of Ceuta, in 1415, he planted himself in his Naval Arsenal at Sagres, close to Lagos town and Cape St. Vincent, and for more than forty years, till his death in 1460, he kept his mind upon the ocean that stretched out from that rocky headland to the unknown West and South. Twice only for any length of time did he come back into political life; for the rest, though respected as the referee of national disputes and the leader and teacher of the people, his time was mainly spent in thinking out his plans of discovery—drawing his maps, adjusting his instruments, sending out his ships, receiving the reports of his captains. His aims were three: to discover, to add to the greatness and wealth of Portugal, and to spread the Christian Faith.

(1.) First of all, he was trying to find a way round Africa to India for the sake of the new knowledge itself and for the power which that knowledge would give. As his mind was above all things interested in the scientific question, it was this side which was foremost in his plans. He was really trying to find out the shape of the world, and to make men feel more at home in it, that the dread of the great unknown round the little island of civilised and habitable world might be lightened. He was working in the mist that so long had hung round Christendom, chilling every enterprise.

Thus the whole question of the world and its shape, its countries and climates, its seas and continents, on every side of practical exploration, was bound to be before Prince Henry as a theorist; the practical question which he helped to solve was only a part of this wider whole. Did this Africa stretching opposite to him in his retreat at Sagres never end till it reached the Southern pole, or was it possible to get round into the Eastern ocean? Since Ptolemy's map had held the field, it had been heresy to suppose this; but in the age of Greek and Phœnician voyages it had been guessed by some, and perhaps even proved by others.

The Tyrians whom Pharaoh Necho sent down the Red Sea more than six hundred years before Christ, brought back after three years a story of their finding Africa an island, and so returning by the west and north through the Straits of Gibraltar.

The same tradition, after a long time of discredit, was now reviving upon the maps of the fourteenth century, and, in spite of the terrible stories of the Arabs, Henry was able in the first years of the fifteenth to find men who would try the forlorn hope of a direct sea-route from Europe to the Indies. We have seen how far the charts and guide-books of the time just before this had advanced Christian knowledge of the world; how the southern coastline of Asia is traced by Marco Polo, and how even Madagascar is named, though not visited, by the same traveller; the Florentine map of 1351 proves that a fairly true guess of the shape of Africa could be made even before persistent exploration began with Henry of Portugal; the Arab settlements on the east coast of Africa and their trade with the Malabar coast, though still kept as a close monopoly for Islam, had thoroughly opened up a line of navigation, that was ready, as it were, for the first Europeans who could strike into it and press the Moorish pilots into a new service. Discovery was thus anticipated when the coasts of West and South had once been rounded.

Beyond this, the vague knowledge of the Guinea coast already gained through the Sahara Caravan Trade was improved by the Prince himself, during his stay at Ceuta, into the certainty that if the great western hump of Africa beyond Bojador could be passed, his caravels would come into an eastern current, passing the gold and ivory coast, which might lead straight to India, and at any rate would be connected by an overland traffic with the Mediterranean.

(2.) Again, Henry was founding upon his work of exploration an empire for his country. At first perhaps only thinking of the straight sea-passage as the possible key of the Indian trade, it became clearer with every fresh discovery that the European kingdom might and must be connected by a chain of forts and factories with the rich countries for whose sake all these barren coasts were passed. In any case, and in the eyes of ordinary men, the riches of the East were the plain and primary reason of the explorations. Science had its own aims, but to gain an income for its work it must promise some definite gain. And the chief hope of Henry's captains was that the wealth now flowing by the overland routes to the Levant would in time, as the prize of Portuguese daring, go by the water way, without delay or fear of plunder or Arab middlemen, to Lisbon and Oporto. This would repay all the trouble and all the cost, and silence all who murmured. For this Indian trade was the prize of the world, and for the sake of this Rome had destroyed Palmyra, and attacked Arabia and held Egypt, and struggled for the mastery of the Tigris. For the same thing half the wars of the Levant had been waged, and by this the Italian republics, Venice, Genoa, and Pisa, had grown to greatness.

(3.) Lastly, Henry was a Crusader with Islam and a missionary with the heathen. Of him fully as much as of Columbus, it may be said, that if he aimed at an empire, it was a Christian one, and from the time of the first voyages his captains had orders not merely to discover and to trade, but to convert. Till his death he hoped to find the land of Prester John, the half-true, half-fabulous Christian Priest-King of the outer world, so long cut off from Christendom by the Mohammedan states.

At this time many things were drawing western Europe towards the East and towards discovery. The progress of science and historic knowledge, the records and suggestions of travellers, the development of the Christian nations, the position of Portugal and the spirit of her people,—all these lines met, as it were, in Henry's time and nation and person, and from that meeting came the results of Columbus and Da Gama and Magellan.

In the earlier chapters we have tried to trace the preparation along these slowly converging paths, for the discoveries of the fifteenth century. We started with that body of knowledge and theory about the world which the Roman Empire bequeathed to Christendom, and which in the earlier Middle Ages was worked upon by the Arabs, and we gained some idea, from the sayings of Moslem geographers and from the doings of Moslem warriors, of the hindrance as well as of the help that Islam gave to European expansion. We saw that during the great struggle of Christianity and of the old Order with barbarism, the chief energy of our Western world in discovery or extension of any sort took the shape of pilgrimage. Then, as time went on, it was possible to see that the Saracens, who had begun as destroyers in the South, were acting as teachers and civilisers upon Europe, and that the Vikings, who as pirates in the North seemed raised up to complete the ruin of Latin civilisation, were really waking it into a new activity.

In the Crusades this activity, which had already founded the kingdom of Russia on one side and touched America on the other, seemed to pass from the Northern seamen into every Christian nation and every class of society, and with the conversion of the Northmen their place as the discoverers and leaders of the Christian world fitted in with the other movements of Mediterranean commerce and war and devotion. Even the pilgrims of the Crusading Age were now no longer distinctive: they were often, as individuals, members of other classes, traders, fighters, or travellers who, after gaining a firm foothold in Syria, began the exploration of the further East.

The three great discovering energies of the thirteenth and fourteenth centuries—in land-travel, navigation, and science—were all seen to be results, in whole or in part, of the Crusades themselves, and in following the more important steps of European travel and trade and proselytism from the Holy Land to China, it became more and more evident that this practical finding out of the treasures of Cathay and the Indies was the necessary preparation for the attempts of Genoese and Portuguese to open up the sea route as another and a safer way to the source of the same treasures.

Lastly, the intermittent and uncertain ventures of the fourteenth-century seamen, Italian, Spanish, French, or English, to coast round Africa or to find the Indies by the Southern route—to reach a definite end without any clear plan of means to that end—and the revival in theoretical geography, which was trying at the same time to fill up the gaps of knowledge by tradition or by probability—seemed to offer a clear contrast and a clear foreshadowing also of Prince Henry's method. Even his nearest forerunners, in seamanship or in map-making[33] were strikingly different from himself. They were too much in the spirit of Ptolemy and of ancient science; they neglected fact for hypothesis, for clever guessing, and so their work was spasmodic and unfruitful, or at least disappointing.

It was true enough that each generation of Christian thought was less in fault than the one before it; but it was not till the fifteenth century, till Henry had set the example, that exploration became systematic and continuous. To Marco Polo and men like him we owe the beginnings of the art and science of discovery among the learned; to the Portuguese is due at least the credit of making it a thing of national interest, and of freeing it from a false philosophy. To find out by incessant and unwearying search what the world really was, and not to make known facts fit in with the ideas of some thinker on what the world ought to be, this we found to be the main difference between Cosmas or even Ptolemy and any true leader of discovery. For a real advance of knowledge, fancy must follow experiment, and no merely hypothetical system or Universe as shewn in Holy Scripture, would do any longer. We have come to the time when explorers were not Ptolemaics or Strabonians or Scripturists, but Naturalists—men who examined things afresh, for themselves.

These various objects are all involved in the one central aim of discovery, but they are not lost in it. To know this world we live in and to teach men the new knowledge was the first thing, which makes Henry what he is in universal history; his other aims are those of his time and his nation, but they are not less a part of his life.

And he succeeded in them all; if in part his work was for all time and in part seemed to pass away after a hundred years, that was due to the exhaustion of his people. What he did for his countrymen was realised by others, but the start, the inspiration, was his own. He persevered for fifty years (1412-60) till within sight of the goal, and though he died before the full result of his work was seen, it was none the less his due when it came.

We find these results put down to the credit of others, but if Columbus gave Castille and Leon a new world in 1492, if Da Gama reached India in 1498, if Diaz rounded the Cape of Tempests or of Good Hope in 1486, if Magellan made the circuit of the globe in 1520-2, their teacher and master was none the less Henry the Navigator.

CHAPTER VIII.

PRINCE HENRY AND THE CAPTURE OF CEUTA.

1415.

We have seen how the kingdom of Portugal itself was almost an offspring of the Crusades. They had left behind them a thirst for wealth and for a wider life on one side, and a broken Moslem power on the other, which opened the way and stirred the enterprise of every maritime state. We know that Lisbon had long been an active centre of trade with the Hanse Towns, Flanders, and England. And now the projected conquest of Ceuta and the appeal of the conqueror of Aljubarrota for a great national effort found the people prepared. A royal prince could do what a private man could not; and Portugal, more fully developed than any other of the Christian kingdoms, was ready to expand abroad without fear at home.

Even before the conquest of Ceuta, in 1410 or 1412, Henry had begun to send out his caravels past Cape Non, which had so long been with C. Bojador the Finisterre of Africa. The first object of these ships was to reach the Guinea coast by outflanking the great western shoulder of the continent. Once there, the gold and ivory and slave trade would pass away from the desert caravans to the European coasters. Then the eastern bend of Africa, along the bights of Benin and Biafra, might be followed to the Indies, if this were possible, as some had thought; if not, the first stage of the work would have to be taken up again till men had found and had rounded the Southern Cape. The outflanking of Guinea proved to be only a part of the outflanking of Africa, but it was far more than half the battle; just as India was the final prize of full success, so the Gold Coast was the reward of the first chapter in that success.

But of these earlier expeditions nothing is known in detail; the history of the African voyages begins with the war of 1415, and the new knowledge it brought to Henry of the Sahara and the Guinea Coast and of the tribes of tawny Moors and negroes on the Niger and the Gambia.

In 1414, when Edward was twenty-three, Pedro twenty-two, and Henry twenty, King John planned an attack on Ceuta, the great Moorish port on the African side of the Straits of Gibraltar. The three princes had all asked for knighthood; their father at first proposed to celebrate a year of tournaments, but at the suggestion of the Treasurer of Portugal, John Affonso de Alemquer, he decided on this African crusade instead. For the same strength and money might as well be spent in conquests from the

Moslem as in sham-fights between Christians. So after reconnoitring the place, and lulling the suspicions of Aragon and Granada by a pretence of declaring war against the Count of Holland, King John gained the formal consent of his nobles at Torres Vedras, and set sail from Lisbon on St. James' Day, July 25, 1415, as foretold by the dying Queen Philippa, twelve days before.

KING JOHN THE GREAT AND QUEEN PHILIPPA.
FROM THEIR TOMB AT BATALHA.

That splendid woman, who had shared the throne for eight and twenty years, and who had trained her sons to be fit successors of her husband as the leaders of Portugal and the "Examples of all Christians," was now cut off by death from a sight of their first victories. Her last thought was for their success. She spoke to Edward of a king's true vocation, to Pedro of his knightly duties in the help of widows and orphans, to Henry of a general's care for his men. On the 13th, the last day of her illness, she roused herself to ask "What wind was blowing so strong against the house?" and hearing it was the north, sank back and died, exclaiming, "It is the wind for your voyage, that must be about St. James' Day." It would have been false respect to delay. The spirit of the Queen, the crusaders felt, was with them, urging them on.

By the night of the 25th of July the fleet had left the Tagus; on the 27th the crusaders anchored in the bay of Lagos and mustered all their forces: "33 galleys, 27 triremes, 32 biremes, and 120 pinnaces and transports," carrying 50,000 soldiers and 30,000 mariners. Some nobles and merchant adventurers from England, France, and Germany took part. It was something like the conquest of Lisbon over again; a greater Armada for a much smaller prey.

On the 10th of August they were off Algeziras, still in Moorish hands, as part of the kingdom of Granada, and on the 12th the lighter craft were over on the African coast; a strong wind nearly carried the heavier into Malaga.

Ceuta, the ancient Septa,[34] once repaired by Justinian, was the chief port of Morocco and a centre of commerce for the trade routes of the South and East, as well as a centre of piracy for the Barbary corsairs. It had long been an outpost of Moslem attack on Christendom; now that Europe was taking the offensive, it would be an outpost of the Spanish crusade against Islam.

The city was built on the ordinary model, in two parts: a citadel and a port-town, which together covered the neck of a long peninsula running out some three miles eastward from the African mainland, and broadening again beyond the eastern wall of Ceuta into a hilly square of country.

It was here, just where the land began to spread and form a natural harbour, that the Portuguese had planned their landing, and to this point Prince Henry, with great trouble, brought up the heavier craft. The strong currents that turned them off to the Spanish coast, proved good allies of the Europeans after all. For the Moors, who had been greatly startled at the first signs of attack, and had hurried to get all the help they could from Fez and the upland, now fancied the Christian fleet to be scattered once for all, and dismissed all but their own garrison; while the Portuguese had been roused afresh to action by the fiery energy of King John, Prince Henry, and his brothers. On the night of the 15th of August, the Feast of the Assumption, the whole armada was at last brought up to the roads of Ceuta; Henry anchored off the lower town with his ships from Oporto, and his father, though badly wounded in the leg, rowed through the fleet in a shallop, preparing all his men for the assault that was to be given at daybreak. Henry himself was to have the right of first setting foot on shore, where it was hoped the quays would be almost bared of defenders. For the main force was brought up against the castle, and every Moor would rush to the fight where the King of Portugal was leading.

While these movements were being settled in the armada, all through that night Ceuta was brilliantly lighted up, as if *en fête*. The Governor in his terror could think of nothing better than to frighten the enemy with the show of an immensely populous city, and he had ordered a light to be kept burning in every window of every house. As the morning cleared and the Christian host saw the beach and harbour lined with Moors, shouting defiance, the attack was begun by some volunteers who forgot the Prince's claim. One Ruy Gonsalvez was the first to land and clear a passage for the rest. The Infantes, Henry and Edward, were not far behind, and after a fierce struggle the Moslems were driven through the gate of the landing-place back to the wall of the city. Here they rallied, under a "negro giant, who fought naked, but with the strength of many men, hurling the Christians to the earth with stones." At last he was brought down by a lance-thrust, and the crusaders forced their way into Ceuta. But Henry, as chief captain on this side, would not allow his men to rush on plundering into the heart of the town, but kept them by the gates, and sent back to the ships for fresh troops, who soon came up under Fernandez d'Ataide, who cheered on the Princes. "This is the sort of tournament for you; here you are getting a worthier knighthood than you could win at Lisbon."

Meantime the King, with Don Pedro, had heard of Henry's first success while still on shipboard, and ordered an instant advance on his side. After a still closer struggle than that on the lower ground, the Moors were routed, and Pedro pressed on through the narrow streets, just escaping death from the showers of heavy stones off the house tops, till he met his brothers in a mosque, or square adjoining, in the centre of Ceuta.

Then the conquerors scattered for plunder, and came very near losing the city altogether. But for the dogged courage of Henry, who twice broke up the Moslem rally with a handful of men, at last holding a gate on the inner wall between the lower town and the citadel, "with seventeen, himself the eighteenth," Ceuta would have been lost after it had been gained. Both Henry and Pedro were reported dead. "Such is the end a soldier must not fear," was all their father said, as he stayed by the ships under the lee of the fortress, waiting, like Edward III. at Creçy, for what his sons would do. But towards evening it was known throughout the army that the Princes were safe, that the port-town had been gained, and that the Moors were slipping away from the citadel.

Henry, Edward, and Pedro held a council, and settled to storm the castle next morning; but after sunset a few scouts, sent out to reconnoitre, reported that all the garrison had fled.

It was true. The Governor, who had despaired all along of holding out, was no sooner beaten out of the lower city than he set the example of a strategic movement up the country, and when the Portuguese appeared at the fortress gate with axes and began to hew it down, only two Moors were left inside. They shouted out that the Christians might save themselves that trouble, for they would open it themselves, and the standard of St. Vincent, Patron of Lisbon, was planted, before dark came, upon the highest tower of Ceuta.

King John offered Henry, for his gallant leadership, the honours of the day and the right to knighted before his brothers, but the Prince, who had offered at the beginning of the storm to resign his command to Edward, as the eldest, begged that "those who were before him in age might have their right, to be first in dignity as well," and the three Infantes received their knighthood in order of birth, each holding in his hands the bare sword that the Queen had given him on her deathbed.

It was the first Christian rite held in the great Mosque of Ceuta, now purified as the Cathedral, and after it the town was thoroughly and carefully sacked from end to end. The plunder, of gold and silver and gems, stuffs and drugs, was great enough to make the common soldiers reckless of other things. The "great jars of oil and honey and spices and all provisions" were flung out into the streets, and a heavy rain swept away what would have kept a large garrison in plenty.

The great nobles and the royal Princes took back to Portugal some princely spoils. Henry's half-brother, now Count of Barcellos, afterwards more famous and more troublesome as Duke of Braganza, chose for his share some six hundred columns of marble and alabaster from the Governor's palace. Henry himself gained in Ceuta a knowledge of inland Africa, of its trade routes and of the Gold Coast, that encouraged him to begin from this time the habit of coasting voyages. His earlier essays in exploration had been attempts, like the unconnected and occasional efforts of Spanish and Italian daredevils. It is from this year that continuous ocean sailing begins; from the time of his stay in Ceuta, Henry works steadily and with foresight towards a nearer goal well foreseen, a first stage in his wider scheme which had been traversed by men he had known and talked with. They had come into Ceuta from Guinea over the sea of the desert; he would send his sailors to *their* starting-point by the longer way, over the desert of the sea.

Thus the victory at Ceuta is not without a very direct influence on our subject; and for the same reason, it was important that the conquerors, instead of razing the place, decided to hold it. When most of the council of war were for a safe and quick return to Portugal, one noble, Pedro de Menezes, a trusted friend of Henry's, struck upon the ground impatiently a stick of orange-wood he had in his hands. "By my faith, with this stick I would defend Ceuta from every Morisco of them all." He was left in command, and thus kept open, as it were, to Europe and to the Prince's view, one end of a great avenue of commerce and intercourse, which Henry aimed at winning for his country. When his ships could once reach Guinea, the other end of that same line was in his hands as well.

GATEWAY OF THE CHURCH OF THE ORDER OF CHRIST AT THOMAR.

The King and the Princes left Ceuta in September of the same year (Sept. 2, 1415), but Henry's connection with his first battle-field was not yet over. Menezes found after three years' sole command, that the Moors were pressing him very hard. The King of Granada had sent seventy-four ships to blockade the city from the sea, and the troops of Fez were forcing their way into the lower town. Henry was hurriedly sent from Lisbon to its relief, while Edward and Pedro got themselves ready to follow him, if needed, from Lagos and the Algarve coast. But Ceuta had already saved itself. As the first succours were sailing through the Straits of Gibraltar, Menezes contrived to send them word of his danger; the Berbers on the land side had mastered Almina, or the eastern part of the merchant town, while the

Granada galleys had closed in upon the port itself. At this news Henry made the best speed he could, but he was only in time to see the rout of the Moors. Menezes and the garrison made a desperate sally directly they sighted the relief coming through the straits; the same appearance struck a panic into the enemy's fleet, and only one galley stayed on the African coast to help their landsmen, who were thus left alone and without hope of succour on the eastern hills of the Ceuta peninsula, cut off by the city from their Berber allies. When Henry landed, Almina had been won back and the last of the Granada Moslems cut to pieces. From that day Ceuta was safe in Christian hands.

But the Prince, after spending two months in the hope that he might find some more work to do in Africa, planned a daring stroke in Europe. Islam still owned in Spain the kingdom of Granada, too weak to reconquer the old Western Caliphate, but too strong, as the last refuge of a conquered and once imperial race, to be an easy prey of the Spanish kingdoms. And in that kingdom, Gibraltar, the rock of Tarik, was the most troublesome of Moorish strongholds. The Mediterranean itself was not fully secured for Christian trade and intercourse while the European Pillar of the Western straits was a Saracen fort. If Portugal was to conquer or explore in northern Africa, Gibraltar was as much to be aimed at as Ceuta. Both sides of the straits, Calpe and Abyla, must be in her hands before Christendom could expand safely along the Atlantic coasts.

So Henry, in the face of all his council, determined to make the trial on his voyage back to Lisbon. But a storm broke up the fleet, and when it could be refitted and re-formed, the time had gone by, and the Prince obeyed his father's repeated orders and returned at once to Court. For his gallantry and skill in the storm of Ceuta, he had been made Duke of Viseu and Lord of Covilham, when King John first touched his own kingdom—after the African campaign—at Tavira, on the Algarve coast. With his brother Pedro, who shared his honours as Duke of Coimbra and Lord of the lands henceforward known as the Infantado or Principality, Henry thus begins the line of Dukes in Portugal, and among the other details of the war, his name is specially joined with that of an English fleet which he had enrolled as a contingent of his armada while recruiting for ships and men in the spring of 1415. In the same way as English crusaders had passed Lisbon just in time to aid in its conquest by Affonso Henriquez, the "great first King" of Portugal in 1147, so now twenty-seven English ships on their way to Syria were just in time to help the Portuguese make their first conquest abroad.

Lastly, the results of the Ceuta campaign in giving positive knowledge of western and inland Africa to a mind like Henry's already set on the finding of a sea-route to India, have been noticed by all contemporaries and followers, who took any interest in his plans, but it was not merely caravan news that he gained in these two visits of 1415 and 1418. Both Azurara, the chronicler of his voyages and Diego Gomez, his lieutenant, the explorer of the Cape Verde Islands and of the Upper Gambia, are quite clear about the new knowledge of the coast now gained from Moorish prisoners.

Not only did the Prince get "news of the passage of merchants from the coasts of Tunis to Timbuctoo and to Cantor on the Gambia, which inspired him to seek the lands by the way of the sea," but also "the Tawny Moors (or Azanegues) his prisoners told him of certain tall palms growing at the mouth of the Senegal or western Nile, by which he was able to guide the caravels he sent out to find that river." By the time Henry was ready to return from Ceuta to Portugal for good and all, in 1418, there were clearly before his mind the five reasons for exploring Guinea given by his faithful Azurara:

First of all was his desire to know the country beyond Cape Bojador, which till that time was quite unknown either by books or by the talk of sailors.

Second was his wish that if any Christian people or good ports should be discovered beyond that cape, he might begin a trade with them that would profit both the natives and the Portuguese, for he knew of no other nation in Europe who trafficked in those parts.

Thirdly, he believed the Moors were more powerful on that side of Africa than had been thought, and he feared there were no Christians there at all. So he was fain to find out how many and how strong his enemies really were.

Fourthly, in all his fighting with the Moors he had never found a Christian prince to help him from that side (of further Africa) for the love of Christ, therefore he wished, if he could, to meet with such.

Last was his great desire for the spread of the Christian Faith and for the redemption of the vast tribes of men lying under the wrath of God.

Behind all these reasons Azurara also believed in a sixth and deeper one, which he proceeds to state with all gravity, as the ultimate and celestial cause of the Prince's work.

"For as his ascendant was Aries, that is in the House of Mars and the Exaltation of the Sun, and as the said Mars is in Aquarius, which is the House of Saturn, it was clear that my lord should be a great conqueror, and a searcher out of things hidden from other men, according to the craft of Saturn, in whose House he was."[35]

CHAPTER IX.

HENRY'S SETTLEMENT AT SAGRES AND FIRST DISCOVERIES.

1418-28.

Whatever the Prince owed to his stay at Ceuta beyond the general suggestion and encouragement to take up a life-profession of discovery, it was at any rate put into practice on his second and last return (1418). From that time to the end of his life he became a recluse from the Court life of Lisbon, though he soon gathered round himself a rival Court, of science and seamanship.

The old "Sacred Cape" of the Romans, then called Sagres, now the "Cape St. Vincent" of Nelson and modern maps, was his chosen home for the next forty years, though he seems to have passed a good deal of his time in his port of Lagos, close by.

In 1419 King John made him Governor for life of the Algarves (the southern province of Portugal) and the new governor at once began to rebuild and enlarge the old naval arsenal, in the neck of the Cape, into a settlement that soon became the "Prince's Town." In Lagos, his ships were built and manned; and there, and in Sagres itself, all the schemes of discovery were thought out, the maps and instruments corrected, and the accounts of past and present travellers compared by the Prince himself. His results then passed into the instructions of his captains and the equipment of his caravels. The Sacred Cape, which he now colonised, was at any rate a good centre for his work of ocean voyaging. Here, with the Atlantic washing the land on three sides, he was well on the scene of action. There were buildings on Sagres headland as old as the eleventh century; Greek geography had made this the starting-point of its shorter and continental measurements for the length of the habitable world, and the Genoese, whose policy was to buy up points of vantage on every coast, were eager to plant a colony there, but Portugal was not ready to become like the Byzantine Empire, a depot for Italian commerce, and Henry had his own reasons for securing a desolate promontory.

On this he now built himself a palace, a chapel, a study, an observatory—the earliest in Portugal—and a village for his helpers and attendants. "In his wish to gain a prosperous result for his efforts, the Prince devoted great industry and thought to the matter, and at great expense procured the aid of one Master Jacome from Majorca, a man skilled in the art of navigation and in the making of maps and instruments, and who was sent for, with certain of the Arab and Jewish mathematicians, to instruct the Portuguese in that science." So at least, says De Barros, the "Livy of Portugal." At Sagres was thus founded anew the systematic study of applied science in Christendom; it was better than the work of the old Greek "University" at Alexandria with which it has been compared, because it was essentially practical. From it "our sailors," says Pedro Nunes, "went out well taught and provided with instruments and rules which all map-makers should know." We would gladly know more of Henry's scientific work; a good many legends have grown up about it, and even his foundation of the Chair of Mathematics in the University of Lisbon or Coimbra, our best evidence of the unrecorded work of his school, has been doubted by some modern critics, even by the national historian, Alexander Herculano. But to Prince Henry's study and science two great improvements on this side may be traced: first in the art of map-making, secondly in the building of caravels and ocean craft.

The great Venetian map of Fra Mauro of the Camaldolese convent of Murano, finished in 1459, one year before the Navigator's death, is evidence for the one; Cadamosto's words, as a practical seaman, of Italian birth, in Henry's service, that the "caravels of Portugal were the best sailing ships afloat," may be proof sufficient of the other.

On both these lines, Henry took up the results of Italians and worked towards success with their aid. As Columbus and the Cabots and Verazzano in later times represented the intellectual leadership of Italy to other nations—Spain, England, and France; but had to find their career and resources not in their own commercial republics, but at the Courts of the new centralised kingdoms of the West, where a paternal despotism gave the best hope of guiding any popular movement, social or religious or political or scientific,—so in the earlier fifteenth century, mariners like Cadamosto and De Nolli, scientific draughtsmen like Fra Mauro and Andrea Bianco, looked from Venice and Genoa to the Court of Sagres and to the service of Prince Henry as their proper sphere, where they would find the encouragement and reward they sought for at home and often sought in vain.

Henry's settlement on Cape St. Vincent was not long without results. The voyage of his captain, John de Trasto, to the "fruitful" district of Grand Canary in 1415 was not in any sense a discovery, as the conquest of John de Béthencourt in 1402 had made these "Fortunate" islands perfectly well known, but the finding of Porto Santo and Madeira in 1418-20 was a real gain. For the Machin story of the English landing in Madeira was a close secret, which by good fortune passed into the Prince's keeping, but not beyond, so that as far as general knowledge went, the Portuguese were now fairly embarked upon the Sea of Darkness.

First came the sighting of the "Holy Haven" in 1418. In this year, says Azurara, two squires of the Prince's household, named John Gonsalvez Zarco and Tristam Vaz, eager for renown and anxious to serve their lord, had set out to explore as far as the coast of Guinea, but they were caught by a storm near Lagos and driven to the island of Porto Santo. This name they gave themselves "at this very time in their joy at thus escaping the perils of the tempest."

Zarco and Vaz returned in triumph to Sagres and reported the new-found island to be well worth a permanent settlement. Henry, always "generous," took up the idea with great interest and sent out Zarco and Vaz with another of his equerries, one Bartholomew Perestrello, to colonise, with two ships and products for a new country; corn, honey, the sugar cane from Sicily, the Malvoisie grape from Crete, even the rabbit from Portugal.

On his first return voyage Zarco had captured the pilot Morales of Seville, and from him the Prince had gained certain news of the English landing in Madeira. So it was with a definite purpose of further discovery that his captains returned to Porto Santo in 1420, with Morales as their guide. Now, as before, Zarco appears as chief in command; he had won himself a name at Ceuta, and if the tradition be true, had just brought in the first use of ship-artillery; the finding of Porto Santo was mainly credited to him.

Sailing from Lagos in June, 1420, he had no sooner reached once again the "Fair Haven" of his first success, than he was called to note a dark line, like a mark of distant land, upon the south-west horizon. The colonists he had left on his earlier visit had watched this day by day till they had made certain of its being something more than a passing appearance of sea or sky, and Morales was ready with his suggestion that this was Machin's island. The fog that hung over this part of the ocean would be natural to a thick and dank woodland like that on the island of his old adventure.

Zarco resolved to try: After eight days' rest in Porto Santo he set sail, and, observing that the fog grew less toward the east of the cloud bank, made for that point and came upon a low marshy cape, which he called St. Lawrence Head. Then, creeping round the south coast, he came to the high lands and the forests of Madeira,—so named here and now, either as De Barros says, "from the thick woods they found there," or, in the form of Machico, from the first discoverer, luckless Robert Machin. For on landing the Portuguese, guided by Morales, soon found the wooden cross and grave of the Englishman and his mistress, and it was there that Zarco, with no human being to dispute his title, "took seizin" of the island in the name of King John, Prince Henry, and the Order of Christ.

Embarking once more, he then coasted slowly round from the "River of the Flint" to "Jackdaw Point," and the "Chamber of the Wolves," where his men started a herd of sea-calves. So he came to the vast plain overgrown with fennel or "Funchal," where the chief town of after days grew up. A party sent inland to explore, reported that on every side the ocean could be seen from the hills; and Zarco, after taking in some specimens of the native wood and plants and birds at Funchal, put back in the last days of August to Portugal.

He was splendidly received at Court, made a count—"Count of the Chamber of the Wolves,"—and granted the command of the island for his own life. A little later, the commandership was made hereditary in his family. Tristam Vaz, the second in the Prince's commission, was rewarded too: the northern half of Madeira was given him as a captaincy, and in 1425 Henry began to colonise in form. Zarco, as early as May, 1421, had returned with wife and children and attendants, and begun to build the "port of Machico," and the "city of Funchal," but this did not become a state affair until four years more had gone by.

But from the first, the island, by its export of wood and dragon's blood and wheat, began to reward the trouble of discovery and settlement. Sugar and wine were brought to perfection in later years, after the great "Seven years' fire" had burnt down the forests and enriched the soil of Madeira. It was soon after Zarco's return to Funchal that he first set fire to the woods behind the fennel fields of the coast, to clear himself a way through the undergrowth into the heart of the island; the fire blazed and smouldered till it had taken well hold of the entire mass of timber that covered the upper country, nothing in the feeble resources of the first settlers could stop it, and Madeira lighted the ships of Henry on their way to the south, like a volcano, till 1428. This was at least the common story as told in Portugal, and it was often joined with another—of the rabbit plague, which ate up all the green stuff of the island in the first struggling years of Zarco's settlement, and so prevented the export of anything but timber. So much of this was brought into Portugal that Henry's lifetime is a landmark in the domestic architecture of Spain, and from the trade of the "Wood Island" is derived the lofty style of building that now began to replace the more modest fashion of the Arabs.

A charter of Henry's, dated 1430, ten years after the rediscovery of Madeira, and reciting the names of some of the first settlers, and his bequest of the island, or rather of its "spiritualties," to the Order of Christ on September 18, 1460, just before his death, are the chief links between this colony and the home country in the next generation—but in the history of institutions there are few more curious facts than the insistence of the Prince on a census for his little "Nation." From the first, the family registers of the colonists were carefully kept, and from these we see something of the wonder of men who were beginning human life, as it were, in a new land. The first children born in Madeira—a son and daughter of Ayres Ferreira, one of Zarco's comrades—were christened Adam and Eve.[36]

CHAPTER X.

CAPE BOJADOR AND THE AZORES.

1428-1441.

But in spite of Zarco's success, Cape Bojador had not yet been passed, though every year, from 1418, caravels had left Sagres, "to find the coasts of Guinea."

In 1428, Don Pedro, Henry's elder brother, had come home from his travels, with all the books and charts he had collected to help the explorers—and it is practically certain that the Mappa Mundi given him in Venice acted as a direct suggestion to the next attempts on west and south—westward to the Azores, southward towards Guinea.

Kept in the royal monastery of Alçobaça till late in the sixteenth century, though now irrecoverably lost, this treasure of Don Pedro's, like his "manuscripts of travel," would seem to have been used at the Sagres school till Prince Henry's death, and at least as early as 1431 its effect was seen in the first Portuguese recovery of the Azores. All the West African islands, plainly enough described in the map of 1428, were half within, half without the knowledge of Christendom, ever and anon being brought back or rediscovered by some accident or enterprise, and then being lost to sight and memory through the want of systematic exploration. This was exactly what the Portuguese supplied. The Azores, marked on the Laurentian Portulano of 1351, were practically unknown to seamen when, after eighty years had passed, Gonzalo Cabral was sent out from Sagres to find them (1431). He reached the Formiga group—the Ant islands,—and next year (1432) returned to make further discoveries, chiefly of the island Santa Maria. But the more important advances on this side were made between 1444-50, after the first colony had been planted twelve or fourteen years, and were the result of the Prince's theoretical correction of his captains' practical oversight. From a comparison of old maps and descriptions with their accounts, he was able to correct their line of sail and so to direct them to the very islands they had searched for in vain.

But as yet these results were far distant, and the slow and sure progress of African coasting towards Cape Bojador was the chief outcome of Pedro's help. In 1430, 1431, and 1432, the Infant urged upon his captains the paramount importance of rounding the Cape, which had baffled all his caravels by its strong ocean currents and dangerous rocks. At last this became the Prince's one command: Pass the Cape if you do nothing beyond; yet the years went by, King John of good memory died in 1433, and Gil Eannes, sent out in the same year with strong hopes of success, turned aside at the Canaries and only brought a few slaves back to Portugal. A large party at Court, in the Army, and among the nobles and merchant classes, complained bitterly of the utter want of profit from Henry's schemes, and there was at this time a danger of the collapse of his movement. For though as yet he paid his own expenses, his treasury could not long have stood the drain without any incoming.

Bojador, the "paunch" or "bulging Cape," 180 miles beyond Cape Non, had been, since the days of the Laurentian Portulano (1351), and the Catalan and Portuguese voyages of 1341 and 1346, the southmost point of Christian knowledge. A long circuit was needed here, as at the Cape of Good Hope, to round a promontory that stretched, men said, fully one hundred miles into the ocean, where tides and shoals formed a current twenty miles across. It was the sight or the fancy of this furious surge which frightened Henry's crews, for it plainly forbade all coasting and compelled the seamen to strike into the open sea out of sight of land. And though the discovery of Porto Santo had proved the feasibility and the gain of venturing boldly into the Sea of Darkness, and though since that time (1418) the Prince had sent out his captains due west to the Azores and south-west to Madeira, both hundreds of miles from the continent, yet in rounding Bojador there were not only the real terrors of the Atlantic, but the legends of the tropics to frighten back the boldest.

Most mariners had heard it said that any Christian who passed Bojador would infallibly be changed into a black, and would carry to his end this mark of God's vengeance on his insolent prying. The Arab tradition of the Green Sea of Night had too strongly taken hold of Christian thought to be easily shaken off. And it was beyond the Cape which bounded their knowledge that the Saracen geographers had fringed the coast of Africa with sea-monsters and serpent rocks and water unicorns, instead of place names, and had drawn the horrible giant hand of Satan raised above the waves to seize the first of his human prey that would venture into his den. If God made the firm earth, the Devil made the unknown and treacherous ocean—this was the real lesson of most of the mediæval maps, and it was this ingrained superstition that Henry found his worst enemy, appearing as it did sometimes even in his most trusted and daring captains.

And then again, the legends of Tropical Africa, of the mainland beyond Bojador, were hardly less terrible than those of the Tropical Ocean. The Dark Continent, with its surrounding Sea of Darkness, was the home of mystery and legend. We have seen how ready the Arabs were to write Uninhabitable over any unknown country—dark seas and lands were simply those that were dark to them, like the Dark Ages to others, but nowhere did their imagination revel in genies and fairies and magicians and all the horrors of hell, with more enthusiastic and genial interest than in Africa. Here only the northern parts could be lived in by man. In the south and central deserts, as we have heard from the Moslem doctors themselves, the sun poured down sheets of liquid flame upon the ground and kept the sea and the rivers boiling day and night with the fiery heat. So any sailors would of course be boiled alive as soon as they got near to the Torrid Zone.

It was this kind of learning, discredited but not forgotten, that was still in the minds of Gil Eannes and his friends when they came home in 1433, with lame excuses, to Henry's Court. The currents and south winds had stopped them, they said. It was impossible to get round Bojador.

The Prince was roused. He ordered the same captain to return next year and try the Cape again. His men ought to have learned something better than the childish fables of past time. "And if," said he, "there were even any truth in these stories that they tell, I would not blame you, but you come to me with the tales of four seamen who perhaps know the voyage to the Low Countries or some other coasting route, but, except for this, don't know how to use needle or sailing chart. Go out again and heed them not, for by God's help, fame and profit must come from your voyage, if you will but persevere."

The Prince was backed by the warm encouragement of the new King, Edward, his eldest brother, who had only been one month upon the throne when he bestirred himself to shew his favour to a national movement of discovery. King John had died on August 14, 1433 (the anniversary of Aljubarrota), and on September 26th, of the same year, by a charter given from Cintra, King Edward granted the islands of Madeira and Porto Santo, with the Desertas, to Henry as Grand Master of the Order of Christ.

With this encouragement the Infant sent out Gil Eannes in 1434 under the strongest charge not to return without a good account of the Cape and the seas beyond. Running far out into the open, his caravel doubled Bojador, and coming back to the coast found the sea "as easy to sail in as the waters at home," and the land very rich and pleasant. They landed and discovered no trace of men or houses, but gathered plants, "such as were called in Portugal St. Mary's roses," to present to Don Henry. Not even the southern Cape of Tempests or Good Hope was so long and obstinate a barrier as Bojador had been, and the passing of this difficulty proved the salvation of the Prince's schemes. Though again and again interrupted by political troubles between 1437 and 1449, the advance at sea went on, and never again was there a serious danger of the failure of the whole movement through general opposition and discontent.

In 1435 Gil Eannes was sent out again to follow up his success with Affonso Baldaya, the Prince's cupbearer, in a larger vessel than had yet been risked in exploration, called a varinel, or oared galley. The two captains passed fifty leagues—one hundred and fifty miles—beyond the Cape, and found traces of caravans, reached as far as an inlet they named Gurnet Bay, from its shoals of fish, and again put back to Lagos, early in the year.

There were still several months left for ocean sailing in 1435, and Henry at once despatched Baldaya again in his varinel, with orders to go as far as he could along the coast, at least till he could find some natives. One of these he was to bring home with him. Baldaya accordingly sailed 130 leagues—390 miles—beyond Cape Bojador, till he reached an estuary running some twenty miles up the country and promising to lead to a great river. This might prove to be the western Nile of the Negroes, or the famous River of Gold, Baldaya thought, and though it proved to be only an inlet of the sea, the name of Rio d'Ouro, then given by the first hopes of the Portuguese, has outlasted the disappointment that found only a sandy reach instead of a waterway to the Mountains of the Moon and the kingdom of Prester John.

Baldaya anchored here, landed a couple of horses which the Infant had given him to scour the country, and set "two young noble gentlemen" upon them to ride up country, to look for signs of natives, and if possible to bring back one captive to the ship. Taking no body-armour, but only lance and sword, the boys followed the "river" to its source, seven leagues up the country, and here came suddenly upon nineteen savages, armed with assegais. They rode up to them and drove them out of the open up to a loose mound of stones; then as evening was coming on and they could not secure a prisoner, they rode back to the sea and reached the ship about the dawn of day. "And of these boys," says the chronicler, "I myself knew one, when he was a noble gentleman of good renown in arms. His name was Hector Homen, and you will find him in our history well proved in brave deeds. The other, named Lopez d'Almeida, was a nobleman of good presence, as I have heard from those who knew him."

This first landing of Europeans on the coasts of unknown Africa, since the days of Carthaginian colonies, is one of the great moments in the story of Western expansion and discovery. For it means that Christendom on her Western side has at last got beyond the first circle of her enemies, the belt of settled Moslem ground, and has begun to touch the wider world outside, on the shore of the ocean as well as along the Eastern trade routes. And it almost seemed to be of little practical value that Marco Polo and the friars and traders who followed him had passed Islam in Asia, and reached even furthest Tartary, for it only made more clear that Asia was not Christian, and that there would have to be a deadly struggle before European influence could be restored on this side to what it had been under Alexander; but on the west, by the Atlantic coasts, once Morocco had been passed, there were only scattered savage tribes to be dealt with. Baldaya had now reached the pagans beyond Islam; the rival civilisation of the Arabs and their converts had been almost outflanked by Don Henry's ships; and the boys who rode up the Rio d'Ouro beach in 1435 were the first pickets of a great army. Their charge upon a body of grown men ten times their number, was a prophecy of the coming conquests of Christian Europe in the new worlds it was now in search of, in south and east and west.

Now Baldaya instantly followed up his pioneers. He took a party in his ship's boat and rode up the stream to the scene of the fight, with the boys on horseback riding by the bank and shewing him the stone-heap where the natives had rallied on the day before. But in the night they had all fled farther up country, leaving most of their miserable goods behind. All these were carried off, and the Portuguese left the Bay of the Horses, as they called this farthest reach of the Rio d'Ouro, and pulled back to the varinel, without any further success than a wholesome disappointment. They must go farther southward if they were to find the western Nile and the way round Africa.

Still Baldaya was not content. He wished to carry back a prisoner, as Henry had charged him, and so he coasted along fifty leagues more, from the Rio d'Ouro to the Port of Gallee, a rock that looked like a galley, where there was a more prominent headland than he had passed since Bojador. Here he landed once again, and found some native nets, made of the bark of trees, but none of the natives who made them.

In the early months of 1436 he and his varinel were again in Portuguese waters; but the land had now been touched that lay three hundred miles beyond the old African Finisterre, and in two years (1434-6) Portugal and all the Christian nations, through Henry's work, had entered on a new chapter of history. The narrower world of the Roman Empire and the Mediæval Church was already growing into the modern globe in the break up of that old terror of the sea which had so long fixed for men the bounds that they must not pass. The land routes had been cleared to Western knowledge, though not mastered, by the Crusades; now the far more dreaded and unknown water-way was fairly entered. For up to this time there is no fair evidence that either Christian or Moorish enterprise had ever rounded Bojador, and the theoretical marking of it upon maps was a very different thing from the experience that it was just like any other cape, and no more an end of the world than Cape St. Vincent itself. Neither Genoese, nor Catalans, nor Normans of Dieppe, nor the Arab wanderers of Edrisi and Ibn Said were before Don Henry now. His discoveries of the

Atlantic islands were findings, rediscoveries; his coast voyages from the year 1433 are all ventures in the true unknown.

But from 1436 to 1441, from Baldaya's second return to the start of Nuno Tristam and Antam Gonsalvez for Cape Blanco, exploration was not successful or energetic. The simple cause of this was the Infant's other business. In these years took place the fatal attempt on Tangier, the death of King Edward, and the troubles of the minority of his child, Affonso V.—Affonso the African conqueror of later years.

True it is, we read in our *Chronicle of the Discovery of Guinea*, that in these years there went to those parts two ships, one at a time, but the first turned back in the face of bad weather, and the other only went to the Rio d'Ouro for the skins and oil of sea wolves, and after taking in a cargo of these, went back to Portugal. And true it is, too, that in the year 1440 there were armed and sent out two caravels to go to that same land, but in that they met with contrary fortune, we do not tell any more of their voyage.

CHAPTER XI.

HENRY'S POLITICAL LIFE. 1433-1441.

The Prince's exile from politics in his hermitage at Sagres could not be absolutely unbroken. He was ready to come back to Court and to the battle field when he was needed. So he appeared at the deathbed of his father in 1433 and of his brother in 1438, at the siege of Tangier in 1437, and during the first years of the Regency (1438-40) he helped to govern for his nephew, Edward's son Affonso. From 1436 till 1441 he did not seriously turn his attention back to discovery.

What is chiefly interesting in the story of these years is the half-religious reverence paid to Henry by his brothers, by Cortés, and the whole people. He was above and beyond his age, but not so much as to be beyond its understanding. He was not a leader where there are no followers; he was one of the fortunate beings who are most valued by those who have lived on the closest terms with them, by father and by brothers.

It was believed throughout the kingdom that King John's last words were "an encouragement to the Infant to persevere in his right laudable purpose of spreading the Christian faith in the lands of darkness"; whether true or not, at any rate it was felt to fit the place and the man, and Henry's brothers, Pedro and Edward, took up loyally their father's commission to keep peace at home and sailing ships on the sea.

But the new reign was short and full of trouble. King Edward had scarcely been crowned when the scheme of an African war was revived by Don Ferdinand, the fourth of the "Famous Infants" of the House of Aviz (1433). Ferdinand, always a Crusader at heart, had refused a Cardinal's hat, that he might keep his strength for killing the enemies of Christ, and in Henry he found a ready listener. It was the Navigator, in fact, who planned and organised the scheme of campaign now pressed upon the King and the country. It was perfectly natural that he should do so. The war of Ceuta had been of the first importance to his work of discovery; it had been largely his own achievement, and his wish to conquer Heathens and Saracens and to make good Christians of them was hardly less strong than his natural bent for discovery and exploring settlement. He now took up Ferdinand's suggestion, made of it a definite project—for a storm of Tangier—and wrung a reluctant consent from Edward and from Cortés. The chief hindrance was lack of money; even the popularity of the Government could not prevent "sore grudging and murmuring among the people." Don Pedro himself was against the whole plan, and from respect to his wishes the question was referred to the Pope. Are we to make war on the infidels or no?

If the infidels in question, answered the Curia, were in Christian land and used Christian churches as mosques of Mohammed, or if they made incursions upon Christians, though always returning to their own land, or if doing none of these things they were idolaters or sinned against nature, the Princes of Portugal would do right to levy war upon them. But this should be done with prudence and piety, lest the people of Christ should suffer loss. Further, it was only just to tax a Christian people for support of an infidel war, when the said war was of necessity in defence of the kingdom. If the war was voluntary, for the conquering of fresh lands from the Heathen, it could only be waged at the King's own cost.

But before this answer arrived, the armament had been made ready, and things had gone too far to draw back; the Queen was eager for the war, and had brought King Edward to a more willing consent. So in the face of bad omens, an illness of Prince Ferdinand's, and the warning words of Don Pedro, the troops were put on board ship, August 17, 1437. On August 22d they set sail, and on the 26th landed at Ceuta, where Menezes still commanded. The European triumphs of 1415 and 1418 were still fresh in the memories of the Moors, and Don Henry was remembered as their hero. So it was to him that the tribes of the Beni Hamed sent offers of submission and tribute on the first news of the invasion. The Prince accepted their presents of gold and silver, cattle and wood, and left them in peace during the war, for the forces he had with him were barely sufficient for the siege of Tangier. Out of fourteen thousand men levied in Portugal, only six thousand answered the roll-call in Ceuta. A great number had shirked the dangers of Africa; and the room on shipboard had in itself been absurdly insufficient. The transports provided were just enough for the battalions that actually crossed, and for a fresh supply they must be sent back to Lisbon. In the council of war most were agreed upon this as the best thing on paper, but the practical difficulties were so great that Henry decided not to wait for reinforcements, but to push forward with the troops in hand.

The direct road to Tangier by way of Ximera was now found impassable, and it was determined to march the army round by Tetuan, while the fleet was brought up along the coast. Ferdinand, who was still suffering and unequal to the land journey, was to go by sea, while his elder brother, as chief captain of the whole armament, undertook to force his way along the inland routes. In this he was successful. In three days he came before Tetuan, which opened its gates at once, and on September 23d, without losing a single man, he appeared before Old Tangier, where Ferdinand was already waiting his arrival.

A rumour was now spread that the Moors were flying from Tangier as they had fled from Ceuta castle two and twenty years before, but Zala ben Zala, who commanded here as he had done there, now knew better how to defend a town, with the desperate courage of his Spanish foes. The attack instantly ordered by Henry on the gates of Tangier was roughly repulsed, and for the next fortnight the losses of the crusaders were so heavy that the siege was turned into a blockade. On September 30th, 10,000 horse and 90,000 foot came down from the upland to the coast for the relief of Tangier. Henry promptly led his little army into the open and ordered an attack, and the vast Moorish host which had taken up its station on a hill within sight of the camp, not daring to accept the challenge, wavered, broke, and rushed headlong to the mountains. But after three days they reappeared in greater numbers and even ventured down into the plain. Again Henry drove them back; again—next day—they returned; at last, after their force had been swollen to 130,000 men, and by overwhelming numbers had compelled the Christians to keep within their trenches, they threw themselves upon the Portuguese outposts. After a desperate struggle they were repulsed and a sally from the town was beaten back at the same time; the Europeans seemed ready to meet any odds. With these victories, Henry was confident that Tangier must soon fall; he ordered another escalade, but all his scaling ladders were burnt or broken and many of his men crushed beneath the overhanging parts of the wall, that were pushed down bodily upon the storming parties. In this final assault of the 5th of October, two Moors were taken who told Henry of immense succours now coming up under the Kings of Fez, of Morocco, and of Tafilet. They had with them, said the captives, at least 100,000 horse; their infantry was beyond count. Sure enough; on the 9th of October, the hills round Tangier seemed covered with the native armies, and it became clear that the siege must be raised. All that was left for Henry was to bring off his soldiers in safety. He tried his best. With quiet energy he issued his orders for all contingents; the marines and seamen were to embark at once; the artillery was given in charge of the Marshal of the Kingdom; Almada, the Hercules of Portugal, was to draw up the foot in line of battle; the Infant himself took his station with the cavalry on a small piece of rising ground.

When the Moors charged, they were well received. In spite of all their strength, one army being held ready to take another's place, as men grew tired, the Portuguese held their own. Henry had a horse killed under him; Cabral, his Master of Horse, fell at his side with five and twenty of his men; the cowardice of one regiment, who fled to the ships, almost ruined the defence; but when night fell, the Moorish columns fell sullenly back and left the Infant one more chance of flight and safety. It was the only hope, and even this was lost through the desertion of a traitor. Martin Vieyra, the apostate priest, once Henry's chaplain, now gave up to the enemy's generals the whole plan of escape.

After a long debate, it was determined, not to massacre the Christian army, but to take sureties from them that Ceuta should be restored with all the Moorish captives in the Prince's hands. These terms were accepted, for it was soon known that escape was hopeless.

But next morning a large party of Moors, with more than the ordinary Moslem treachery, made a last fierce attempt to surprise the camp. For eight hours, eight separate attacks went on; when all had failed, the retreating Berbers tried to set fire to the woodwork of the entrenchments. With the greatest trouble, Henry saved his timbers, and under cover of night fortified a new and smaller camp close to the shore. Food and water had both run short, and the besiegers, who were now become the besieged, had to kill their horses and cook them, with saddles for fuel. They were saved from a fatal drought by a lucky shower of rain, but their ruin was only a matter of time, for it was hopeless to try an embarkation under the walls of the city with all the hosts of Morocco waiting for the first chance of a successful storm; but the losses of the native kings and chiefs had been so great that they were ready to sign a written truce and to keep their cut-throats to the terms of it.

On the 15th of October, Don Henry, for the Portuguese, agreed that Ceuta, with all the Moorish prisoners kept in guard by Menezes, should be given up and that no further attack should be made by the King of Portugal on any side of Barbary for one hundred years. The arms and baggage of the crusaders were to be surrendered at once: directly this was done they were to embark, with none of the honours of war, and to sail back at once to Europe. Don Ferdinand was left with twelve nobles as hostages for the treaty till Ceuta was restored; on the other side Zala ben Zala's eldest son was all the security given. Even after this, a plot was laid to massacre the "Christian dogs" as they passed through the streets of Tangier, on their free passage to the harbour which the treaty secured them. Henry got wind of this just in time, and instantly embarked his men by boats from the shore outside the walls, but his rearguard was set upon just as they were leaving the land and about sixty were killed.

It was a terrible disaster. Although his losses were but some five hundred killed and disabled, Henry was overcome with the disgrace. As he thought of his brother among the Moors, he refused to show his face in Portugal and shut himself up in Ceuta. Here, as he worried himself to find some means of saving Ferdinand, he fell dangerously ill, till fresh hope came to him with the arrival of Don John, whom Edward had sent to the help of his brothers with some reserves from Algarve. Henry and John consulted about Ferdinand's ransom and at last offered their chief hostage, Zala ben Zala's boy, as an exchange for the Infant. It was the only ransom, they told the Moors, that would ever be thought of; Ceuta would never be surrendered.

Don John's mission was a failure, as might have been expected, and both the Princes were now recalled to Portugal, where Henry steadily refused to go to Court, staying at Sagres in an almost complete retirement from his usual interests, till King Edward's death forced him again into action. It was the unavoidable shame of the only choice given to himself and the kingdom that paralysed his energy, and made him moody and helpless through this time of inaction and disgrace.

"Captive he saw his brother, bright FernandThe Saint, aspiring high with purpose brave,Who as a hostage in the Saracen's handBetrayed himself his 'leagured host to save.Lest bought with price of Ceita's potent townTo public welfare be preferred his own."[37]

The mere failure to storm Tangier was brilliantly atoned for by the bravery of the army and the repeated victories over immensely superior force. But now either Ceuta must be exchanged for Ferdinand, or the youngest and favourite brother of the House of Aviz must be left to die among the Berbers. Many, if not most of the Cortés, summoned in 1438 to Leiria to discuss the ransom, were in favour of letting Ceuta go; but all the chiefs of the Government, except the King himself, "thought it not just to deliver a whole people to the fury of the infidels for the liberty of one man." Even Henry at last agreed in this with Don Pedro and Don John.

Edward was in despair; he was willing to pay almost any price to recover Ferdinand, and in hope of finding support he now appealed from his own royal house and his nobles to the Pope, the cardinals, and the crowned heads of Europe. All agreed that a Christian city must not be bartered even for a Christian Prince; Edward's offers of money and "perpetual peace" were scornfully rejected by the Moors, who held to their bond "Ceuta or nothing"—and their wretched captive, treated to all the filthy horrors of Mussulman imprisonment and slavery and torture, died under his agony in the sixth year of his living death and the forty-first of his age, 5th June, 1443.

Before this his loss had dragged down to the same fate his eldest brother, King Edward, and but for the inspiration of a great purpose, which again put meaning into his life, Henry might have died of the same "illness of soul." Every Portuguese burned to revenge the Constant Prince; the Pope was called upon to approve a new crusade, levies were made and vessels built, when the plague broke out with terrible violence, and ravaged every class and every district as it had not since the days of the Black Death. The King, seized by it in his misery and weakness and bitter disappointment, fell a victim. The wreck of all his hopes left him with hardly a wish to live, and on September 9, 1438, at the age of forty-seven, and after a reign of five years, he died at Thomar, in the act of breaking open a letter, but not before Henry had come to his side.

To the last he kept on working for his people, and it was in the fatigue of travelling from one plague-stricken town to another that he caught the pest. Among all the kings of Christendom there was never a better, or nobler, or more luckless, an Alfred with the fortune of "Unready" Ethelred.

By his last will there was fresh trouble provided for Don Henry and Don Pedro and the Cortés. His successor—the child Affonso V., now six years of age—was strictly charged to rescue Ferdinand even at the price of Ceuta; this was nothing to practical politics; but in naming his wife, Leonor of Aragon, along with Don Pedro and Don Henry, as guardian of his children and regent of the kingdom, he put power in the wrong place.

The Portuguese were always intensely suspicious of foreign government, and after the age of Leonora Telles they might well refuse a female Regent. On the other side King Edward's Queen, who had won his absolute trust as a wife and a mother, was not willing to stand aside for Pedro or for Henry. She began to organise a party, and she worked on her side, the nobles and the patriots counterworked on theirs. Don John was the first of her husband's brothers to take his natural place as a leader of the national opposition; Henry for a time seemed to waver between friendship and loyalty; all who knew the Queen loved her, but the people hated the very notion of a foreign female reign. Like John Knox they could not be fair to the Monstrous Regiment of Women, and their voices grew clearer and clearer for Don Pedro and his rights, real or supposed. The eldest of the young King's uncles, the right-hand man of the State since his return from travel in 1428, he was the proper guardian of the kingdom; Henry was a willing exile from most of Court life, though his support was the greatest moral strength of any government; John had begun the movement of discontent, but no one thought of him before his brothers; while they lived his only part was in helping them on their way.

Donna Leonor recognised her chief danger in Don Pedro, and tried to win him over. When she summoned Cortés, she pressed him to sign the royal writs; then she offered to betroth his daughter Isabel to her son; Pedro secured a written promise, and waited for the opening of the National Assembly in 1439. Here a fierce outcry was raised by a party of the nobles against the marriage-settlement of their King, but Don Pedro was too strong to be put down. He moved on by slow and steady intrigue towards the Regency he claimed. Henry had now appeared as peacemaker, and in his brother's interests arranged a compromise. The Queen was to keep the actual charge of her children, and to train the little King for his duties; Pedro was to govern the state as "Defender of the Kingdom and of the King"; the Count of Barcellos, soon to be Duke of Braganza, the leader of the factious and fractious party, was to be bought off with the Administration of the Justice of the Interior.

The Queen at first struggled on against this dethronement; fortified herself in Alemquer, and sent for help from her old home in Aragon. At this the mob rose in fury and only Henry was able to prevent a massacre and a war that would have stopped the expansion of Portugal abroad for many a day. He went straight to Alemquer (1439), talked Queen Leonor into reason, and brought her back with him to Lisbon, where she introduced Affonso to his people and his Parliament. For another year Henry stayed at Court, completing his work of settlement and reconciliation, and towards the end of 1440 that work seemed fairly safe. The fear of civil war was over; Don Pedro's government was well started; Henry could now go back to Sagres to his other work of discovery.

It was time to do something on this side. For in the past five years scarcely any progress had been made to Guinea and the Indies.

CHAPTER XII.

FROM BOJADOR TO CAPE VERDE.

1441-5.

But with the year 1441 discovery begins again in earnest, and the original narratives of Henry's captains, which old Azurara has preserved in his chronicle, become full of life and interest. From this point to the year 1448, where ends the *Chronica*, its tale is exceedingly picturesque, as it was written down from the remembrance of eye-witnesses and actors in the discoveries and conquests it records. And though the detail may be wearisome to a modern reader as a wordy and emotional and unscientific history, yet the story told is delightfully fresh and vivid, and it is told with a simple naïveté and truth that seems now almost lost in the self-consciousness of modern literature.

"It seems to me, says our author" (Azurara's favourite way of alluding to himself), "that the recital of this history should give as much pleasure as any other matter by which we satisfy the wish of our Prince; and the said wish became all the greater, as the things for which he had toiled so long, were more within his view. Wherefore I will now try to tell of something new," of some progress "in his wearisome seedtime of preparation."

"Now it was so that in this year 1441, as the affairs of the kingdom had now some repose, though it was not to be a long one, the Infant caused them to arm a little ship, which he gave to Antam Gonsalvez, his chamberlain, a young captain, only charging him to load a cargo of skins and oil. For because his age was so unformed, and his authority of needs so slight, he laid all the lighter his commands upon him and looked for all the less in performance."

But when Antam Gonsalvez had performed the voyage that had been ordered him, he called Affonso Goterres, another stripling of the Infant's household and the men of his ship, who were in all twenty-one, and said to them, Brothers and friends, it seems to me to be shame to turn back to our Lord's presence, with so little service done; just as we have received the lest strict orders to do more than this, so much more ought we to try it with the greater zeal. And how noble an action would it be, if we who came here only to take a cargo of such wretched merchandise as these sea wolves, should be the first to bring a native prisoner before the presence of our Lord. In reason we ought to find some hereabout, for it is certain there are people, and that they traffic with camels and other beasts, who bear their merchandise; and the traffic of these men must be chiefly towards the sea and back again; and since they have yet no knowledge of us, they will be scattered and off their guard, so that we can seize them; with all which our Lord the Infant will be not a little content, as he will thus have knowledge of who and what sort of people are the dwellers in this land. Then what shall be our reward, you know well enough from the great expense and trouble our Prince has been at, in past years, only to this one end.

The crew shouted a hearty "Do as you please; we will follow," and in the night following Antam Gonsalvez set aside nine men, who seemed to him most fit, and went up from the shore about three miles, till they came on a path, which they followed, thinking that by this they might come up with some man or woman, whom they might catch. And going on nine miles farther they came upon a track of some forty or fifty men and boys, as they thought, who had been coming the opposite way to that our men were going. Now the heat was very great and by reason of that, as well as of the trouble they had been at, the long tramp they had on foot and the failure of water, Antam Gonsalvez saw the weariness of his men, that it was very great. So let us turn back and follow after these men, said he, and turning back toward the sea, they came upon a man stark naked, walking after and driving a camel, with two spears in his hand, and of our men, as they rushed on after him, there was not one who kept any remembrance of his great weariness. As for the native, though he was quite alone, and saw so many coming down upon him, he stood on his defence, as if wishing to show that he could use those weapons of his, and making his face by far more fierce than his courage was warrant for. Affonso Goterres struck him with a dart and the Moor, frightened by his wounds, threw down his arms like a conquered thing and so was taken, not without great joy of our men. And going on a little farther they saw upon a hill the people whose track they followed. And they did not want the will to make for these also, but the sun was now very low and they very weary, and thinking that to risk more might bring them rather damage than profit, they determined to go back to their ship.

But as they were going, they came upon a blackamoor woman, a slave of the people on the hill, and some were minded to let her alone, for fear of raising a fresh skirmish, which was not convenient in the face of the people on the hill, who were still in sight and more than twice their number. But the others were not so poor-spirited as to leave the matter thus, Antam Gonsalvez crying out vehemently that they should seize her. So the woman was taken and those "on the hill made a show of coming down to her rescue; but seeing our men quite ready to receive them, they first retraced their steps and then made off in the opposite direction." And so Antam Gonsalvez took the first captives.

And for that the philosopher saith, resumes the next chapter of the chronicle, "that the beginning is two parts of the whole matter," great praise should be given to this noble squire, who now received his knighthood, as we shall tell. For now we have to see how Nuno Tristam, a noble knight, valiant and zealous, who had been brought up from boyhood at the Infant's Court, came to that place where was Antam Gonsalvez, bringing with him an armed caravel with the express order of his lord that he was to go to the port of Gallee and as far beyond as he could, and that he should try and make some prisoners by every means in his power. And you may imagine what was the joy of the two captains, both natives of one and the self-same realm and brought up in one and the self-same household, thus to meet so far from home. And now Nuno Tristam said that an Arab he had brought with him, a servant of the Infant, should speak with Gonsalvez' prisoners, and see if he understood their tongue, and that if he understood it, it would profit them much thus to know all the state and conditions of the people of that land. But the tongue of the Arab was very different from that of the captives, so that they could not understand each other.

And when Nuno Tristam perceived that he could not learn any more of the manner of that land, he would fain be gone, but envy made him wish to do something before the eyes of his fellows that should be good for all.

You know, he said to Antam Gonsalvez, that for fifteen years the Infant has been seeking in vain for certain news of this land and its people, in what law or lordship they do live. Now let us take twenty men, ten from each of the crews, and go up country in search of those that you found. Not so, said the other, for those whom we saw will have warned all the others, and peradventure when we are looking out to capture them, we may in our turn become their prisoners. But where we have gained a victory let us not return to suffer loss. Nuno Tristam said this counsel was good, but there were two squires whose longing to do well outran all besides. Gonsalo de Cintra was the first of these, whose valour we shall know more of in the progress of this history, and he counselled that as soon as it was night they should set out in search of the natives, and so it was determined. And such was their good fortune that they came early in the night to where the people lay scattered in two dwellings; now the place between the two was but small, and our men divided themselves in three parties and began to shout at the top of their voice "Portugal," "St. James for Portugal," the noise of which threw the enemy into such confusion, that they began to run without any order, as ours fell upon them. The men only made some show of defending themselves with assegais, especially two who fought with Nuno Tristam till they received their death. Three others were killed and ten were taken, of men, women, and children. But without question, many more would have been killed or taken if all our men had rushed in together at the first. And among those who were taken was one of their chiefs, named Adahu, who shewed full well in his face that he was nobler than the rest.

Then, when the matter was well over, all came to Antam Gonsalvez and begged him to be made a Knight, while he said it was against reason that for so small a service he should have so great an honour, and that his age would not allow it, and that he would not take it without doing greater things than these, and much more of that sort. But at last, by the instant demand of all others, Nuno Tristam knighted Antam Gonsalvez, and the place was called from that time "Port of the Cavalier."

When the party got back to the ships, Nuno Tristam's Arab was set to work again, with no better success, "for the language of the captives was not Moorish but Azaneguy of Sahara," the tongue of the great desert zone of West Africa, between the end of the northern strip of fertile country round Fez and Morocco, and the beginning of the rich tropical region at the Senegal, where the first real blacks were found. The Portuguese were in despair of finding a prisoner who could "tell the lord Infant what he wanted to know," but now the chief, "even as he shewed that he was more noble than the other captives, so now it appeared that he had seen more than they, and had been to other lands where he had learnt the Moorish tongue so that he understood our Arab and answered to whatever was asked of him."

And so to make trial of the people of the land and to have of them more certain knowledge, they put that Arab on shore and one of the Moorish women their captives with him, who were to speak to the natives if they could, about the ransom of those they had taken and about exchange of merchandise.

And at the end of two days there came down to the shore quite one hundred and fifty Moors on foot, and thirty-five mounted on camels and horses, and though they seemed to be a race both barbarous and bestial, there was not wanting in them a certain sharpness, with which they could cheat their enemies, for at first there only appeared three of them on the beach, and the rest lay in ambush till our men should land and they could rush out and master them, which thing they could easily have done, so many were they, if our men had been a whit less sharp than themselves. But when the Moors saw that our boats did not land, but turned back again to the ship, they discovered their treachery, and all came down in a body upon the beach, hurling stones and making gestures of defiance, shewing us the Arab we had sent to them as a captive in their hands.

So our men came back to the ship and made their division of the prisoners, according to the lot of each. And Antam Gonsalvez turned back because he had now loaded his caravel with the cargo that the Infant had ordered him, but Nuno Tristam went on, as he for his part had in charge. But as his vessel was in need of repair, he put to shore and careened and refitted it as well as he could, keeping his tides as if he were before the port of Lisbon, at which boldness of his many wondered greatly. And sailing on again, he passed the port of "Gallee," and came to a cape which he called "The White" (Cape Blanco), where the crew landed to see if they could make any captures. But after finding only the tracks of men and some nets, they turned back, seeing that for that time they could not do any more than they had already done.

Antam Gonsalvez came home first with his part of the booty and then arrived Nuno Tristam, "whose present reception and future reward were answerable to the trouble he had borne, like a fertile land that with but little sowing answers the husbandman."

The chief, or "cavalier" as he is called, whom Antam Gonsalvez brought home was able to "make the Infant understand a great deal of the state of that land where he had been," though as for the rest, they were pretty well useless, except as slaves, "for their tongue could not be understood by any other Moors who had been in that land." But the Prince was so encouraged by the sight of the first captives that he at once began to think "how it would be necessary to send to those parts many a time his ships and crews well armed, where they would have to fight with the infidels. So he determined to send at once to the Holy Father and ask of him that he should give him of the treasures of Holy Church, for the salvation of the souls of those who in this conquest should meet their end."

Pope Eugenius IV., then reigning, if not governing, in the great Apostolic See of the West, answered this appeal "with great joy" and with all the rhetoric of the Papal Register. "As it hath now been notified to us by our beloved son Henry, Duke of Viseu, Master of the Order of Christ, that trusting firmly in the aid of God, for the confusion of the Moors and enemies of Christ in those lands that they have desolated, and for the exaltation of the Catholic Faith,—and because that the Knights and Brethren of the said Order of Christ against the said Moors and other enemies of the Faith have waged war with the Grace of God, under the banner of the said Order,—and to the intent that they may bestir themselves to the said war with yet greater fervour, we do to each and all of those engaged in the said war, by Apostolic authority and by these letters, grant full remission of all those sins of which they shall be truly penitent at heart and of which they have made confession by their mouth. And whoever breaks, contradicts, or acts against the letter of this mandate, let him lie under the curse of the All-Mighty God and of the Blessed Apostles Peter and Paul."

And besides, adds the chronicle, rather quaintly, of more temporal and material benefits, the Infant D. Pedro, then Regent of the kingdom, gave to his brother Henry a charter, granting him the whole of the fifth of the profits which appertained to the King, and, considering that it was by him alone that the whole matter of the discovery was carried out at infinite trouble and expense, he ordered further that no one should go to those parts without D. Henry's licence and express command.

The chronicle, which has told us how Antam Gonsalvez made the first captives, now goes on to say how the same one of the Prince's captains made the first ransom. For the captive chief, "that cavalier of whom we spoke," Henry's first prize from the lands beyond Bojador, pined away in Europe, "and many times begged of Antam Gonsalvez that he would take him back to his own land, where, as he said, they would give for him five or six blackamoors, and he said, too, that there were two boys among the other captives for whom they would get a like ransom." So the Infant sent him back with Gonsalvez to his own people, "as it was better to save ten souls than three, for though they were black, yet had they souls like others, all the more as they were not of Moorish race, but Heathen and so all the easier to lead into the way of salvation. From the negroes too it would be possible to get news of the land beyond them. For not only of the Negro land did the Infant wish to know more certainly, but also of the Indies and of the land of Prester John."

So Gonsalvez sailed with his ransom, and in his ship went a noble stranger, like Vallarte the Dane, whom we shall meet later on, one of a kind which was always being drawn to Henry's Court. This was Balthasar the Austrian, a gentleman of the Emperor's Household, who had entered the Infant's service to try his fortune at Ceuta, where he had got his knighthood, and who now "was often heard to say that his great wish was to see a storm, before he left that land of Portugal, that he might tell those who had never seen one what it was like.

"And certainly his fortune favoured him. For at the first start, they met with such a storm that it was by a marvel they escaped destruction."

Again they put out to sea, and this time reached the Rio d'Ouro in safety, where they landed their chief prisoner, "very well vested in the robes that the Infant had ordered to be given him," under promise that he would soon come back and bring his tribe with him.

"But as soon as he got safely off, he very soon forgot his promises, which Antam Gonsalvez had trusted, thinking that his nobility would hold him fast and not let him break his word, but by this deceit all our men got warning that they could not trust any of the natives save under the most certain security."

The ships now went twelve miles up the Rio d'Ouro, cast anchor, and waited seven days without a sign of anybody, but on the eighth there came a Moor, on top of a white camel, with fully one hundred others who had all joined to ransom the two boys. Ten of the tribe were given in exchange for the young chiefs, "and the man who managed this barter was one Martin Fernandez, the Infant's own Ransomer of Captives, who shewed well that he had knowledge of the Moorish tongue, for he was understood by those people whom Nuno Tristam's Arab, Moor though he was by nation, could not possibly get speech with, except only the one chief, who had now escaped."

With the "Blackamoors," Antam Gonsalvez got as ransom what was even more precious, a little gold dust, the first ever brought by Europeans direct from the Guinea Coast, which more thoroughly won the Prince's cause at home and brought over more enemies and scoffers and indifferentists to his side than all the discoveries in the world.

"Many ostrich eggs, too," were included in the native ransom, "such that one day men saw at the Infant's table three dishes of the same, as fresh and as good as those of any other domestic fowls." Did the Court of Sagres suppose the ostrich to be some large kind of hen?

What was still more to the Prince's mind, "those same Moors related, that in those parts there were merchants who trafficked in that gold that was found there among them"—the same merchants, in fact, whose caravels Henry had already known on the Mediterranean coast, and whose starting-point he had now begun to touch. Ever since the days of the first Caliphs, this Sahara commerce had gone on under the control of Islam; for centuries these caravans had crossed the valleys and plains to the south of Morocco and sold their goods—pepper, slaves, and gold dust—in Moslem Ceuta and Moslem Andalusia; now, after seven hundred years of monopoly, this Moslem trade was broken in upon by the Europeans, who, in fifty years' time, broke into the greater monopoly of the Indian Seas, when Da Gama sailed from Lisbon to Malabar (1497-9).

Next year (1443) came Nuno Tristam's turn once more. People were now eager to sail in the Infant's service, after the slaves, and still more the gold dust, had been really seen and handled in Portugal, and "that noble cavalier," for each and all of the three reasons of his fellows—"to serve his lord," "to gain honour," "to increase his profit,"—was eager to follow up his first successes.

Commanding a caravel manned in great part from the Prince's household, he went out straight to Cape Blanco, the white headland, which he had been the first to reach in 1441. Passing twenty-five leagues, seventy-five miles beyond, into the bank or bight of Arguin, he saw a little island, from which twenty-five canoes came off to meet him, all hollowed out of logs of wood, with a host of native savages, "naked not for swimming in the water, but for their ancient custom." The natives hung their legs over the sides of their boats, and paddled with them like oars, so that "our men, looking at them from a distance and quite unused to the sight, thought they were birds that were skimming so over the water." As for their size, the sailors expected much greater marvels in those parts of the world, where every map and traveller's tale made the sea swarm with monsters as big as a continent.

"But as soon as they saw they were men, then were their hearts full of a new pleasure, for that they saw the chance of a capture." They launched the ship's boat at once, chased them to the shore, and captured fourteen; if the boat had been stronger, the tale would have been longer, for with a crew of seven they could not hold any more prisoners, and so the rest escaped.

With this booty they sailed on to another island, "where they found an infinite number of herons, of which they made good cheer, and so returned Nuno Tristam very joyfully to the Prince."

This last piece of discovery was of much more value than Nuno thought. He saw in it a first-rate slave hunting-ground, but it became the starting-point for trade and intercourse with the Negro States of the Senegal and the Gambia, to the south and east. It was here, in the bay of Arguin, where the long desert coast of the Sahara makes its last bend towards the rich country of the south,—that Henry built in 1448 that fort which Cadamosto found, in the next ten years, had become the centre of a great European commerce, which was also among the first permanent settlements of the new Christian exploration, one of the first steps of modern colonisation.

And now the volunteer movement had fairly begun. Where in the beginning, says Azurara, people had murmured very loudly against the Prince's enterprise, each one grumbling as if the Infant was spending some part of *his* property, now when the way had been fairly opened and the fruits of those lands began to be seen in Portugal in much greater abundance, men began, softly enough, to praise what they had so loudly decried. Great and small alike had declared that no profit would ever come of these ventures, but when the cargoes of slaves and gold began to arrive, all were forced to turn their blame into flattery, and to say that the Infant was another Alexander the Great, and as they saw the houses of others full of new servants from the new discovered lands and their property always increasing, there were few who did not long to try their fortune in the same adventures.

The first great movement of the sort came after Nuno's return at the end of 1443. The men of Lagos took advantage of Henry's settlement so near them in his town of Sagres, to ask for leave to sail at their own cost to the Prince's coast of Guinea. For no one could go without his licence.

One Lançarote, a "squire, brought up in the Infant's household, an officer of the royal customs in the town of Lagos, and a man of great good sense," was the spokesman of these merchant adventurers. He won his grant very easily, "the Infant was very glad of his request, and bade him sail under the banner of the Order of Christ," so that six caravels started in the spring of 1444 on the first exploring voyage that we can call national since the Prince had begun his work.

So, as the beginning of general interest in the Crusade of Discovery which Henry had now preached to his countrymen for thirty years, as the beginning of the career of Henry's chief captain, the head of his merchant allies, as the beginning, in fact, of a new and bright period, this first voyage of Lançarote's, this first Armada sent out to find and to conquer the Moors and Blacks of the unknown or half-known South, is worth more than a passing notice.

And this is not for its interest or importance in the story of discovery pure and simple, but as a proof that the cause of discovery itself had become popular, and as evidence that the cause of trade and of political ambition had become thoroughly identified with that of exploration. The expansion of the European *nations*, which had languished since the Crusades, had begun again. What was more unfortunate, from a modern standpoint, the African slave trade, as a part of European commerce, begins here too. It is useless to try to explain it away.

Henry's own motives were not those of the slave-driver; it seems true enough that the captives, when once brought home to Spain, were treated, under his orders, with all kindness; his own wish seems to have been to use this man-hunting traffic as a means to Christianise and civilise the native tribes, to win over the whole by the education of a few prisoners. But his captains did not always aim so high. The actual seizure of the captives—Moors and Negroes—along the coast of Guinea, was as barbarous and as ruthless as most slave-drivings. There was hardly a capture made without violence and bloodshed; a raid on a village, a fire and sack and butchery, was the usual course of things—the order of the day. And the natives, whatever they might gain when fairly landed in Europe, did not give themselves up very readily to be taught; as a rule, they fought desperately, and killed the men who had come to do them good, whenever they had a chance.

The kidnapping, which some of the Spanish patriot writers seem to think of as simply an act of Christian charity, "a corporal work of mercy," was at the time a matter of profit and money returns. Negro bodies would sell well, Negro villages would yield plunder, and, like the killing of wild Irish in the sixteenth century, the Prince's men took a Black-Moor hunt as the best of sport. It was hardly wonderful, then, that the later sailors of Cadamosto's day (1450-60) found all the coast up in arms against them, and that so many fell victims to the deadly poisoned arrows of the Senegal and the Gambia. Every native believed, as they told one of the Portuguese captains in a parley, that the explorers carried off their people to cook and eat them.

In most of the speeches that are given us in the chronicle of the time, the masters encourage their men to these slave-raids by saying, first, what glory they will get by a victory; next, what a profit can be made sure by a good haul of captives; last, what a generous reward the Prince will give for people who can tell him about these lands. Sometimes, after reprisals had begun, the whole thing is an affair of vengeance, and thus Lançarote, in the great voyage of 1445, coolly proposes to turn back at Cape Blanco, without an attempt at discovery of any sort, "because the purpose of the voyage was now accomplished." A village had been burnt, a score of natives had been killed, and twice as many taken. Revenge was satisfied.

It was only here and there that much was said about the Prince's purpose of exploration, of finding the western Nile or, Prester John, or the way round Africa to India; most of the sailors, both men and officers, seem to know that this, or something towards this, is the "will of their Lord," but it is very few who start for discovery only, and still fewer who go straight on, turning neither to right hand nor left, till they have got well beyond the farthest of previous years, and added some piece of new knowledge to the map of the known world out of the blank of the unknown.

What terrified ignorance had done before, greed did now, and the last hindrance was almost worse than the first. So one might say, impatiently, looking at the great expense, the energy, and time and life spent on the voyages of this time, and especially of the years 1444-8. More than forty ships sail out, more than nine hundred captives are brought home, and the new lands found are all discovered by three or four explorers. National interest seems awakened to very little purpose. But what explains the slow progress of discovery, explains also the fact that any progress, however slow, was made at all, apart from the personal action of Henry himself. Without the mercantile interest, the Prince's death would have been the end and ruin of his schemes for many a year.

But for the hope of adventure and of profitable plunder, and the certainty of reward; but for the assurance, so to say, of such and such a revenue on the ventures of the time, Portuguese "public opinion" would not probably have been much ahead of other varieties of the same organ. In deciding the abstract question to which the Prince had given his life, the mob of Lisbon or of Lagos would hardly have been quicker than modern mobs to rise to a notion above that of personal gain. If the cause of discovery and an empire to come had been left to them, the labour leaders might have said then in Spain, as some of them have said to-day in England, "What is all this talk about the Empire? What is it to us working men? We don't want the Empire, we want more wages." And so when the great leader was dead, and the people were left to carry out his will, his spiritual foresight of great scientific discoveries, his ideas of conversion and civilisation, were not the things for the sake of which ordinary men were reconciled to his scheme and ready to finish his work. If they thought or spoke or toiled for the finding of the way to India, it was to find the gold and spices and jewels of an earthly paradise.

This is not fancy. It is simply impossible to draw any other conclusion from the original accounts of these voyages in Azurara's chronicle, for Azurara himself, though one of Henry's first converts, a man who realised something of the grandeur of his master's schemes and their reach beyond a merely commercial ideal through discovery to empire, yet preserves in the speeches and actions of captains and seamen alike, proof enough of the thoroughly commonplace aims of most of the first discoverers.

On the other hand, the strength of the movement lay of course in the few exceptions. As long as all or nearly all the instruments employed were simply buccaneers, with a single eye to trade profits, discovery could not advance very fast or very far. Till the real meaning of the Prince's life had impressed his nearest followers with something of his own spirit, there could be no exploration, except by accident, though without this background of material gain no national interest could have been enlisted in exploration at all.

Real progress in this case was by the slow increase of that inner circle which really shared Henry's own ambition, of that group of men who went out, not to make bargains or do a little killing, but to carry the flag of Portugal and of Christ farther than it had ever been planted before, "according to the will of the Lord Infant." And as these men were called to the front, and only as they were there at all, was there any rapid advance. If two sailors, Diego Cam and Bartholomew Diaz, could within four years, in two voyages, explore the whole south-west coast of Africa from the Equator to the Cape of Tempests or of Good Hope, was it not absurd that the earlier caravels, after Bojador was once passed should hang so many years round the north-west shores of the Sahara?

Even some of the more genuine discoverers, the most trusted of the Prince's household, men like Gil Eannes, the first who saw the coasts beyond the terrible Bojador, or Diniz Diaz, or Antam Gonsalvez, or Nuno Tristam, as they come before us in Azurara's chronicle, are more like their men than their master.

He thought of the slaves they brought home "with unspeakable pleasure, as to the saving of their souls, which but for him, would have been for ever lost." They thought a good deal more, like the crowd that gathered at the slave market in Lagos, of the "distribution of the captives," and of the money they would get for each. At those sales, which Azurara describes so vividly, Henry had the bearing of one who cared little for amassing plunder, and was known, once and again, to give away his fifth of the spoil, "for his spoil was chiefly in the success of his great wishes." But his suite seems to have been as keenly on the look-out for such favours as their lord was easy in bestowing them.

To return to Lançarote's voyage:

"For that the Infant knew, by certain Moors that Nuno Tristam had carried off, that in the Isle of Naar, in the Bay of Arguin, and in the parts thereabout, were more than two hundred souls," the six caravels began with a descent on that island. Five boats were launched and thirty men in them, and they set off from the ships about sunset. And rowing all that night, we are told, they came about the time of dawn to the island that they sought. And as day was breaking they got up to a Moorish village close to the shore, where were living all the people in the island. At sight of this the boats' crews drew up, and the leaders consulted whether to go on or turn back. It was decided to attack. Thirty "Portugals" ought to be a match for five or six times as many natives; the sailors landed and rushed upon the villagers and "saw the Moors with their women and children coming out of their huts as fast as they could, when they caught sight of their enemy; and our men, crying out 'St. James, St. George, Portugal,' fell upon them, killing and taking all they could. There you might have seen mothers catch up their children, husbands their wives, each one trying to fly as best he could. Some plunged into the sea, others thought to hide themselves in the corners of their hovels, others hid their children underneath the shrubs that grew about there, where our men found them.

"And at last our Lord God, who gives to all a due reward, to our men gave that day a victory over their enemies, in recompence for all their toil in His service, for they took, what of men, women, and children, one hundred and sixty-five, without counting the slain."

Then finding from the captives that there were other well-peopled islands near at hand, they raided these for more prisoners. In their next descent they could not catch any men, but of women and little boys, not yet able to run, they seized seventeen or eighteen; soon after this they did meet the "Moormen bold," who were drawing together on all sides to defend themselves; a great power of three hundred savages chased another raiding party to their boats.

That the whole expedition had no thought of discovery was plain enough from the fact that Lançarote did not try to go beyond the White Cape (Blanco), which had been already passed several times, but turned back directly he found the hunting grounds becoming deserted, and a descent producing no prize, except one girl, who had chosen to go to sleep when the rest of the people fled up country at the first sight of the Christian boats.

The voyage was a slave chase from first to last, and two hundred and thirty-five Blacks were the result. Their landing and their sale at Lagos was a day of great excitement, a long remembered 8th of August. "Very early in the morning, because of the heat (of the later day) the sailors began to land their captives, who as they were placed all together in the field by the landing-place, were indeed a wonderful sight; for among them there were some that were almost white, of beautiful form and face; others were darker; and others again as black as moles and so hideous, alike in face and body, that they looked, to any one who saw them, the very images of a Lower Hemisphere."

But what heart so stern, exclaims the chronicler, as not to be pierced with pity to see that company. For some held down their heads, crying piteously, others looked mournfully upon one another, others stood moaning very wretchedly, sometimes looking up to the height of Heaven, calling out with shrieks of agony, as if invoking the Father of Nature; others grovelled upon the ground, beating their foreheads with their hands, while others again made their moan in a sort of dirge, in their own way, for though one could not understand the words, the sense of all was plain in the agony of those who uttered it.

But most terrible was that agony when came the partition and each possessor took away his lot. Wives were divided from husbands, fathers from sons, brothers from brothers, each being forced to go where his lot might send him. Parents and children who had been ranged opposite one another, now rushed forward to embrace, if it were for the last time; mothers, holding their little children in their arms, threw themselves down, covering their babes with their own bodies.

And yet these slaves were treated with kindness, and no difference was made between them and other and freeborn servants. The younger captives were taught trades, and those who showed that they could manage property were set free and married. Widow ladies treated the girls they bought like their own daughters, and often left them dowries by will, that they might marry as entirely free. Never have I known one of these captives, says Azurara, put in irons like other slaves, or one who did not become a Christian. Often have I been present at the baptisms or marriages of these slaves, when their masters made as much and as solemn a matter of it as if it had been a child or a parent of their own.

During Henry's life the action of buccaneers on the African coast was a good deal kept in check by the spirit and example and positive commands of the Infant, who sent out his men to explore, and could not prevent some outrages in the course of exploration. Again and again he ordered his captains to act fairly to the natives, to trade with them honourably, and to persuade them by gentler means than kidnapping to come to Europe for a time. In the last years of his life he did succeed in bettering things; by establishing a regular Government trade in the bay of Arguin he brought a good deal more under control the unchained deviltry of the Portuguese freebooters; Cadamosto and Diego Gomez, his most trusted lieutenants of this later time, were real discoverers, who tried to make friends of the natives rather than slaves.

In the early days of Portuguese exploration, it may also be said, information, first-hand news of the new countries and their dangers, was absolutely needed, and if the Negroes and the Azaneguy Moors could not or would not speak some Christian tongue and guide the caravels to Guinea, they must be carried off and made fit and proper instruments for the work.

It would be out of place here to justify or condemn this excuse or to enter on the wider question of the right or wrong of the slave-trade in general. It is enough to see how brutally the work of "saving the Heathen," was carried out by the average explorer, when discovery was used as a plea for traffic.

No one then questioned the right of Christians to make slaves of Heathen Blacks; Henry certainly did not, for he used slavery as an education, he made captives of "Gentiles" for the highest ends, as he believed, to save their souls, and to help him in the way of doing great things for his country and for Christendom. He knew more of the results than of the incidental cruelty, more of the hundreds taken than of the hundreds more killed and maimed and made homeless in the taking. For centuries past Moors had brought back slaves from the south across the Sahara to sell on the coast of

Tunis and Morocco; no Christian doubted the right and—more than the right—the merit of the Prince in bringing black slaves by sea from Guinea to Lisbon, where they might be fairly saved from the grasp of "Foul Mahumet."

So if it is said that Henry started the African slave-trade of European nations, that must not be understood as the full-blooded atrocity of the West Indian planters, for the use he made of his prisoners was utterly different, though his action was the cause of incessant abuse of the best end by the worst of means.

At the time the gold question was much more important than the slave-trade, and most Portuguese, most Europeans—nobles, merchants, burghers, farmers, labourers—were much more excited by the news and the sight of the first native gold dust than by anything else whatever. It was the first few handfuls of this dust, brought home by Gonsalvez in 1442, that had such a magical effect on public opinion, that spread the exploring interest from a small circle out into every class, and that brought forward volunteers on every side. For a Guinea voyage was now the favourite plan of every adventurer.

But however they may be explained, however natural and even necessary they may seem to be, as things stood in Portugal and in Latin Christendom, the slave-trade and the gold hunger hindered the Prince's work quite as much as they helped it. If further discovery depended upon trade profits, native interpreters, and the attractions of material interest, there was at least a danger that the discoverers who were not disposed to risk anything, and only went out to line their own pockets, would hang about the well known coasts till they had loaded all the plunder they could hold, and would then simply reappear at Sagres with so many more souls for the good Prince to save, but without a word or a thought of "finding of new lands." And this, after all, was the end. Buccaneering on the north-west coast of Africa was not what Henry aimed at.

So he gave a caravel to one of his household, Gonsalo de Cintra, "who had been his stirrup-boy," and "bade him go straight to the Land of Guinea, and that for no cause whatever should he do otherwise." But when De Cintra got to the White Cape (Blanco) it struck him that "with very little danger he could make some prisoners there."

So with a cheerful impudence, in the face of the Infant's express commands, he put his ship about and landed in that bay of Arguin, where so many captures had been made, but he was cut off from the rest of the men, and killed with seven others by a host of more than two hundred Moors, and the chronicle which tells of all such details at the greatest length, stops to give seven reasons for this, the first serious loss of life the

Europeans had suffered in their new African piracies. And for the rest, "May God receive the soul that He created and the nature that came forth from Him, as it is His very own. *Habeat Deus animam quam creavit et naturam, quod suum est.*" (*Azurara*, ch. 27).

Three other caravels, which quickly followed De Cintra, sailed with special orders to Christianise and civilise the natives wherever and however they could, and the result of this was seen in the daring venture of Joan Fernandez. This man, the pattern of all the Crusoes of after time, offered to stay on shore among the Blacks "to learn what he could of the manners and speech and customs of the people," and so was left along with that "bestial and barbarous" nation for seven months, on the shores of the Bank of Arguin, while in exchange for him an old Moor went back to Portugal.

Yet a third voyage was made in this spring of 1445 by Nuno Tristam. And of this, says Azurara, I know nothing very exact or at first hand, because Nuno Tristam was dead before the time that King Affonso (D. Henry's nephew) commanded me to write this history. But this much we do know, that he sailed straight to the Isle of Herons in Arguin, that he passed the sandy wilderness and landed in the parts beyond, in a land fertile and full of palm trees; and having landed he took a score of prisoners. And so Nuno Tristam was the first to see the country of the real Blacks. In other words, Nuno reached Cape Palmar, far beyond Cape Blanco, where he saw the palms and got the all-important certainty that the desert did end somewhere, and that beyond, instead of a country unapproachable from the heat, where the very seas were perpetually boiling as if in a cauldron, there was a land richer than any northern climate, through which men could pass to the south.

Still further was this proved by the next voyage, which reached the end of the great western trend of the African coast, and found that instead of the continent stretching out farther and farther to an infinite breadth, there was an immense contraction of the coast.

Diniz Diaz, the eldest of that family which gave to Portugal some of her greatest men and makers, now begged a caravel from the Prince with the promise of "doing more with it than any had done before." He had done well under old King John, and now he kept his word.

Passing Arguin and Cape Blanco and Cape Palmar, he entered the mouth of the Senegal, the western Nile, which was now fixed as the northern limit of Guinea, or Blackman's Land. "Nor was this a little honour for our Prince, whose mighty power was thus brought to bear upon the peoples so far distant from our land and so near to that of Egypt." For Azurara like Diaz, like Henry himself, thought not only that the Senegal was the Niger, the western Nile of the Blacks, but that the caravels of Portugal were far nearer to India than was the fact,—were getting close to the Mountains of the Moon and the sources of the Nile.

But Diaz was not content with this. He had reached and passed, as he thought, the great western stream up which men might sail, in the belief of the time, to the mysterious sources of the world's greatest river, and so down by the eastern and northern course of the same to Cairo and the Christian seas. He now sailed on "to a great cape, which he named Cape Verde," a green and beautiful headland covered with grass and trees and dotted with native villages, running out into the Western Ocean far beyond any other land, and beyond which, in turn, there was no more western coast, but only southern and eastern. From this point Diaz returned to Portugal.

"But great was the wonder of the people of the coast in seeing his caravel, for never had they seen or heard tell of the like, but some thought it was a fish, others were sure it was a phantom, others again said it might be a bird that had that way of skimming along the surface of the sea." Four of them picked up courage to venture out in a canoe and try to settle this doubt. Out they went in their little boat, all made from one hollow tree, but when they saw that there were men on board the caravel they fled to the shore and "the wind falling our men could not overtake.

"And though the booty of Diniz Diaz was far less than what others had brought home before him, the Prince made very much of his getting to that land of Negroes and Cape Verde and the Senegal," and with reason, for these discoveries assured the success of his work, and from this time all trouble and opposition were at an end. Mariners now went out to sail to the golden country that had been found or to the spice land that was now so near; men passed at once from extreme apathy or extreme terror to an equally extreme confidence. They seemed to think the fruit was within reach for them to gather, before the tree had been half climbed. Long before Fernando Po had been reached, while the caravels were still off the coasts of Sierra Leone, men at home, from King Affonso to the common seamen of the ports, "thought the line of Tunis and even of Alexandria had been long passed." The difficult first steps seemed all.

Now three volunteers, Antam Gonsalvez, and two others who had already sailed in the Prince's service, applied for the command of ships for the discovery and conquest of the lands of Guinea, and to bring back Joan Fernandez from his exile. Sailing past Cape Blanco they set up there a great wooden cross and "much would it have amazed any one of another nation that should have chanced to pass that way, not knowing of our voyages along that coast," says Azurara gleefully, giving us proof enough in every casual expression of this sort, often dropped with perfect simplicity and natural truthfulness, that to his knowledge and that of his countrymen, to the Europe of 1450, the Portuguese had had no forerunners along the Guinea Coast.

A little south of the Bight of Arguin the caravels sighted a man on the shore making signals to the ships, and coming closer they saw Fernandez who had much to tell. He had completely won over the natives of that part during his seven months' stay, and now he was able to bring the caravels to a market where trinkets were exchanged for slaves and gold with a Moorish chief—"a cavalier called Ahude Meymam." Then he was taken home to tell his story to the Prince, the fleet wasting some time in descents on the tribes of the bay of Arguin.

When he was first put on shore, Joan Fernandez told Don Henry, the natives came up to him, took his clothes off him and made him put on others of their own make. Then they took him up the country, which was very scantily clothed with grass, with a sandy and stony soil, growing hardly any trees. A few thorns and palms were the only relief to the barren monotony of this African prairie, over which wandered a few nomade shepherds in search of pasture for their flocks. There were no flowers, no running streams to light up the waste, so Fernandez thought at first, till he found one or two exceptions that proved the rule. The natives got their water from wells, spoke a tongue and wrote a writing that was different from that of the other Moors, though all these people, in the upland, were Moslems, like the Berbers nearer home. For they themselves were a tribe, the Azaneguy tribe, of the great Berber family, who had four times—in the eleventh, twelfth, thirteenth, and fourteenth centuries—come over to help the Moslem power in Spain.

Yet, said Fernandez, these Moors of the west are quite barbarous: they have neither law nor lordship; their food is milk and the seeds of wild mountain herbs and roots; meat and bread are both rare luxuries; and so is fish for those on the upland, but the Moors of the coast eat nothing else, and for months together I have seen those I lived among, their horses and their dogs, eating and drinking only milk, like infants. 'T is no wonder they are weaker than the negroes of the south with whom they are ever at war, fighting with treachery and not with strength. They dress in leather— leather breeches and jackets, but some of the richer wear a native mantle over their shoulders—such rich men as keep good swift horses and brood mares. It was about the trade and religion of the country that Fernandez was specially questioned, and his answers were not encouraging on either point. The people were bigoted, ignorant worshippers of the abominations of Mahumet, he said, and their traffic in slaves and gold was a small matter after all. The only gold he saw in their country was in ankle rings on the women of the chiefs; the gold dust and black bodies they got from the negroes they took to Tunis and the Mediterranean coast on camels. Their salt, on which they set great store, was from the Tagazza salt quarries, far inland. The chief, Ahude Meymam, who had been so kind to Fernandez, lived in the upland; the Christian stranger had been induced to ride up from the coast, and had reached the Court only after tortures of thirst. The water failed them on the way, and for three days they had nothing to drink.

Altogether, Fernandez' report discouraged any further attempts to explore by land, where all the country as far as could be reached seemed to yield nothing but desert with a few slender oases. It was not indeed till the European explorers reached the Congo on their coasting voyages to the south that they found a natural and inviting pathway into the heart of Africa. The desert of the north and west, the fever-haunted swamps and jungle of the Guinea Coast only left narrow inlets of more healthy and passable country, and these the Portuguese did their best to close by occasional acts of savage cruelty and impudent fraud in their dealings with the natives.

Another expedition, and that an unlucky one, under Gonsalo Pacheco, a gentleman of Lisbon, followed this last of Antam Gonsalvez. Pacheco got leave to make the voyage, equipped a caravel that he had built for himself, and got two others to share the risk and profits with him. And so, says Azurara, hoisting the banners of the Order of Christ, they made their way to Cape Blanco. Here they found, one league from the Cape, a village, and by the shore a writing, that Antam Gonsalvez had set up, in which he counselled all who passed that way not to trouble to go up and sack the village, as it was quite empty of people. So they hung about the Bank of Arguin, making raids in various places, and capturing some one hundred and twenty natives, all of which is not of much interest to any one, though as Pacheco and his men had to pay themselves for their trouble, and make a profit on the voyage, these man-hunts were the chief thing they thought about and the main thing in their stories when they got home.

Men like Pacheco and his friends were not explorers at all. They stopped far short of the mark that Diniz Diaz had made for the European Furthest, and their only discovery was of a new cape one hundred miles and more beyond the Bank of Arguin. Sailing south, because the natives fled at their approach and left the coast land all bare, "they came to a headland which they called Cape St. Anne, by which an arm of the sea ran four leagues up the country," where they hunted for more prisoners.

Still in search of slaves and gold they sailed on two hundred and fifty miles—eighty leagues—to Negroland, where Diaz had been before, and where they saw a land, to the north of the Great Western Cape, all green, peopled with men and cattle, but when they tried to near the shore and land a storm drove them back. For three days they struggled against it, but at last they found themselves near Cape Blanco, more than three hundred miles to the north, where they gave up all thought of trying to push into the unknown south, and turned cheerfully to their easier work of slave-hunting. In one of these raids, a party of seven, in a boat away from all the rest, was overpowered and killed like De Cintra's men by a large body of natives, "whose souls may God in His mercy receive in the Habitation of the Saints." The Moors carried off the boat and broke it up for the sake of its nails, and Azurara was told by some that the bodies of the dead were eaten by their brutal conquerors. 'T is certain at least, he adds, that their custom is to eat the livers of their victims and to drink their blood, when they are avenging the death of parents or brothers or children, as they do it to have full vengeance on such as have so greatly injured them.

CHAPTER XIII.

THE ARMADA OF 1445.

While Gonsalo Pacheco had been wasting time and men and the good name of Europe and Christendom in his plunderings between C. Bojador and C. Blanco, the memory of the death of Gonsalo de Cintra was kept alive in Lagos, and the men of the town came in solemn deputation to the Prince, before the summer of this same year (1445) was out, to beg him for permission to take full, perfect, and sufficient vengeance. In other words, they offered to equip the largest fleet that had ever sailed on an ocean voyage—as it now began to be called, a Guinea voyage—since the Prince began his work. As far as we know, this was also one of the greatest armadas that had been sent out into the new-discovered or re-discovered or undiscovered seas and lands since the European nations had begun to look at all beyond their own narrow limits.

Neither the fleet of 1341, which found the Canaries, and of which Boccaccio tells us, nor the Genoese expedition of 1291, nor the Catalan venture of 1346, nor De Béthencourt's armament of 1402, for the conquest of the Fortunate Isles, was anything like this armada of 1445. For this last was a real sign of national interest in a work which was not only discovery, but profit and a means to more; it proved that in Portugal, in however base and narrowly selfish a way, there was now a spirit of general enterprising activity, and till this had been once awakened, there was not much hope of great results from the efforts of individuals.

The first contingent now equipped in Lagos—for the Prince at once approved of his men's idea—numbered fourteen caravels—fourteen of the best sailing ships afloat, as Cadamosto said a little later; but this was only the central fleet, under Lançarote as Admiral. Three more ships came from Madeira, one of them under Tristam Vaz, the coloniser of Funchal; Diniz Diaz headed another contingent from Lisbon; Zarco, the chief partner in the discovery and settlement of Madeira, sent his own caravel in command of his nephew; in all there were seven and twenty ships—caravels, galleys, and pinnaces. Since the Carthaginians sent out their colonists under Hanno beyond the Pillars of Hercules, a larger and braver fleet had not sailed down that desolate West of Africa.

Gil Eannes, who had rounded Bojador, was there, with the Diaz, who had passed the Green Headland and come first to the land of the Negroes, and the list of captains was made up of the most daring and seasoned of Spanish seamen. Scarcely a man who had ventured on the ocean voyages of the last thirty years was still alive and able-bodied who did not sail on the 10th August, 1445.

At the start Cape Blanco was appointed as the rendezvous; with favouring wind and tide the ships raced out as far as Arguin. Lawrence, a younger brother of the Diaz family, drew ahead, and was the first to fall in with Pacheco's three caravels, which were slowly crawling home after their losses. Now, hearing of the great fleet that was coming after to take vengeance, they turned about to wait for them, "as it was worth while to have revenge though one had to live on short rations." So, now, thirty European ships and their crews were included in the fleet. The pioneer, Lawrence Diaz, and the rest, lay to at the Isle of Herons in the Bank of Arguin; while waiting there they saw some wonderful things in birds, and Azurara tells us what they told him, though rather doubtfully. The great beaks of the Marabout, or Prophet Bird, struck them most,—"a cubit long and more, three fingers' breadth across, and the bill smooth and polished, like a Bashaw's scabbard, and looking as if artificially worked with fire and tools,"—the mouth and gullet so big that the leg of a man of the ordinary size would go into it. On these birds particularly, says Azurara, our men refreshed themselves during their three days' stay.

Slowly but surely, two by two, three by three, nine caravels mustered at C. Blanco, and as the flagship of Lançarote was among them, an attack was made at once with two hundred and seventy-eight men picked from among the crews, the footmen and lancers in one boat and the archers in another, with Lançarote himself and the men-at-arms behind. They were steered by pilots who had been on the coast before and knew it, and it was hoped they would come upon the natives of Tider Island with the first light of dawn. But the way was longer than the pilots reckoned, the night was pitchy dark, without moon or stars, the tide was on the ebb, and at last the boats were aground. It was well on in the morning before they got off on the flood and rowed along the coast to find a landing-place. The shore was manned with natives, not at all taken by surprise, but dancing, yelling, spitting, and throwing missiles in insolent defiance. After a desperate struggle on the beach, they were put to flight with trifling loss—eight killed, four taken,— but when the raiders reached the village, they found it empty; the women and children had been sent away, and all their wretched little property had gone with them. The same was found true of all the villages on that coast; but in a second battle on the next day, fifty-seven Moors were captured, and the army went back on shipboard once more.

And now the fleet divided. Lançarote, holding a council of his captains, declared the purpose of the voyage was accomplished. They had punished the natives and taken vengeance for Gonsalo de Cintra and the other martyrs; now it was for each crew and captain to settle whether they would go farther. All the prisoners having now been divided like prize-money between the ships, there was nothing more to stay for.

Five caravels at once returned to Portugal after trying to explore the inlet of the sea at C. Blanco; but they only went up in their boats five leagues, and then turned back. One stayed in the Bay of Arguin to traffic in slaves, and lost one of the most valuable captives by sheer carelessness,—a woman, badly guarded, slipped out and swam ashore.

But there was a braver spirit in some others of the fleet. The captain of the King's caravel, which had come from Lisbon in the service of the King's uncle, swore he would not turn back. He, Gomes Pires, would go on to the Nile; the Prince had ordered him to bring him certain word of it. He would not fail him. Lançarote for himself said the same, and another, one Alvaro de Freitas, capped the offers of all the rest. He would go on beyond the Negro-Nile to the Earthly Paradise, to the farthest East, where the four sacred rivers flowed from the tree of life. "Well do you all know how our Lord the Infant sets great store by us, that we should make him know clearly about the land of the Negroes, and especially the River of Nile. It will not be a small guerdon that he will give for such service."

Six caravels in all formed the main body of the Perseverants, and these coasted steadily along till they came to Diaz's Cape of Palms, which they knew was near the Senegal and the land of the Negroes, "and so beautiful did the land now become, and so delicious was the scent from the shore, that it was as if they were by some gracious fruit garden, ordained to the sole end of their delights. And when the men in the caravels saw the first palms and towering woodland, they knew right well that they were close upon the River of Nile, which the men there call the Sanaga." For the Infant had told them how little more than twenty leagues beyond the sight of those trees they would see the river, as his prisoners of the Azanegue tribes had told him. And as they looked carefully for the signs of this, they saw at last, two leagues from land, "a colour of the water that was different from the rest, for that was of the colour of mud."

And understanding this to mean that there were shoals, they put farther out to sea for safety, when one took some of the water in his hand and put it to his mouth, and found that it was sweet. And crying out to the others, "Of a surety," said they, "we are now at the River of Nile, for the water of the river comes with such force into the sea as to sweeten it." So they dropped their anchors in the river's mouth, and they of the caravel of Vincent Diaz (another brother of Diniz and Lawrence) let down a boat, into which jumped eight men who pulled ashore.

Here they found some ivory and elephant hide, and had a fierce battle with a huge negro whose two little naked children they carried off,—but though the chronicle of the voyages stops here for several chapters of rapturous reflection on the greatness of the Nile, and the valour and spirit of the Prince who had thus found a way to its western mouth, we must follow the captains as they coast slowly along to Cape Verde, "for that the wind was fair for sailing." Landing on a couple of uninhabited islands off the Cape, they found first of all "fresh goat-skins and other things," and then the arms of the Infant and the words of his motto, *Talan de bien faire*, carved upon trees, and they doubted, like Azurara when writing down his history from their lips; "whether the great power of Alexander or of Cæsar could have planted traces of itself so far from home," as these islands were from Sagres. For though the distance looks small enough on a full map of all the world, on the chart of the Then Known it was indeed a lengthy stretch— some two thousand miles, fully as great a distance as the whole range of the Mediterranean from the coast of Palestine to the Straits of Gibraltar.

Now by these signs, adds the chronicler, they understood right well that other caravels had been there already—and it was so; for it was the ship of John Gonsalvez Zarco, Captain of Madeira, which had passed this way, as they found for a fact on the day after. And wishing to land, but finding the number of the natives to be such that they could not land by day or night, they put on shore a ball and a mirror and a paper on which was drawn a cross.

And when the natives came and found them in the morning, they broke the ball and threw away the pieces, and with their assegais broke up the mirror into little bits, and tore the paper, showing that they cared for none of these things.

Since this is so, said Captain Gomes Pires to the archers, draw your bows upon these rascals, that they may know we are people who can do them a damage.

But the negroes returned the fire with arrows and assegais—deadly weapons, the arrows unfeathered and without a string-notch, but tipped with deadly poison of herbs, made of reed or cane or charred wood with long iron heads, and the assegais poisoned in like manner and pricked with seven or eight harpoons of iron, so that it was no easy matter to draw it out of the flesh.

So they lost heart for going farther, with all the coast-land up in arms against them, and turned back to Lagos, but before they left the Cape they noticed in the desert island, where they had found the Prince's arms, trees so large that they had never seen the like, for among them was one which was 108 palms round at the foot. Yet this tree, the famous baobab, was not much higher than a walnut; "of its fibre they make good thread for sewing, which burns like flax; its fruit is like a gourd and its kernels like chestnuts."

And so, we are told, all the captains put back along the coast, in a mind to enter the aforesaid River of Nile, but one of the caravels getting separated from the rest and not liking to enter the Senegal alone, went straight to Lagos, and another put back to water in the Bay of Arguin and the Rio d'Ouro estuary, where there came to them at once the Moors on board the caravel, full of confidence because they had never had any dealings before with the merchants of Spain, and sold them a negro for five doublons, and gave them meat and water from their camels, and came in and out on board the ship, so that there was great fear of treachery, but at last without any quarrel they were all put on shore, under promise that next July their friends would come again and trade with them in slaves and gold to their hearts' content. And so, taking in a good cargo of seal-skins, they made their way straight home.

Meantime two of the other caravels and a pinnace, which had been separated early in the voyage from the main body, under the pilotage of the veteran Diniz Diaz, had also made their way to C. Verde, had fought with the natives in some desperate skirmishes—one knight had his "shield stuck as full with arrows as the porcupine with quills," and had turned back in the face of the same discouragements as the rest; and so would have ended the whole of this great enterprise but for the dauntless energy of one captain and his crew.

Zarco of Madeira had given his caravel to his nephew with a special charge that, come what might, he was not to think of profit and trading, but of doing the will of the Prince his lord. He was not to land in the fatal Bay of Arguin, which had been the end of so many enterprises; he was to go as Diniz Diaz had first gone, straight to the land of the Negroes, and pass beyond the farthest of earlier sailors. Now the caravel, says Azurara proudly, was well equipped and was manned by a crew that was ready to bear hard ship, and the captain was full of energy and zeal, and so they went on steadily, sailing through the great Sea of Ocean till they came to the River of Nile, where they filled two pipes with water, of which they took back one to the city of Lisbon. And not even Alexander, though he was one of the monarchs of the world, ever drank of water that had been brought from so far as this.

"But now, still going on, they passed C. Verde and landed upon the islands I have spoken of, to see if there were any people there, but they found only some tame goats without any one to tend them; and it was there that they made the signs that the others found on coming after, the arms of the Infant with his device and motto. And then drawing in close to the Cape, they waited to see if any canoes would come off to them, and anchored about a mile off the shore. But they had not waited long before two boats, with ten negroes in them, put off from the beach and made straight for the caravel, like men who came in peace and friendship. And being near, they began to make signs as if for a safe-conduct, which were answered in like manner, and then at once, without any other precaution, five of them came on board the caravel, where the captain made them all the entertainment that he could, bidding them eat and drink, and so they went away with signs of great contentment, but it appeared after, that in their hearts they meditated treachery. For as soon as they got to land they talked with the other natives on shore, and thinking that they could easily take the ship, with this intent there now set out six boats, with five and thirty or forty men, arrayed as those who come to fight, but when they came close they were afraid and stayed a little way off, without daring to make any attack. And seeing this, our men launched a boat on the other side of the caravel, where they could not be seen by the enemy, and manned it with eight rowers, who were to wait till the canoes came nearer to the ship. At last the negroes were tired of waiting and watching, and one of their canoes came up closer, in which were five strong warriors, and at once our boat rowed round the caravel and cut them off. And because of the great advantage that we had in our style of rowing, in a trice our men were upon them, and they having no hope of defence, threw themselves into the water, and the other boats made off for the shore. And our men had the greatest trouble in catching those that were swimming away, for they dived not a whit worse than cormorants, so that we could scarcely catch hold of them. One was taken, not very easily, on the spot, and another, who fought as desperately as two men, was wounded, and with these two the boat returned to the caravel.

"And for that they saw that it would not profit them to stay longer in that place, they resolved to see if they could find any new lands of which they might bring news to the Infant their lord. And so, sailing on again, they came to a cape, where they saw 'groves of palm trees dry and without branches, which they called the Cape of Masts.'" Here, a little farther along the coast, a reconnoitring party of seven landed and found four negro hunters sitting on the beach, armed with bows and arrows, who fled on seeing the strangers. "And as they were naked and their hair cut very short, they could not catch them," and only brought away their arrows for a trophy.

This Cape of Masts, or some point of the coast a little to the south-east, was the farthest now reached by Zarco's caravel. "From here they put back and sailed direct to Madeira, and thence to the city of Lisbon, where the Infant received them with reward enough. For this caravel, of all those who had sailed at this time (1445), had done most and reached farthest."

There was one contingent of the great armada yet unaccounted for, but they were sad defaulters. Three of the ships on the outward voyage which had separated from the main body and Lançarote's flagship, had the cowardice or laziness to give up the purpose of the voyage altogether; "they agreed to make a descent on the Canary Islands instead of going to Guinea at all that year."

Here they stayed some time, raiding and slave-hunting, but also making observations on the natives and the different natural features of the different islands, which, as we have them in the old chronicle, are not the least interesting part of the story of the Lagos Armada of 1445.[38]

CHAPTER XIV.

VOYAGES OF 1446-8.

And yet, but for the enterprise of Zarco's crew, this expedition of 1445 that began with so much promise, and on which so much time and trouble had been spent, was almost fruitless of "novelties," of discoveries, of the main end and object of all the Prince's voyages.

The next attempt, made by Nuno Tristam in 1446, ended in the most disastrous finish that had yet befallen the Christian seamen of Spain. Nuno, who had been brought up from boyhood at the Prince's court, "seeing how earnest he was that his caravels should explore the land of the Negroes, and knowing how some had already passed the River of Nile, thought that if he should not do something of right good service to the Infant in that land, he could in no wise gain the name of a brave knight.

"So he armed a caravel and began sail, not stopping anywhere that he might come straight to the Black Man's land. And passing by Cape Verde he sailed on sixty leagues and found a river, where he judged there ought to be some people living. So he bade them lower two small boats and put ten men in the one and twelve in the other, which pulled straight towards some huts they sighted ahead of them. But before they could jump on shore, twelve canoes came out on the other side, and seventy or eighty Blackmoors in them, with bows in their hands, who began to shoot at our people." As the tide rose, one of the Guinea boats passed them and landed its crew, "so that our men were between a fire from the land and a fire from the boats." They pulled back as hard as they could, but before they could get on board, four of them were lying dead.

"And so they began to make sail home again, leaving the boats in that they were not able to take charge of them. For of the twenty-two who went to land in them there did not escape more than two; nineteen were killed, for so deadly was the poison that with a tiny wound, a mere scratch that drew blood, it could bring a man to his last end. But above and beyond these was killed our noble knight, Nuno Tristam, earnestly desiring life, that he might die not a shameful death like this, but as a brave man should." Of seven who had been left in the caravel, two had been struck by the poisoned arrows as they tried to raise the anchors, and were long in danger of death, lying a good twenty days at the last gasp, without the power to raise a finger to help the others who were trying to get the caravel home, so that only five were left to work the ship.

Nuno's men were saved by the energy and skill of one—a mere boy, a page of the Infant's House—who took charge of the ship, and steered its course due north, then north by east, so that in two months' time they were off the coast of Portugal. But they were absolutely helpless and hopeless, knowing nothing of their whereabouts, for in all those two months they had had no glimpse of land,—so that when at last they caught sight of an armed fusta, they were "much troubled," supposing it to be a Moorish cruiser. When it came near and shewed itself to be a Gallician pirate, the poor fellows were almost wild with delight, still more when they found they were not far from Lagos. They had had a terrible time; first they were almost poisoned by the dead bodies of Nuno Tristam and the victims of the savages' poisoned arrows; then, when at last they had "thrown their honour to the winds and those bodies to the fishes," shamefaced and utterly broken in spirit, the five wretchedly ignorant seamen, who were now left alone, drifted, with the boundless and terrible ocean on one side, and the still more dangerous and unknown coast of Africa on the other, for sixty days. A common sailor, "little enough skilled in the art of sailing"; a groom of the Prince's chamber, the young hero who saved the ship; a negro boy, who was taken with the first captives from Guinea; and two other "little lads small enough,"—this was the crew. As for the rest, Beati mortui qui in Domino moriuntur, Blessed are the dead that die in the Lord, cries the chronicler in that outburst of bewildered grief with which he ends his story. There were widows and orphans left for the Prince to care for, and "of these he took especial charge."

But all people were not so unlucky as Nuno Tristam. The caravel of Zarco of Madeira, which under Zarco's nephew, Alvaro Fernandez, had already passed beyond every other in the year of the great armada, 1445, was sent back again on its errand "of doing service in the unknown lands of Guinea to the Lord Don Henry," in the black year, 1446. Its noble and valiant owner now "charged the aforesaid" Alvaro Fernandez, with the ship well armed, to go as far as he could, and to try and make some booty, that should be so new and so splendid that it would be a sign of his good-will to serve the Lord who had made him. So they sailed on straight to Cape Verde, and beyond that to the Cape of Masts (or Spindle Palms), their farthest of the year before, but they did not turn back here, in spite of unfriendly natives and unknown shores. Still coasting along, they found tracks of men, and a little farther on a village, "where the people came out as men who shewed that they meant to defend their homes; in front of them was a champion, with a good target on his arm and an assegai in his hand. This fellow our captain rushed upon, and with a blow of his lance struck him dead upon the ground. Then, running up, he seized his sword and spear, and kept them as trophies to be offered to the Lord Infant." The negroes fled, and the conquerors turned back to their ship and sailed on.

Next day they came to a land where they saw certain of the women of those negroes, and seized one who was of age about thirty, with her child a baby of two, and another, a young girl of fourteen, "the which had a good enough presence and beauty for that country"; but the strength of the woman was so wonderful, that she gave the three men who held her trouble enough to lift her into the boat. And seeing how they were kept struggling on the beach, they feared that some of the people of the country might come down upon them. So one of them put the child into the boat, and love of it forced the mother to go likewise, without much more pushing.

Thence they went on, pursues the story, till they came to a river, into which they made an entrance with a boat, and carried off a woman that they found in a house. But going up the river somewhat farther, with a mind to make some good booty, there came out upon them four or five canoes full of negroes, armed as men who would fight for their country, whose encounter our men in the boat did not wish to await in face of the advantage of the enemy, and fearing above all the great peril of poisoned arrows. So they began to pull down stream as hard as they could towards the caravel; but as one of the canoes distanced the others and came up close to them, they turned upon it and in the fight one of the negroes shot a dart, that wounded the captain, Alvaro Fernandez, in the foot. But he, as he had been already warned of the poison, drew out the arrow very quickly and bathed it with acid and oil, and then anointed it well with theriack, and it pleased God that he passed safely through a great trouble, though for some days he lay on the point of death. And so they got back to the caravel.

But though the captain was so badly wounded, the crew did not stop in following the coast and went on (all this was over quite new ground) till they came to a certain sand-spit, directly in front of a great bay. Here they launched a boat, and rowed out to see the land they had come to, and at once there came out against them full 120 negroes, some with bows, others with shields and assegais, and when they reached the edge of the sea, they began to play and dance about, "like men clean wearied of all sadness, but our men in the boat wishing to be excused from sharing in that festival of theirs, turned and rowed back to the ship."

Now all this was a good 110 leagues,—320 miles beyond Cape Verde, "mostly to the south of the aforesaid cape" (that is, about the place of Sierra Leone on our maps), and this caravel remained a longer time abroad and went farther than any other ship of that year, and but for the sickness of the wounded captain they would not have stopped there. But as it was they came straight back to the Bank of Arguin, "where they met that chief Ahude Meymam, of whom we have spoken before," in the story of Joan Fernandez. And though they had no interpreter, by whom they might do their business, by signs they managed so that they were able to buy a negress, in exchange for certain cloths that they had with them. And so they came safe home. There was not much trouble now in getting volunteers for the work of discovery, and a reward of 200 doubloons—100 from Prince Henry, 100 more from the Regent Don Pedro—to the last bold explorers who had got fairly round Senegambia, added zest to enterprise.

In this same year 1446-7, no fewer than nine caravels sailed to Guinea from Portugal in another armada, on the track of Zarco's successful crew. At Madeira they were joined by two more, and the whole fleet sailed through the Canary island group to Cape Verde. Eight of them passed sixty leagues, 180 miles, beyond, and found a river, the Rio Grande, "of good size enough," up which they sailed, except one ship, belonging to a Bishop—the Bishop of Algarve—"for that this happened to run upon a sand-bank, in such wise, that they were not able to get her off, though all the people on board were saved with the cargo. And while some of them were busy in this, others landed and found the country just deserted by its inhabitants, and going on to find them, they soon perceived that they had found a track, which they had chanced on near the place where they landed."

They followed this track recklessly enough, and nearly met the fate of Nuno Tristam. "For as they went on by that road, they came to a country with great sown fields, with plantations of cotton trees and rice plots, in a land full of hills like loaves, after which they came to a great wood," and as they were going into the wood, the Guineas came out upon them in great numbers, with bows and assegais and saluted them with a shower of poisoned arrows. The first five Europeans fell dead at once, two others were desperately wounded, the rest escaped to the ships, and the ships went no farther that year.

Still worse was the fate of Vallarte's venture in the early months of 1448. Vallarte was a nobleman of the Court of King Christopher of Denmark, who had been drawn to the Court of Henry at Sagres by the growing fame of the Prince's explorations, and who came forward with the stock request, "Give me a caravel to go to the land of the negroes."

A little beyond Cape Verde, Vallarte went on shore with a boat's crew and fell into the trap which had caught the exploring party of the year before. He and his men were surrounded by negroes and were shot down or captured to a man. But one escaped, swimming to the ship, and told how as he looked back over his shoulder to the shore, again and again, he saw Vallarte sitting a prisoner in the stern of the boat.

"And when the chronicle of these voyages was in writing at the end of the self-same year, there were brought certain prisoners from Guinea to Prince

Henry, who told him that in a city of the upland, in the heart of Africa, there were four Christian prisoners." One had died, three were living, and in these four, men in Europe believed they had news of Vallarte and his men.

But between the last voyage of Zarco's caravel in 1446 and the first voyage of Cadamosto in 1455, there is no real advance in exploration.

The "third armada," as it was called, that is the fleet of the nine caravels of 1446-7, the voyage of Gomes Pires to the Rio d'Ouro at the same time, the trading ventures of the Marocco coast which were the means of bringing the first lion to Portugal in 1447, the expeditions to the Rio d'Ouro and to Arguin in the course of the same year, are not part of the story of discovery, but of trade. There is hardly a suspicion of exploring interest about most of them. Even Vallarte's venture in 1448 has nothing of the novelty which so many went out to find "for the satisfaction of the Lord Henry." Guinea voyages are frequent, almost constant, during these years, and this frequency has at any rate the point of making Europeans thoroughly familiar with the coast already explored, if it did little or nothing to bring in new knowledge.

But the value and meaning of Henry's life and work was not after all in commerce, except in a secondary sense; and these voyages of purely trading interest, with no design or at any rate no result of discovery, do not belong to our subject. Each one of them has its own picturesque beauty in the pages of the old chronicle of the Conquest of Guinea, but measured by its importance to the general story of the expansion of Europe, there is no lasting value in any one of the last chapters of Azurara's voyages,—his description of the Canaries, and of the "Inferno" of Teneriffe, "of how Madeira was peopled, and the other islands that are in that part, of how the caravel of Alvaro Dornellas took certain of the Canarians, of how Gomes Pires went to the Rio d'Ouro and of the Moors that he took, of the caravel that went to Meça (in Marocco) and of the Moors that were taken, of how Antam Gonsalvez received the island of Lançarote in the name of the Prince."

Only the chronicler's summary of results, up to the year 1446, the year of Nuno Tristam's failure, is of wider interest. "Till then there had been fifty-one caravels to those parts, which had gone 450 leagues (1350 miles) beyond the Cape (Boyador). And as it was found that the coast ran southward with many points, the Prince ordered these to be added to the sailing chart. And here it is to be noted, that what was clearly known before of the coast of the great sea was 200 leagues (600 miles), which have been increased by these 450. Also what had been laid down upon the Mappa Mundi was not true but was by guess work, but now 't is all from the survey by the eyes of our seamen. And now seeing that in this history we have given account sufficient of the first four reasons which brought our noble Prince to his attempt, it is time we said something of the accomplishment of his fifth object, the conversion of the Heathen, by the bringing of a number of infidel souls from their lands to this, the which by count were nine hundred and twenty-seven, of whom the greater part were turned into the true way of salvation. And what capture of town or city could be more glorious than this."

CHAPTER XV.

THE AZORES.

1431-1460.

We have now come very nearly to the end of the voyages that are described in the old *Chronicle of the Discovery and Conquest of Guinea*, and setting aside the story of the famous Venetian Cadamosto, this is also the end of the African mainland-coasting of Henry's seamen. Though he did not die till 1460, and we have now only reached the year 1448, for Azurara's solemn catalogue of negroes brought to Europe is reckoned only up to that year—"nine hundred and twenty-seven who had been turned into the true path of salvation,"—yet there is no more exploration in the last ten years of Henry's life worth noting, except what falls into this and two of the following chapters.

The first of these is Cadamosto's own record of his two voyages along the Guinea coast, in which he is supposed to have reached Cape Palmar, some five hundred miles beyond Cape Verde, and certainly reached the Gambia, whose great mouth, "like an arm of the sea," is well described in his journal.

The second is the "true account of the finding of the Cape Verde islands by Diego Gomez, servant of Don Henry," who writes the story of the Prince's death and was as faithful a servant as he had at his Court. But there is one other chapter of the exploration directed from Sagres and described by Azurara, which must find its place, and is best spoken of here and now, in the interval between the two most active periods of African coasting voyages. This is the story of the colonisation of the Azores, of the Western or Hawk islands, known to map-makers at least as early as 1351, for they figure clearly enough on the great Florentine chart of that year, though not reclaimed for Europe and Christendom till somewhere about 1430. These islands were found, says a legend, on the Catalan map of 1439, by Diego de Sevill, pilot of the King of Portugal, in 1427. But these islands were after all only two groups of the Archipelago, and the rediscovery or finding of the rest fell between the years 1432 and 1450.

The voyage of Diego de Sevill and Gonzalo Velho Cabral to the Azores, that is to the island of St. Mary and the Formigas, has been alluded to as among the earliest of Prince Henry's successes. But as it was out of this first attempt that the discovery of the whole group resulted, it has been necessary to refer to it again. Cabral, rewarded by his lord with the gift of his discoveries and living in St. Mary's island as "Captain Donatory" or

Lord of the Land, was in charge of the colonisation of the islands he had already found, and of as many others as might come to light. He spent three years (1433-6) collecting men and means in Portugal and then settled in the "Western Isles" with some of the best families in this country.

With this, discovery seemed to have come to a standstill, but years after, somewhere about 1440-1 an odd chance started exploration westward once more. There was a hunt after a runaway slave, a negro, of course, from the continent, who had escaped to the top of the highest mountain in St. Mary. The weather was of the clearest, and he fancied that he saw far off on the horizon the outline of an unknown land. Was it another island? He knew his masters were there as explorers quite as much as colonisers, and he must often have heard their talk about the finding of new lands, and the will of their Lord the Prince that those new lands should at all costs be found, was no secret. That will had sent them there; that same will would secure their slave's pardon, if he came back from hiding with the news of a real discovery.

So he reasoned to himself; and he was right. The Prince, hearing the news, instantly consulted his ancient maps and found that these hinted at lands in the same direction as the slave had pointed out. He ordered Cabral to start at once in search of them. Cabral tried and missed. Then came a wonderful test of Henry's knowledge; he who had never been within a thousand miles of the place, proved to his captain that he had passed between St. Mary and the unknown land, and correcting his course sent him out again, to seek and to find.

On the 8th of May, 1444, the new island was found "on the day of the apparition of St. Michael," and named after the festival. It is our modern "St. Michael of the Oranges."

As with the other islands so with this, colonisation followed discovery. On the 29th of September, 1445, Cabral returned with Europeans, having before left only a few Moors to open up the country. Now on his return he found these wretched men frightened almost to death by the earthquakes that had kept them trembling since they first landed. "And if they had been able to get a boat, even the lightest, they would certainly have escaped in it." Cabral's pilot also, who had been with him before to that same island, declared that of the two great mountain peaks which he had noticed at the two ends of the island, east and west, only the Eastern was now standing. The slang name of "Azores" or "Hawks" now began to take the place of the old term of "Western" islands, from the swarms of hawks or kites that were found in the new discovered St. Michael, and in the others which came to light soon after. For the Third Group, "Terceira," was sighted between 1444-50, and added to the Portugal that was thus creeping slowly out towards the unknown West, as if in anticipation of Columbus, throwing its outposts farther and farther into the ocean, as its pioneers grew more and more sure of their ground outside the Straits of Gibraltar. Some seamen of Prince Henry's, returning from "Guinea" to Spain, some adventurer trying to "win fame for himself with the Lord Infant," some merchants sent out to try their luck on the western side as so many had tried on the southern, some African coasters driven out of sight of land by contrary winds;—it may have been any of these, it must have been some one of them, who found the rest of the Azores, Terceira or the island of Jesus, St. George, Graciosa, Fayal, Flores, and Corvo.

Who were the discoverers is absolutely unknown. At this day we have only a few traces of the first colonisation, but of two things we may be pretty certain. First, that the Azores were all found and colonised in Henry's lifetime, and for the most part between 1430 and 1450. Second, that no definite purpose was formed of pushing discovery beyond this group across the waste of waters to the west, and so of finding India from the "left" hand. Henry and all his school were quite satisfied, quite committed, to the south-east route. By coasting round the continent, not by venturing across the ocean, they hoped and meant to find their way to Malabar and Cathay. As to the settlement of these islands, a copy is still left of Henry's grant of the Captaincy of Terceira to the Fleming Jacques de Bruges.

The facts of the case were these. Jacques came to the Prince one day with a little request about the Hawk islands—that "within the memory of man the aforesaid islands had been under the aggressive lordship of none other than the Prince, and as the third of these islands called the island of Jesu Christ, was lying waste, he the said Jacques de Bruges begged that he might colonise the same. Which was granted to him with the succession to his daughters, as he had no heirs male."

For Jacques was a rich Fleming, who had come into the Prince's service, it would seem, with the introduction of the Duchess of Burgundy, Don Henry's niece. Since then he had married into a noble house of Portugal, and now he was offering to take upon himself all the charges of his venture. Such a man was not lightly to be passed over. His design was encouraged, and more than this his example was followed. An hidalgo named Sodré—Vincent Gil Sodré—took his family and adherents across to Terceira, the island of Jesu Christ, and from thence went on and settled in Graciosa, while another Fleming, Van der Haager, joining Van der Berge or De Bruges in Terceira with two ships "fitted out at his own cost and filled with his own people and artisans, whom he had brought to work as in a new land," tried though unsuccessfully to colonise the island of St. George.

The first Captain Donatory of Fayal was another Fleming—Job van Heurter, Lord of Moerkerke—and there is a special interest in his name. For it is through him that we get in 1492 the long and interesting notice of the first settlement of the Azores on the globe of Martin Behaim, now at Nuremberg, the globe which was made to play such a curious part, as undesigned as it was ungenerous, in the Columbus controversy.

"These islands," says the tablet attached to them on the map, "these Hawk islands, were colonised in 1466, when they were given by the King of Portugal to his sister Isabel, Duchess of Burgundy, who sent out many people of all classes, with priests and everything necessary for the maintenance of religion. So that in 1490 there were there some thousands of souls, who had come out with the noble knight, Job de Heurter, my dear father-in-law, to whom the islands were given in perpetuity by the Duchess.

"Now in 1431, Prince Henry provisioned two ships for two years and sent them to the lands beyond Cape Finisterre, and they, sailing due west for some five hundred leagues, found these islands, ten in number, all desert without quadrupeds or men, only tenanted by birds, and these so tame that they could be caught by the hand. So they called these 'the Islands of the Hawks' (Azores).

"And next year (1432), by the King's orders, sixteen vessels were sent out from Portugal with all kinds of tame animals, that they might breed there."

Of the first settlement of Flores and Corvo, the two remaining islands of the group, still less is known, but in any case it seems not to have been fully carried out till the last years of the Prince's life, possibly it was the work of his successor in the Grand Mastership of the Order of Christ, which now took up a sort of charge to colonise outlying and new discovered lands. For among the Prince's last acts was his bequest of the islands, which had been granted to himself by his brother, King Edward, in 1433, to Prince Ferdinand, his nephew, whom he had adopted with a view of making him his successor in aims as well as in office, in leading the progress of discovery as well as in the headship of the Order of Christ.

CHAPTER XVI.

THE TROUBLES OF THE REGENCY AND THE FALL OF DON PEDRO.

1440-9.

Don Pedro had been nominated sole Regent of Portugal on November 1, 1439, and by the end of the next year all the unsettlement consequent on the change at court seemed to be at an end. But a deep hatred continued between the various parties.

First of all, the Count of Barcellos, natural son of John I., created Duke of Braganza by Affonso V., had taken up a definite policy of supplanting the Regent. The Queen Mother had not forgotten or forgiven Don Pedro's action at Edward's death, and the young King himself, though engaged to the Regent's daughter, was already distrustful, was fitting himself to lead the Barcellos party against the Prince.

On February 18, 1445, died the Queen Leonor, with suspicions of poison, diligently fostered by the malcontents. Next year (1446) Affonso, now fourteen, came of age, and his uncle proposed at once to resign all actual power and retire to his estates as Duke of Coimbra. But the King was either not yet prepared to part with him, or still felt some gratitude to his guardian, "the wisest head in Spain."

He begged him to keep the chief direction of affairs, thanked him for the past, and promised to help him in the future. More than this, he protested that he wished to be married to his cousin, Pedro's daughter Isabel. They had been formally betrothed four years; now Affonso called on his nobles and the deputies of Cortés to witness the marriage.

In May, 1447, this royal wedding was celebrated, but coldly and poorly, as nephew and uncle had now drifted quite apart. The more the younger disliked and suspected the elder, the more vehement became his protestations of regard. But he bitterly resented the Duke's action in holding him to his promise, and he made up his mind before the marriage that he would henceforth govern as well as reign.

The Regent just prevented his dismissal by laying down his offices; the King seemed almost to relent in parting from his guardian, who had kept the kingdom in such perfect peace and now resigned so well discharged a duty; but even his wife could not prevent the coming storm. She struggled hard to reconcile her father and her husband, but the mischief-makers were too hard for her. Persuaded that the Duke was a traitor, the King allowed himself to be used to goad him into revolt. "Your father wishes to be punished," he said fiercely to the Queen, "and he shall be punished."

HENRY IN MORNING DRESS, WITH GREAT HAT.

If Henry, who in the last six years had only once left Sagres, to knight Don Pedro's eldest son at Coimbra in 1445, had now been able, in presence as well as writing, to stand by his brother in this crisis, the Regent might have been saved. As it was, Pedro had hardly settled down in his exile at Coimbra, when he found himself charged with the secret murders of King Edward, Queen Leonor, and Prince John. The more monstrous the slander, the more absurd and self-contradictory it might be, the more eagerly it was made.

Persecution as petty and grinding as that which hunted Wolsey to death, at last drove Pedro to take arms. His son, knighted by Henry himself for the high place of Constable of the Realm, had been forced into flight, the arms of Coimbra Arsenal seized for the King's use, his letters to his nephew opened and answered, it was said by his enemies, who wrote back in the sovereign's name, as he would write to an open rebel. All this the Prince bore, but when he heard that his bastard brother of Braganza, who had betrayed and maligned and ruined him, was on the march to plunder his estates, like an outlaw's, he collected a few troops and barred his way. At this Affonso was persuaded to declare war.

Only one great noble stood by the fallen Regent, but this was his friend Almada, the Spanish Hercules, his sworn brother in arms and in travels, one of the Heroes of Christendom, who had been made a Count in France and a Knight of the Garter in England. It was he who now escaped from honourable imprisonment at Cintra, joined Pedro in Coimbra, and proposed to him that they should go together to Court and demand justice and a fair trial, but sword in hand and with their men at their back. Was it not better to die as soldiers than as traitors without a hearing?

So on May 5, 1449, the Duke left Coimbra with his little army of vassals, 1000 horse and 5000 foot and passed by Batalha, where he stopped to revisit the great church and the tombs of his father and his brothers. Thence he marched straight on Lisbon, which the King covered from Santarem with 30,000 men. At the rivulet of Alfarrobeira the armies met; a lance thrust or a cross-bow shot killed the Infant; a common soldier cut off his head and carried it to Affonso in the hope of knighthood. Almada, who fought till he could not stand from loss of blood, died with his friend. Hurling his sword from him, he threw himself on the ground, with a scornful, "Take your fill of me, Varlets," and was cut to pieces.

Though at first leave could hardly be got to bury Don Pedro's body, as time went on his name was cleared. His daughter bore a son to the King, and the proofs of his loyalty, the indignant warnings of foreign Courts, the entreaties of the Queen, at last brought Affonso to something like repentance and amendment. He buried the Regent at Batalha and pardoned his friends, those who were left from the butchery of Alfarrobeira.

CHAPTER XVII.

CADAMOSTO.

1455-6.

We have now come to the voyages of the Venetian Cadamosto, in the service of Prince Henry. And though these were far from being the most striking in their general effect, they are certainly the most famous, the best known, of all the enterprises of these fifty years (1415-1460). It is true that Cadamosto fairly reached Sierra Leone and, passing the farthest mark of the earlier Portuguese caravels, coasted along many miles of that great eastern bend of the West African coast which we call the Gulf of Guinea. But it is to his general fame as a seaman, his position in Italy, and the interest he aroused by his written and published story that he owed his greater share of attention.

When I first set my mind, begins his narrative, on sailing the ocean between the Strait of Cadiz and the Fortunate Islands, the one man who had tried to enter the aforesaid ocean, since the days of our Father Adam, was the Infant Don Henry of Portugal, whose illustrious and almost countless deeds I pass over, excepting only his zeal for the Christian faith and his freedom from the bonds of matrimony. For his father, King John, had not given up the ghost before he had warned his son Henry with saving precepts, that the aforesaid Holy Faith he should foster with a dauntless mind and not fail in his vows of warring down the foes of Christ.

Therefore every year did Don Henry, as it were, challenging and hurling defiance at the Moors, persist in sending out his caravels as far as the headland called the Cape of Non (Not), from the belief that beyond the said Cape there is "*No*" return possible. And as for a long time the ships of the Prince did not dare to pass that point, Henry roused himself to accomplish this feat, seeing that his caravels did much excel all other sailing ships afloat, and strictly enjoined his captains not to return before they had passed the said Cape. Who steadily pressing on, and never leaving sight of the shore, did in truth pass near one hundred miles beyond, finding nothing but desert land.

Beyond this again, for the space of one hundred and fifty miles, the Prince then sent another fleet, which fared no better, and finding no trace of men or of tillage, returned home. And Don Henry, growing ever keener for discovery, and excited by the opposition as it were of nature, sent out again and again till his sailors had reached beyond the Desert Coast to the land of the Arabs and of those new races called Azaneguys, people of a tawny colour.

And finally there appeared to these bold mariners the land of Æthiopia, which lies upon the shore of the Southern ocean, and here again from day to day the explorers discovered new races and new lands.

"Now I, Luigi Ca da Mosto, who had sailed nearly all the Mediterranean coasts, once leaving Venice for 'Celtogallia' (France), but being caught by a storm off C. St. Vincent, had to take refuge in the Prince's town, near the said Cape, and was here told of the glorious and boundless conquests of the Prince, whence accrued such gain that from no traffic in the world could the like be had.

"The which," continues the candid trader, "did exceedingly stir my soul, eager as it was for gain above all things else; and so I made suit to be brought before the Prince, if so be that I might gain leave to sail in his service, for since the profit of this voyage is subject to his pleasure, he doth guard his monopoly with no small care."

With the Prince, at last, Cadamosto made terms: either that he, the adventurer, should furnish the ships at his own cost, and take the whole risk upon himself, and of the merchandise that he might gain a fourth part to go to his lord; or that the Prince should bear the cost of equipment and should have half the profits. But in any case, if there was no profit, the whole expense should fall upon the trader. The Prince added that he would heartily welcome any other volunteers from Venice, and on Cadamosto himself he urged an immediate start. "As for me," repeats the sailor, "my age, my vigour, my skill equal to any toil, above all my passionate desire to see the world and explore the unknown, set me all on fire with eagerness. And especially the fact that no countryman of mine had ever tried the like, and my certainty of winning the highest honour and gain from such a venture, made me forward to offer myself. I only stayed to enquire from veteran Portuguese what merchandise was the most highly prized among the Æthiopians and people of the furthest South, and then went home to find the best light craft for the ocean coasting that I had in mind." Meantime the Prince ordered a caravel to be equipped, which he gave to one Vincent, a native of Lagos, as captain, and caused to be armed to the teeth, as was required, and on the 21st of March, 1455, Cadamosto sailed for Madeira. On the 25th they were off Porto Santo, and the Venetian stops to give us a description of the island, which, he says in passing, had been found and colonised by the Prince's seamen twenty-seven years before. It was worth the settling. Every kind of grain and fruit was easily raised, and there was a great trade in dragon's blood, "which is made from the tears of a tree."

On March 27th, Cadamosto sailed from Porto Santo to Madeira, forty miles distant, and easily seen from the first island when the weather was cloudy, and here the narrative stops some time to describe and admire sufficiently. Madeira had been colonised under the lead and action of the Prince four and twenty years before, and was now thickly peopled by the Portuguese settlers. Beyond Portugal its existence was hardly known. Its name was "from its woodland,"—here Cadamosto repeats the traditional falsehood about the place,—but the first settlers had destroyed most of this in trying to clear an open space by fire. The whole island had once been in flames, the colonists only saved their lives by plunging into the rivers, and even Zarco, the chief discoverer, with his wife and children had to stand in a torrent bed for two whole days and nights before they could venture on dry land again.

The island was forty miles round; like Porto Santo, it was without a harbour, but not without convenient roads for ships to lie in; the soil was fertile, well watered by eight rivers that flowed through the island. "Various kinds of carved wood are exported, so that almost all Portugal is now adorned with tables and other furniture made from these woods."

"Hearing of the great plenty of water in the island, the Prince ordered all the open country to be planted with sugar-cane and with vines imported from Crete, which do excellent well in a climate so well suited to the grape; the vine staves make good bows, and are exported to Europe like the wine, red and white alike, but especially the red. The grapes are ripe about Easter in each year," and this vintage, as early as Cadamosto's day, was evidently the main interest of the islanders, who had all the enthusiasm of a new venture in their experiment, "for no one had ever tried his hand upon the soil before."

From Madeira the caravel sailed on 320 miles to the Canaries, of which says our Venetian, there are ten, seven cultivated and three still desert; and of the seven inhabited four are Christian, three Heathen, even now, fifty years after De Béthencourt's conquest. Neither wine nor grain can be produced on this soil, and hardly any fruit, only a kind of dye, used for clothes in Portugal; goat's flesh and cheese can also be exported, and something, Cadamosto fancies, might be made of the wild asses that swarm in the islands.

Each of these Canary islands being some forty miles from the next, the people of one do not understand the speech of their neighbours. They have no walls, but open villages; watch towers are placed on the highest mountains to guard the people of one village from the attacks of the next, for a guerilla warfare, half marauding, half serious civil war, is the order of the day.

Speaking of the three heathen islands, "which were also the most populous," Cadamosto stops a little over the mention of Teneriffe, "wonderful among the islands of the earth, and able to be seen in clear weather for a distance of seventy Spanish leagues, which is equal to two hundred and fifty miles. And what makes it to be seen from so far, is that on the top is a great rock of adamant, like a pyramid, which stone blazes like the mountain of Ætna, and is full fifteen miles from the plain, as the natives say."

These natives have no iron weapons, but fight with stones and wooden daggers; they go naked except for a defensive armour of goat-skins, which they wear in front and behind. Houses they have none, not even the poorest huts, but live in mountain caves, without faith, without God. Some indeed worship the sun and moon, and others planets, reverence certain idols; in their marriage customs the chiefs have the first right by common consent, and at the graves of their dead chiefs are most of their religious sacrifices; the islanders have only one art, that of stone-slinging, unless one were to count their mountain-climbing and skill in running and in all bodily exercises, in which nature has created these Canarians to excel all other mortals.

They paint their bodies with the juice of plants in all sorts of colours and think this the highest point of perfection, to be decked out on their skins like a garden bed.

From the Canaries, Cadamosto sails to the White Cape, C. Blanco, on the mainland, some way beyond Bojador, "towards Æthiopia," passing the bay and isles of Arguin on the way, where the crews found such quantities of sea-birds that they brought home two ship-loads. And here it is to be noticed, says the narrative, that in sailing from the parts of Cadiz to that Æthiopia which faces to the south, you meet with nothing but desert lands till you come to Cape Cantin, from which it is a near course to C. Blanco. These parts towards the south do run along the borders of the negroes' land, and this great tract of white and arid land, full of sand, very low lying at a dead level, it would be a quick thing to cross in sixty days. At C. Blanco some hills begin to rise out of the plain, and this cape was first found by the Portuguese, and on it is nothing but sand, no trace of grass or trees; it is seen from far, being very sharply marked, three-sided, and having on its crest three pyramids, as they may be called, each one a mile from its neighbour. A little beyond this great desert tract is a vast sea and a wondrous concourse of rivers, where only explorers have reached. At C. Blanco there is a mart of Arab traders, a station for the camels and caravans of the interior, and those pass by the cape who are coming from Negro-land and going to the Barbary of North Africa. As one might expect on such a barren stony soil, no wine or grain can be raised; the natives have oxen and goats, but very few; milk of camels and others is their only drink; as for religion, the wretches worship Mahomet and hate Christians right bitterly. What is of more interest to the Venetian merchant, the traders of these parts have plenty of camels which carry loads of brass and silver, and even of gold, brought from the negroes to the people of our parts.

The natives of C. Blanco are black as moles, but dress in white flowing robes, after the Moorish fashion, with a turban wound round the head; and indeed plenty of Arabs are always hovering off the cape and the bay of Arguin for the sake of trade with the Infant's ships, especially in silver, grain, and woven stuffs, and above all in slaves and gold. To protect this commerce, the Prince some time since (1448), built a fort in the bay, and every year the Portuguese caravels that come here lie under its protection and exchange the negro slaves that they have captured farther south for Arab horses, one horse against ten or fifteen slaves, or for silks and woven stuffs from Morocco and Granada, from Tunis and the whole land of Barbary. The Arabs on their side sell slaves, that they have driven from the upland, to the Portuguese at Arguin, in all nearly a thousand a year, so that the Europeans, who used to plunder all this coast as far as the Senegal, now find it more profitable to trade.

The mention of the Senegal brings Cadamosto to the next stage of his voyage, to the great river, "which divides the Azaneguys, Tawny Moors, from the First Kingdom of the Negroes."

The Azaneguys, Cadamosto goes on to define more exactly as a people of a colour something between black and ashen hue, whom the Portuguese once plundered and enslaved but now trade with peacefully enough. "For the Prince will not allow any wrong-doing, being only eager that they should submit themselves to the law of Christ. For at present they are in a doubt whether they should cleave to our faith or to Mahomet's slavery." But they are a filthy race, continues the traveller, all of them mean and very abject, liars and traitorous knaves, squat of figure, noisome of breath, though of a truth they cover their mouths as of decency, saying that the mouth is a very cesspool and sewer of impurity. They oil their hair with a foul-smelling grease, which they think a great virtue and honour. Much do they make also of their gross fat women, whose breasts they deform usually, that they may hang out the more, straining their bodies (when) at seventeen years of age with ropes.

Ignorant and brutal as they are, they know no other Christian people but the Portuguese, who have enslaved and plundered them now fourteen years. This much is certain, that when they first saw the ships of Don Henry sailing past, they thought them to be birds coming from far and cleaving the air with white wings. When the crews furled sail and drew in to the shore, the natives changed their minds and thought they were fishes; some, who first saw the ships sailing by night, believed them to be phantoms gliding past. When they made out the men on board of them, it was much debated whether these men could be mortal; all stood on the shore, stupidly gazing at the new wonder.

The centre of power and of trade in these parts was not on the coast, but some way inland. Six days' journey up the country is the place called Tagaza, or the Gold-Market, whence there is a great export of salt and metals which are brought on the camels of the Arabs and Azaneguys down to the shore. Another route of merchants is inland to the Negro Empire of Melli and the city of Timbuctoo, where the heat is such that even animals cannot endure to labour and no green thing grows for the food of any quadruped, so that of one hundred camels bearing gold and salt (which they store in two hundred or three hundred huts) scarce thirty return home to Tagaza, for the journey is a long one, 'tis forty days from Tagaza to Timbuctoo and thirty more from Timbuctoo to Melli.

"And how comes it," proceeds Cadamosto, "that these people want to use so much salt?" and after some fanciful astrological reasoning he gives us his practical answer, "to cool their blood in the extreme heat of the sun": and so much is it needed that when they unload their camels at the entrance of the kingdom of Melli, they pack the salt in blocks on men's heads and these last carry it, like a great army of footmen, through the country. When one negro race barters the salt with another, the first party comes to the place agreed on, and lays down the salt in heaps, each man marking his own heap by some token. Then they go away out of sight, about the time of midday sun, when the second party comes up, being most anxious to avoid recognition and places by each heap so much gold as the buyer thinks good. Then they too go away. The sellers come back in the evening, each one visits his pile, and where the gold is enough for the seller's wishes, he takes it, leaves the salt and goes away for good; where it is not enough, he leaves gold and salt together and only goes away to wait again till the buyers have paid a second visit. Now, the second party coming up again, take away the salt where the gold has been accepted, but where it still lies, refused, they either add more or take their money away altogether, according to what they think to be the worth of the salt.

Once the King of Melli, who sent out a party with salt to exchange for gold, ordered his men to make captive some of the negroes who concealed themselves so carefully. They were to wait till the buyers should come up to put down their gold; then they were to rush out and seize all they could. In this way one man and only one was taken, who refused all food and died on the third day after his capture, without uttering a word, "whereby the King of Melli did not gain much," but which induced the men of Melli to believe that the other people were naturally dumb. The captors described the appearance of those who escaped their hands, "men of fine build and height, more than a palm's length greater than their own, having the lower lip brought out and hung down even to the breast, red and bleeding and disclosing their teeth which were larger than the common, their eyes black, prominent, and fierce-looking."

For this treachery the trade was broken off three whole years, till the great want of salt compelled the injured negroes to resume, and since then the business had gone on as before.

The gold thus gained is carried by the men of Melli to their city, and then portioned out in three parts; one part goes by the caravan route towards Syria, the other two thirds go to Timbuctoo, and are there divided once again, part going to Tunis, the head of Barbary, and part to the regions of Marocco, over against Granada, and without the strait of the Pillars of Hercules (Gibraltar). And to those parts come Christian merchants, and especially Italians, to buy the gold in exchange for merchandise of every sort. For among the negroes and Azaneguys there is no coinage of gold or of silver, no money token of metal, but the whole is simply matter for exchange.

From the trade, Cadamosto changes to discourse of the politics of the natives, their manners and customs. Their government for the most part is not monarchy, but a tyranny of the richest and most powerful caste. Their wars are waged only with offensive arms, light spears and swords; they have no defensive armour, but use horses, which they sit as the Moors do. Their ordinary garments are of cotton.

The plague of excessive drought during all the year, except from August to October, is aggravated at certain seasons by the worse plague of locusts, "and I myself have seen them flying by troops upon the sea and shore like an army, but of countless number." After this long digression Cadamosto comes back to the Gulf of Senegal. "And this," says he, "is the chief river of the Region of the Negroes, dividing them from the Tawny Moors." The mouth of the estuary is a mile wide, but an island lying in mid-channel divides the river into two parts just where it enters the sea. Though the central channel is deep enough, the entrance is made difficult to strangers by the shallows and sand banks on either side; every six hours the river rises and falls with the flow and ebb of the ocean, and where it pours out its waters into the sea, the flux and reflux of waters reaches to a distance of sixty miles, as say the Portuguese who have watched it. The Senegal is nearly four hundred miles beyond Cape Blanco; a sandy shore stretches between the two; up to the river the sailor sees from the shore only the wandering Azaneguys, tawny, squat, and miserable savages; across the stream to the south are the real Blacks, "well built noble-looking men," and after so long a stretch of arid and stony desert, there is now a beautiful green land, covered with fruit-bearing trees, the work of the river, which, men say, comes from the Nile, being one of the four most glorious rivers of earth that flow from the Garden of Eden and earthly paradise. For as the eastern Nile waters Egypt, so this doth water Æthiopia.

Now the land of these negroes is at the entering in of Æthiopia, from which to Cape Verde the land is all level, where the King of Senegal, reigning over people that have no cities, but only scattered huts, lives by the presents that his subjects bring him. Such are oxen, goats, and horses, which are much valued for their scarceness, but used without saddle, bridle, or trappings. To these presents the King adds what he can plunder by his own strength, especially slaves, of which the Blacks have a great trade with the Azaneguys. Their horses they sell also to the Christian traders on the coast. The King can have as many wives as he likes (and always keeps well above his minimum of thirty), to each of whom is assigned a certain estate with slaves and cattle, but not equal; to some more, to others less. The King goes the round of these farms at will, and lives upon their produce. Any day you may see hosts of slaves bringing fruits of all sorts to the King, as he goes through the country with his motley following, all living at free quarters.

Of the negroes of these parts most go naked, but the chiefs and great men use cotton shirts, as the country abounds in this sort of stuff. Cadamosto describes in great detail the native manufacture of garments, and the habits of the women; barefoot and bare-headed they go always, dressed in linen, elegant enough in apparel, vile in life and diet, always chattering, great liars, treacherous and deceitful to the last degree. Bloody and remorseless are the wars the princes of these barbarians carry on against one another. They have no horsemen or body armour, but use darts and spears, barbed with many poisonous fangs, and several kinds of arrows, as with us. From the beginning of the world they knew nothing of ships before the Portuguese came; they only used light canoes or skiffs, each of which can be carried by three men, and in which they fish and go from place to place on the river.

The boundaries of the kingdom of Senegal are the ocean on the west, the land of Gambra on the south, the inland Blackman's country on the east, and on the north the River Niger (Senegal), which, "as I have said before, divides the Azaneguys from the First Kingdom of the Negroes. And the said river," concludes Cadamosto, "five years before my coming, had been explored by the Portuguese, who hoped to open up a great commerce in those parts. So that every year from that time their ships had been off that coast to trade."

Cadamosto determined to push farther up the river than any had done before, and so to come to the land of Budomel, one of the great negro princes and kingdoms, for it was the name both of place and person. When he came there he found an "Emperor so honest that he might have been an example to any Christian," who exchanged his horses, wool-fells, and linen goods for the strangers' merchandise and slaves, with deeds as honourable as his words. Our adventurer was so taken with "Lord Budomel" that he gladly went with him two hundred and fifty miles up country, on his promising a supply of negro slaves, black but comely, and none of them more than twelve years old.

On this adventurous journey, of which we are next given a full account, Cadamosto is taken charge of by Bisboror, the Prince's nephew, "through whom I saw many things worth noting." The Venetian was not anxious to put off to sea, as the weather was very rough, so rough indeed that no boat could venture off from the bank at the river's mouth to where the ships lay, and the captain had to send word to his crews by negro swimmers, who could pass any surf, "for that they excel all other living men in the water and under it, for they can dive an hour without rising."

It is not worth while to follow Cadamosto in all his long account of what he saw and heard of negro life in the course of this journey; it is as unsavoury as it is commonplace. He repeats very much of what he has said before about the Azaneguys, of their servility to their Princes, "who are to them as mortal Gods"; of the everlasting progresses and wanderings of those Princes round their kingdoms, from kraal to kraal, living on the stores each wife has provided; of the kraals themselves, no towns or castles, as people at home might think, says Cadamosto, but merely collections of forty and fifty huts, with a hedge of living trees round, intertwined, and the royal palace in the middle.

The Prince of Budomel has a bodyguard of two hundred men, besides the volunteer guard of his innumerable children, who are broken up in two groups, one always at Court, "and these are made the most of," the other scattered up and down the country, as a sort of royal garrison. The wretched subjects, who "suffer more from their King with a good will than they would from any stranger under force," are punished with death for the smallest things. Only two small classes have any privileges: ministers of religion share with the greatest nobles the sole right of access to the person of the "Mortal God."

Cadamosto set up a mart in the upland and made what profits he could from their miserable poverty, making exchanges with cottons, cloths, oil, millet, skins, palm-leaves, and vegetables, and above all, of course, with gold, what little there was to be had. "Meantime the negroes came stupidly crowding about me, wondering at our Christian symbols; our white colour, our dress and shape of body, our Damascenes, garments of black silk and robes of blue cloth or dyed wool, all amazed them; some insisted that the white colour of the strangers was not natural but put on"; as with Cook and so many others the savages now behaved with Cadamosto. They spat upon his arm and tried to rub off the white paint; then they wondered more than ever when they found the flesh itself was white.

Of gold after all not much was to be got, and the exploring party was not long in returning to the caravels and pushing on beyond Cape Verde. To the last the ships and their instruments were the chief terror and delight of the negroes and above all of the negro women; the whole thing was the work of demons, they said, not of men, seeing that our engines of war could fell one hundred men at one discharge; the trumpets sounding they took to be the yells of a living and furious beast of prey. Cadamosto gave them a trumpet that they might see it was made by art; they changed their minds accordingly, and decided that such things were directly made by God himself, above all admiring the different tones, and crying loudly that they had never seen anything so wonderful.

The women looked through every part of the ship—masts, helm, anchors, sails, and oars. The eyes painted on the bow excited them: the ship had eyes and could see before it, and the men who used it must be wonderful enchanters like the demons. "This specially they wondered, that we could sail out of all sight of land and yet know well enough where we were, all which, said they, could not happen, without black art. Scarcely less was their wonder at the sight of lighted candles, as they had never before seen any light but that of fire, when I shewed them how to make candles from wax which before they had always thrown aside as worthless, they were still more amazed, saying there was nothing we did not know."

And now Cadamosto was ready to put off from the coast into the ocean and strike south for the kingdom of Gambro, as he had been charged by the Prince, who had told him it was not far from the Senegal, as the negroes had reported to him at Sagres. And that kingdom, he had been told, was so rich in gold that if Christians could reach it they would gain endless riches.

So with two aims, first to find the golden land, and second to make discoveries in the unknown, the Venetian was just beginning to start afresh, when he was joined by two more ships from Portugal, and they agreed to round Cape Verde together. It was only some forty miles beyond Budomel and the caravels reached it next day.

Cape Verde gets its name from its green grass and trees, like C. Blanco from its white sand. Both are very prominent, lofty, and seen from a great distance, as they run out far into the sea, but Cape Verde is more picturesque, dotted as it is with little native villages on the side of the ocean, and with three small desert islands a short distance from the mainland, where the sailors found birds' nests and eggs in thousands, of kinds unknown in Europe, and, above all, enormous shell-fish (turtles), of twelve pounds' weight.

Soon after passing C. Verde, the coast makes a great sweep to the east, still covered with evergreen trees, coming down in thick woods to within a bowshot of the sea, so that from a distance the forest line seems to touch the high-water mark, "as we thought at first looking on ahead from our ships. Many countries have I been in to East and West, but never did I see a prettier sight."

From the place the description again changes to the people, and we are told once more with wearisome repetitions about the people beyond C. Verde, in most ways like the negroes of the Senegal but "not obedient to that kingdom and abhorring the tyranny of the negro Princes, having no King or laws themselves, worshipping idols, using poisoned arrows which kill at once, even though they drew but little blood,"—in short a most truculent folk, but very fine of stature, black and comely. The whole coast east of C. Verde was found unapproachable, except for certain narrow harbours, till "with a south wind we reached the mouth of a river, called Ruim, a bowshot across at the mouth. And when we sighted this river, which was sixty miles beyond C. Verde, we cast anchor at sunset in ten or twelve paces of water, four or five miles from the shore, but when it was day, as the look-out saw there was a reef of rocks on which the sea broke itself, we sailed on and came to the mouth of another river as large as the Senegal, with trees growing down to the water's edge and promising a most fertile country." Cadamosto determined to land a scout here, and caused lots cast among his slave-interpreters which was to land. "And of these slaves, negroes whom the native kings in the past had sold to Portuguese and who had then been trained in Europe I had many with me who were to open the country for our trade and to parley between us and the natives. Now the lot fell upon the Genoese caravel (which had joined the explorers), to draw into the shore and land a prisoner, to try the good will of the natives before any one else ventured." The poor wretch, instructed to enquire about the races living on the river and their manners, polity, King's name and capital, gold supply, and other matters of commerce, had no sooner swum ashore than he was seized and cut to pieces by some armed savages, while the ships sailed on with a south wind, making no attempt to avenge their victim, till after a lovely coast, fringed with trees, low-lying, and rich exceedingly, they came to the mouth of the Gambra, three or four miles across, the haven where they would be, and where Cadamosto expected his full harvest of gold and pepper and aromatics.

The smallest caravel started at once the very next morning after the discovery to go upstream, taking a boat with it, in case the stream should suddenly get too shallow for anything larger, while the sailors were to keep sounding the river with their poles all the way. Everybody too kept a sharp look-out for native canoes. They had not long to wait. Two miles up the river three native "Almadias" came suddenly out upon them and then stopped dead, too astonished at the ship and the white men in it to offer to do more, though they had at first a threatening look and were now invited to a parley by the Europeans with every sign that could be thought of.

As the natives would not come any nearer, the caravel returned to the mouth of the river, and next morning at about nine o'clock the whole fleet started together upstream to explore "with the hope of finding some more friendly natives by the kind care of Heaven." Four miles up the negroes came out upon them again in greater force, "most of them sooty black in colour, dressed in white cotton, with something like a German helmet on their heads, with two wings on either side and a feather in the middle. A Moor stood in the bow of each Almadia, holding a round leather shield and encouraging his men in their thirteen canoes to fight and to row up boldly to the caravels. Now their oars were larger than ours and in number they seemed past counting." After a short breathing space, while each party glared upon the other, the negroes shot their arrows and the caravels replied with their engines, which killed a whole rank of the natives. The savages then crowded round the little caravel and set upon her; they were at last beaten off with heavy loss and all fled; the slave interpreters shouting out to them as they rowed away that they might as well come to terms with men who were only there for commerce, and had come from the ends of the earth to give the King of Gambra a present from his brother of Portugal, "and for that we hoped to be exceeding well loved and cherished by the king of Gambra. But we wanted to know who and where their king was, and what was the name of this river. They should come without fear and take of us what they would, giving us in return of theirs."

The negroes shouted back that they could not be mistaken about the strangers, they were Christians. What could they have to do with them; they knew how they had behaved to the King of Senegal. No good men could stand Christians who ate human flesh. What else did they buy negro slaves for? Christians were plundering brigands too and had come to rob them. As for their king, he was three days' journey from the river, which was called Gambra.

When Cadamosto tried to come to closer quarters, the natives disappeared, and the crews refused to venture any farther upstream. So the caravels turned back, sailed down the river, and coasted away west to Cape Verde, and so home to Portugal. But before the Venetian ends his journal, he tells us how near Prince Henry's ships had now come to the Equator. "When we were in the river of Gambra, once only did we see the North Star, which was so low that it seemed almost to touch the sea." To make up for the loss of the Pole Star—sunk to "the third part of a lance's length above the edge of the water,"—Cadamosto and his men had a view of six brilliant stars, "in form of a cross," while the June night was "of thirteen hours and the day of eleven."

Cadamosto only went home to refit for a second voyage. Though at first he had been baffled by the "savagery of the men of Gambra" from finding out much about them, he resolved to try again, sailed out the very next year by way of the Canaries and Cape Blanco, and found, after three days' more sailing, certain islands off Cape Verde, where no one had been before. The lookouts saw two very large islands, towards the larger of which they sailed at once, in the hope of finding good anchorage and friendly natives. But no one, friend or foe, seemed to live there.

So next morning, says Cadamosto, that I might satisfy my own mind, I bade ten of my men, armed with missiles and cross-bows, to explore the inland. They crossed the hills that cut off the interior from the coast, but found nothing except doves, who were so tame that they could be caught in any number by the hand.

And now from another side of the first island they caught sight of three others towards the north, and of two more towards the west, which could not be clearly seen because of the great distance. "But for the matter of that, we did not care to go out of our way to find what we now expected, that all these other islands were desolate like the first. So we went on our way (due south) and so passed another island, and, coming to the mouth of a river, landed in search of fresh water and found a beautiful and fruitful country covered with trees. Some sailors who went inland found cakes of salt, white and small, by the side of the river, and immense numbers of great turtles, with shells of such size that they could make very good shields for an army."

Here they stayed a couple of days, exploring in the country and fishing in the river, which was so broad and deep that it would easily bear a ship of one hundred and fifty tons burden and a full bowshot would not carry across it. Then, naming their first discovered island Boa Vista, and the largest of the group St. James, because it was on the feast of the Apostle they found it, they sailed on along the coast of the mainland, till they came to the Place of the Two Palms, between the Senegal and Cape Verde, "and since the whole land was known to us before, we did not stay, but boldly rounded C. Verde and ran along to the Gambra." Up this they at once began to steer.

No canoes came out upon them this time, and no natives appeared, except a few who hung about some way off and did not offer to stop them. Ten miles up they found a small island, where one of the sailors died of a fever, and they called the new discovered land "St. Andrew," after him. The natives were now much more approachable and Cadamosto's men conversed with the bolder ones who came close up to the caravel. Like the men of Senegal, two things above all astonished and confounded them, the white sails of the ships and the white skins of the sailors. After much debate, carried on by yelling from boat to boat, one of the negroes came on board the caravel and was loaded with presents, to make him more communicative. The ruse was successful. The string of his tongue was quite loosed and he chattered along freely enough. The country, like the river, was called "Gambra"; its king, Farosangul, lived ten days' journey toward the south, but he was himself under the Emperor of Melli, chief of all the negroes.

Was there no one nearer than Farosangul? Oh, yes, there was Battimansa, "King Batti," and a good many other princes who lived quite close to the river. Would he guide them to Battimansa? Yes, safe enough, his country was only some forty miles from the mouth of the Gambra.

"And so we came to Battimansa, where the river was narrowed down to about a mile in breadth," where Cadamosto offered presents to the King, and made a great speech before the negro magnates, which is abridged in the narrative, "lest the matter should become a great Iliad." King Batti returned the Portuguese presents with gifts of slaves and gold, but the Europeans were sadly disappointed with the gold. It was not at all equal to what they expected, or what the people of Senegal had talked of; "being poor themselves, they had fancied their neighbours must be rich." On the other hand, the negroes of Gambra would give almost any price for trinkets and worthless toys, because they were new. Fifteen days, or nearly that, did the Portuguese stay there trading, and immense was the variety of their visitors in that time. Most came on board simply from wonder and to stare at them, others to sell their cotton cloths, nets, gold rings, civet and furs, baboons and marmots, fruit and especially dates. Each canoe seemed to differ in its build and its crew from the last. The river, crowded with this light craft, was "like the Rhone, near Lyons," but the natives worked their boats like gondolas, standing, one rowing and another steering with oars, that were like half a lance in shape, a pace and a half long, with a round board like a trencher tied at the end. "And with these they make very good pace, being great coasting voyagers, but not venturing far out to sea or away from their own country, lest they should be seized and sold for slaves to the Christians."

After the fortnight's stay in Battimansa's country, the crews began to fall ill and Cadamosto determined to drop down the river once more to the coast, noting as he did so all the habits of the natives. Most of them were idolaters, nearly all had implicit faith in charms, some worshipped "Mahmoud most vile," and some were Nomades like the Gypsies of Europe. For the most part the people of the Gambra lived like those of the Senegal, dressing in cotton and using the same food, except that they ate dog's flesh and were all tattooed, women as well as men.

We need not follow Cadamosto in his accounts of the great trees, the wild elephants, great bats and "horse-fish" of the country. A chief called Gnumi-Mansa, "King Gnumi," living near the mouth of the Gambra, took him on an elephant-hunt, in which he got the trophies, foot, trunk, and skin, that he took home and presented to Prince Henry.

On descending the Gambra, the caravel tried to coast along the unexplored land, but was driven by a storm into the open sea. After driving about some time and nearly running on a dangerous coast, they came at last to the mouth of a great river which they called Rio Grande, "for it seemed more like a gulf or arm of the sea than a river, and was nearly twenty miles across, some twenty-five leagues beyond the Gambra." Here they met natives in two canoes, who made signs of peace, but could not understand the language of the interpreters. The new country was absolutely outside the farthest limits of earlier exploration, and discovery would have to begin afresh. Cadamosto had no mind to risk anything more. His crew were sick and tired, and he turned back to Lisbon, observing, before he left the Ra or Rio Grande, as he noticed in his earlier voyage, that the North Star almost touched the horizon and that "the tides of that coast were very marvellous. For instead of flow and ebb being six hours each, as at Venice, the flow here was but four, and the ebb eight, the tide rising with such force that three anchors could hardly hold the caravel."

CHAPTER XVIII.

VOYAGES OF DIEGO GOMEZ.

1458-60.

The last voyage of Henry's lifetime was that of his faithful servant, Diego Gomez, by which the Cape Verde islands first became clearly and fully known. It followed close upon Cadamosto's venture.

"No long time after, the Prince equipped at Lagos a caravel, called the *Wren*, and set over it Diego Gomez, with two other caravels, of which the same Gomez was captain-in-chief. Their orders were to go as far as they could.

"But after passing a great river beyond the Rio Grande, we met such strong currents in the sea that no anchor could hold. The other captains and their men were much alarmed, thinking we were at the end of the ocean, and begged me to put back. In the mid-current the sea was very clear and the natives came off from the shore and brought us their merchandise, cotton cloth, ivory, and a quart measure of malaguette pepper, in grain and in its pods as it grows, which delighted us.

"As the current prevented our going farther, and even grew stronger, we put back and came to a land where there were groves of palms near the shore with their branches broken, so tall that from a distance I thought they were the masts or spars of negroes' vessels.

"So we went there and found a great plain covered with hay and more than five thousand animals like stags, but larger, who shewed no fear of us. Five elephants came out of a small river that was fringed by trees, three full grown, with two young ones, and on the shore we saw holes of crocodiles in plenty. We went back to the ships and next day made our way from Cape Verde and saw the broad mouth of a great river, three leagues in width, which we entered and guessed to be the Gambia. Here wind and tide were in our favour, so we came to a small island in mid-stream and rested there the night. In the morning we went farther in, and saw a crowd of canoes full of men, who fled at the sight of us, for it was they who had killed Nuno Tristam and his men. Next day we saw beyond the point of the river some natives on the right-hand bank, who welcomed us. Their chief was called Frangazick and he was the nephew of Farosangul, the great Prince of the Negroes. There they gave us one hundred and eighty pounds worth of gold, in exchange for our goods. The lord of the country had a negro with him named Buka, who knew the tongue only of Negroland, and finding him perfectly truthful, I asked him to go with me to Cantor and promised him all he needed. I made the same promise to his chief and kept it.

THE BORGIAN MAP OF 1450.
(SEE LIST OF MAPS)

"We went up the river as far as Cantor, which is a large town near the riverside. Farther than this the ships could not go, because of the thick growth of trees and underwood, but here I made it known that I had come to exchange merchandise, and the natives came to me in very great numbers. When the news spread through the country that the Christians were in Cantor, they came from Tambucatu in the North, from Mount Gelu in the South, and from Quioquun, which is a great city, with a wall of baked tiles. Here, too, I was told, there is gold in plenty and caravans of camels cross over there with goods from Carthage, Tunis, Fez, Cairo and all the land of the Saracens. These are exchanged for gold, which comes from the mines on the other side of Sierra Leone. They said that range ran southwards, which pleased me very greatly, because all the rivers coming from thence, as far as could be known, ran westward, but they told me that other very large rivers ran eastward from the other side of the ridge.

"There was also, they said, East of these mountains, a great lake, narrow and long, on which sailed canoes like ships. The people on the opposite sides of this lake were always at war; and those on the eastern side were white. When I asked who ruled in those parts, they answered that one chief was a negro, but towards the East was a greater lord who had conquered the negroes a short time before.

"A Saracen told me he had been all through that land and had been present at the fighting, and when I told this to the Prince, he said that a merchant in Oran had written him two months before about this very war, and that he believed it.

"Such were the things told me by the negroes at Cantor; I asked them about the road to the gold country, and who were the lords of that country. They told me the King lived in Kukia, and was lord of all the mines on the right side of the river of Cantor, and that he had before the door of his palace a mass of gold just as it was taken from the earth, so large that twenty men could hardly move it, and that the King always fastened his horse to it and kept it as a curiosity on account of its size and purity. The nobles of his Court wore in their nostrils and ears ornaments of gold.

"The parts to the East were full of gold mines, but the men who went into the pits to get gold did not live long, because of the foul air. The gold sand was given to women to wash the gold from it.

"I enquired the road from Cantor to Kukia and was told the road ran eastward; where was great abundance of gold; as I can well believe, for I saw the negroes who went by those roads laden with it.

"While I was thus trafficking with these negroes of Cantor, my men became worn out with the heat and so we returned towards the ocean. After I had gone down the river fifty leagues, they told me of a great chief living on the South side, who wished to speak with me.

"We met in a great wood on the bank, and he brought with him a vast throng of people armed with poisoned arrows, assegais, swords and shields. And I went to him, carrying some presents and biscuit and some of our wine, for they have no wine except that made from the date-palm, and he was pleased and extremely gracious, giving me three negroes and swearing to me by the one only God that he would never again make war against Christians, but that they might trade and travel safely through all his country.

"Being desirous of putting to proof this oath of his, I sent a certain Indian named Jacob whom the Prince had sent with us, in order that in the event of our reaching India, he might be able to hold speech with the natives, and I ordered him to go to the place called Al-cuzet, with the lord of that country, to find Mount Gelu and Timbuctoo through the land of Jaloffa. A knight had gone there with him before.

"This Jacob, the Indian, told me that Al-cuzet was a very evil land, having a river of sweet water and abundance of lemons; and some of these he brought to me. And the lord of that country sent me elephants' teeth and four negroes, who carried one great ivory tusk to the ship.

"Now the houses here are made of seaweed, covered with straw, and while I stayed here (at the river mouth) three days, I learned that all the mischief that had been done to the Christians had been done by a certain king called Nomimansa, who has the country near the great headland by the mouth of the river Gambia. So I took great pains to make peace with him, and sent him many presents by his own men in his own canoes, which were going for salt along the coast to his own country, for this salt is plentiful there and of a red colour. Now Nomimansa was in great fear of the Christians, lest they should take vengeance upon him.

"Then I went on to a great harbour where I had many negroes come to me, sent by Nomimansa to see if I should do anything, but I always treated them kindly. When the King heard this, he came to the river side with a great force and sitting down on the bank, sent for me. And so I went and paid him all respect. There was a Bishop there of his own faith who asked me about the God of the Christians, and I answered him as God had given me to know; and then I questioned him about Mahomet, whom they believe. At last the King was so pleased with what I said that he sprang to his feet and ordered the Bishop to leave his country within three days, and swore that he would kill any one who should speak the name of Mahomet from that day forward. For he said he trusted in the one only God and there was no other but He, whom his brother Prince Henry worshipped.

"Then calling the Infant his brother, he asked me to baptize him and all his lords and women. He himself would have no other name than Henry, but his nobles took our names, like James and Nuno. So I remained on shore that night with the King but did not baptize him, as I was a layman. But next day I begged the King with his twelve chief men and eight of his wives to dine with me on my caravel; and they all came unarmed and I gave them fowls and meat and wine, white and red, as much as they could drink, and they said to one another that no people were better than the Christians.

"Then again on shore the King asked me to baptize him but I said I had not leave from the Pope; but I would tell the Prince, who would send a priest. So Nomimansa at once wrote to Prince Henry to send him a priest and some one to teach him the faith, and begged him to send him a falcon with the priest, for he was amazed when I told him how we carried a bird on the hand to catch other birds. And with these he asked the Prince to send him two rams and sheep and geese and ganders and a pig, and two men to build houses and plan out his town. And all these wishes of his I promised him that the Prince would grant. And he and all his people made a great noise at my going but I left the King at Gambia and started back for Portugal. One caravel I sent straight home, but with the others I sailed to Cape Verde.

"And as we came near the sea-shore we saw two canoes putting out to sea; but we sailed between them and the shore, and so cut them off. Then the interpreter came to me and said that Bezeghichi, the lord of the land and an evil man, was in one of them.

"So I made them come into the caravel and gave them to eat and drink with a double share of presents, and making as if I did not know him to be the chief, I said 'Is this the land of Bezeghichi?' He answered 'Yes, it is.' And I, to try him, exclaimed 'Why is he so bitter against the Christians? He would do far better to have peace with them, so that they might trade in his land

and bring him horses and other things, as they do for other lords of the negroes. Go and tell your lord Bezeghichi that I have taken you and for love of him have let you go.'

"At this he was very cheerful and he and his men got into their canoes, as I bade them, and as they all were standing by the side of the caravel, I called out 'Bezeghichi, Bezeghichi, do not think I did not know thee. I could have done to thee what I would, and now, as I have done to thee, do thou also to our Christians.'

"So they went off, and we came back to Arguin and the Isle of the Herons, where we found flocks of birds of every kind, and after this came home to Lagos, where the Prince was very glad of our return.

"Then after this for two years no one went to Guinea, because King Affonso was at war in Africa and the Prince was quite taken up with this. But after he had come back from Alcaçer, I reminded him of what King Nomimansa had asked of him; and the Prince sent him all he had promised, with a priest, the Abbot of Soto de Cassa, and a young man of his household named John Delgado. This was in 1458.

"Two years afterwards King Affonso equipped a large caravel and sent me out as captain, and I took with me ten horses and went to the land of the Barbacins, which is near the land of Nomimansa. And these Barbacins had two kings, but the King of Portugal gave me power over all the shores of that sea, that any ships I might find off the coast of Guinea should be under me, for he knew that there were those who sold arms to the Moors, and he bade me to seize such and bring them bound to Portugal.

"And by the help of God I came in twelve days to this land (of the Barbacins), and found two ships there,—one under Gonzalo Ferreira, of Oporto, of the Household of Prince Henry, that was conveying horses; the other was under Antonio de Noli, of Genoa. These merchants injured our trade very much, for the natives used to give twelve negroes for one horse, and now gave only six.

"And while we were there, a caravel came from Gambia, which brought us news that a captain called De Prado was coming with a richly laden ship, and I ordered Ferreira to go to Cape Verde and look for that ship and seize it, on pain of death and loss of all his goods. And he did so, and we found a great prize, which I sent home with Ferreira to the King. And then I and Antonio de Noli left that coast, and sailed two days and one night towards Portugal, and we sighted islands in the ocean, and as my ship was lighter and faster than the rest, I came first to one of those islands, to a good harbour, with a beach of white sand, where I anchored. I told all my men and the other captains that I wished to be first to land, and so I did.

"We saw no trace of natives, and called the island Santiago, as it is still known. There were plenty of fish there and many strange birds, so tame that we killed them with sticks. And I had a quadrant with me, and wrote on the table of it the altitude of the Arctic Pole, and I found it better than the chart, for though you see your course of sailing on the chart well enough, yet if once you get wrong, it is hard by map alone to work back into the right course.

"After this we saw one of the Canary islands, called Palma, and so came to the island of Madeira; and then adverse winds drove me to the Azores, but Antonio de Noli stayed at Madeira, and, catching the right breeze, he got to Portugal before me, and begged of the King the captaincy of the island of Santiago, which I had found, and the King gave it him, and he kept it till his death.

"But De Prado, who had carried arms to the Moors, lay in irons and the King ordered him to be brought out. And then they martyrised him in a cart, and threw him into the fire alive with his sword and gold."

COIMBRA UNIVERSITY OF WHICH HENRY WAS THE OFFICIAL PATRON.

CHAPTER XIX.

HENRY'S LAST YEARS AND DEATH.

1458-60.

While Cadamosto and Diego Gomez were carrying the Prince's flag farther from the shores of Europe "than Alexander or Cæsar had ever ventured," the Prince himself was getting more and more absorbed in the project of a new Holy War against the Infidel.

The fall of Constantinople in 1453 into the hands of the Ottoman Turks, had at least the effect of frightening and almost of rousing Western Christendom at large. In the most miserably divided of Latin states there was now a talk about doing great things, though the time, the spirit for actually doing them, had long passed by, or was not yet come. Spain, the one part of the Western Church and State, which was still living in the crusading fervour of the twelfth century, was alone ready for action. The Portuguese kingdom in particular, under Affonso V., had been keeping up a regular crusade in Marocco, and was willing and eager to spend men and treasure in a great Levantine enterprise. So the Pope's Legate was welcomed when he came in 1457 to preach the Holy War. Affonso promised to keep up an army of twelve thousand men for war against the Ottoman, and struck a new gold coinage—the Cruzado—to commemorate the year of Deliverance.

But Portugal by itself could not deliver New Rome or the Holy Land, and when the other powers of the West refused to move, Affonso had to content himself with the old crusade in Africa, but he now pushed on even more zealously than before his favourite ambition, a land empire on both sides of the Straits, and Prince Henry's last appearance in public service was in his nephew's camp in the Marocco campaign of 1458. In the siege of Alcaçer the Little, the "Lord Infant" forced the batteries, mounted the guns, and took charge of the general conduct of the siege. A breach was soon made in the walls, and the town surrendered on easy terms, "for it was not," said Henry, "to take their goods or force a ransom from them that the King of Portugal had come against them, but for the service of God." They were only to leave behind in Alcaçer their Christian prisoners; for themselves, they might go, with their wives, their children, and their property.

The stout-hearted veteran Edward Menezes became governor of Alcaçer, and held the town with his own desperate courage against all attempts to recover it. When the besiegers offered him terms, he offered them in return his scaling ladders that they might have a fair chance; when they were raising the siege he sent them a message, Would they not try a little longer? It had been a very short affair.

Meantime Henry, returning to Europe by way of Ceuta, re-entered his own town of Sagres for the last time. His work was nearly done, and indeed, of that work there only remains one thing to notice. The great Venetian map, known as the Camaldolese Chart of Fra Mauro, executed in the convent of Murano just outside Venice, is not only the crowning specimen of mediæval draughtsmanship, but the scientific review of the Prince's exploration. As Henry himself closes the middle age of exploration and begins the modern, so this map, the picture and proof of his discoveries, is not only the last of the older type of plan, but the first of the new style— the style which applied the accurate and careful methods of Portolano-drawing to a scheme of the whole world. It is the first scientific atlas.

But its scale is too vast for anything of a detailed account: it measures six feet four inches across, and in every part it is crammed with detail, the work of three years of incessant labour (1457-9) from Andrea Bianco and all the first coasters and draughtsmen of the time. In general, there is an external carefulness as well as gorgeousness about the workmanship; the coasts, especially in the Mediterranean and along the west coast of Europe, would almost suit a modern Admiralty Chart, while its notice, the first notice, of Prince Henry's African and Atlantic discoveries is the special point of the whole work.

There is a certain disposition to exaggerate the size of rivers, mountains, towns, and the whole proportion of things, as we get farther away from the well-known ground of Europe; Russia and the north and north-east of Asia are somewhat too large, but along the central belt, it is fair to say that the whole of the country west of the Caspian is thoroughly sound, the best thing yet done in any projection.

No one could look at Fra Mauro's map and fail to see at a glance a picture of the Old World; and the more it is looked at, the more reliable it will prove to be, by the side of all earlier essays in this field. No one can look at the Arabic maps and their imitations in mediæval Christendom, whether conscious or unconscious (as in the Spanish example of 1109), without despair. It is almost hopeless to try and recognise in these anything of the shape, the proportions, or the distribution of the parts of the world which are named, and which one might almost fancy it was meant to represent at the time.

Place the map of 1459 by the side of the Hereford map of 1300 or of Edrisi's scheme of 1130 (made at the Christian Court of Sicily), or in fact beside any of the theoretical maps of the thousand years that had gone to make the Italy and the Spain of Fra Mauro and Prince Henry, and it will seem to be almost absurd to ask the question: Do these belong to the same civilisation, in any kind of way? What would the higher criticism answer, out of its infallible internal evidence tests? Of course, these are quite different. The one is merely a collection of the scratchings of savages, the other is the prototype of modern maps. Yet the Christian world is answerable for both kinds; it had struggled through ignorance and superstition and tradition into clearer light and truer knowledge.

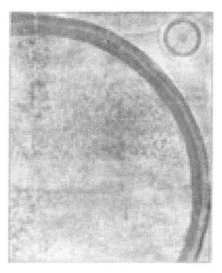

WESTERN SECTION OF THE MAPPE-MONDE OF FRA MAURO.
1457-9.
(SEE LIST OF MAPS)

And when Greek geography came to be reprinted and revived, this was in part at least a consequence of that revival of true science which had begun in that very dark time, the night of the twelfth century, where we are not likely to see any signs of dawn till we look, not so much at what is written now, as at what the poor besotted savages of the ages of Abelard and Bernard and Aquinas and Dante have left to bear witness of themselves.

Between Henry's return from Alcaçer and his death, while the great Venetian map was in making, two years went by, years in which Diego Gomez was finding the Cape Verde islands and pushing the farthest south of European discovery still farther south, but of the Prince's own working, apart from that of his draughtsmen, we have little or nothing, but a set of charters. These charters were concerned with the trade profits of the Guinea commerce and the settlers in the new found lands off the continent—Madeira, the Azores, the Canaries,—and have an interest as being a sort of last will and testament of the Prince to his nation, settling his colonies, providing for the working of the lands he had explored, before it should be too late. Already on the 7th June, 1454, Affonso had granted to the Order of Christ, for the explorations "made and to be made at the expense of the aforesaid Order," the spiritual jurisdiction of Guinea, Nubia, and Ethiopia, with all rights as exercised in Europe and at the Mother house of Thomar.

Now on the 28th December, 1458, Prince Henry granted "in his town" that "the said Order should receive one twentieth of all merchandise from Guinea," slaves, gold and all other articles; the rest of the profit to fall to the Prince's successor in this "Kingdom of the Seas." In the same way on the 18th September, 1460, the Prince grants away the Church Revenues of Porto Santo and Madeira to the Order of Christ, and the temporalities to the Crown of Portugal. It was his to give, for by Royal Decree of September 15, 1448, the whole control of the African and ocean trade and colonies had been expressly conferred upon the Infant. No ships as we have seen could sail beyond Bojador without his permit; whoever transgressed this forfeited his ship; and all ships sailing with his permit were obliged to pay him one fifth or one tenth of the value of their freight.

But the end was in sight. The Prince was now sixty-six, and he had spent himself too strenuously for there to be much hope of a long life in him. Of late years, pressed by the increasing claims of his work, he had borrowed enormous sums from his half brother, the millionaire Duke of Braganza. Now his body failed him like his treasures.

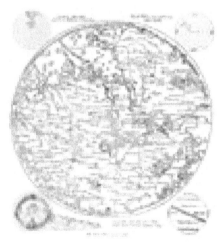

SKETCH-MAP OF FRA MAURO'S MAPPE-MONDE.
(SEE LIST OF MAPS)

What we know of his death is mainly from his body servant, Captain Diego Gomez, who was with him at the last. "In the year of Christ 1460, the Lord Infant Henry fell sick in his own town, on Cape St. Vincent, and of that sickness he died on Thursday, November 13th, in the selfsame year. And King Affonso, who was then at Evora with all his men, made great mourning on the death of a Prince so mighty, who had sent out so many fleets, and had won so much from Negro-land, and had fought so constantly against the Saracens for the Faith.

"And at the end of the year, the King bade me come to him. Now till then I had stayed in Lagos by the body of the Prince my lord, which had been carried into the Church of St. Mary in that town. And I was bidden to look and see if the body of the Prince were at all corrupted, for it was the wish of the King to remove it to the Monastery of Batalha which D. Henry's father King John had built. But when I came and looked at the body, I found it dry and sound, clad in a rough shirt of horse-hair. Well doth the Church repeat 'Thou shalt not suffer thine Holy One to see corruption.'

"For how the Lord Infant had been chaste, a virgin to the day of his death, and what and how many good deeds he had done in his life, is to be remembered, though it is not for me here to speak of this. For that would be a long tale. But the King Affonso had the body of his uncle carried to Batalha and laid in the chapel that King John had built, where also lie buried the aforesaid King John and his Queen Phillipa, mother of my lord the Prince, and all the five brothers of the Infant."

He was brawny and large of frame, says Azurara, strong of limb as any. His complexion was fair by nature, but by his constant toil and exposure of himself it had become quite dark. His face was stern and when angry, very terrible. Brave as he was in heart and keen in mind, he had a passion for the doing of great things. Luxury and avarice never found lodgment within him. For from a youth, he quite left off the use of wine, and more than this, as it was commonly reported, he passed all his days in unbroken chastity. He was so generous that no other uncrowned Prince in Europe had so noble a household, so large and splendid a school for the young nobles of his country.

For all the best men of his nation and still more those who came to him from foreign lands were welcomed at his Court, so that often the medley of tongues and peoples and customs to be heard and seen there was a wonder. And none who worthily came to him left the Court without some proof of his kindness.

THE RECUMBENT STATUE OF PRINCE HENRY.
FROM HIS TOMB IN BATALHA CHURCH.

Only to himself was he severe. All his days were spent in work, and it would not easily be believed how often he passed the night without sleep, so that by his untiring industry he conquered the impossibilities of other men. His virtues and graces it is too much to reckon up; wise and thoughtful, of wonderful knowledge and calm bearing, courteous in language and manner and most dignified in address, yet no subject of the lowest rank could show more obedience and respect to his sovereign than this uncle to his nephew, from the very beginning of his reign, while King Affonso was still a minor. Constant in adversity and humble in prosperity, my Lord the Infant never cherished hatred or ill will against any, even though they had grievously offended him, so that some, who spoke as if they knew everything, said that he was wanting in retributive justice, though in all other ways most impartial. Thus they complained that he forgave some of his soldiers who deserted him in the attack on Tangier, when he was in the greatest danger. He was wholly given up to the public service, and was always glad to try new plans for the welfare of the Kingdom at his own expense. He gloried in warfare against the Infidels and in keeping peace with all Christians. And so he was loved by all, for he loved all, never injuring any, nor failing in due respect and courtesy towards any person however humble, without forgetting his own position. A foul or indecent word was never heard to issue from his lips.

To Holy Church, above all, he was most obedient, attending all its services and in his own chapel causing them to be rendered as solemnly as in any Cathedral Church. All holy things he reverenced, and he delighted to shew honour and to do kindness to all the ministers of religion. Nearly one half of the year was passed by him in fasting, and the hands of the poor never went out empty from his presence. His heart never knew fear except the fear of sin.

CHAPTER XX.

THE RESULTS OF PRINCE HENRY'S WORK.

Henry's own life is in one way the least important part of him. We have seen how many were the lines of history and of progress—in Christendom, in Portugal, in Science—that met in him; how Greek and Arabic geography, both knowledge and practical exploration, was as much a part of what he found to work with as the memoirs of Christian pilgrims, traders, and travellers for a thousand years; how the exploring and expanding energy which the Northmen poured into Europe, leading directly to the Crusading movement, was producing in the Portugal of the fifteenth century the very same results as in the France and Italy and England of the twelfth and thirteenth: and now, on the failure of the Syrian crusades, the Spanish counterpart of those crusades, the greatest of social and religious upheavals in the Middle Ages, had reached such a point of success that the victorious Christians of Spain could look out for new worlds to conquer. Again we have seen how the twelfth, thirteenth, and fourteenth century progress in science, especially in geographical maps and plans, the great extension of land travel and the new beginnings of ocean voyaging during the same time, must be taken into any view of the Prince's life and work. We have now to look for a moment at the immense results of that same life which had so vast and so long a preparation.

For just as we cannot see how that work of his could have been done without each and every part of that many-sided preparation in the history of the past, so it is quite as difficult to see how the great achievements of the generation that followed him and of the century, that wonderful sixteenth century, which followed the age of Henry's courtiers and disciples, could have been realised without the impetus he had given and the knowledge he had spread.

For it was not merely that his seamen had broken down the middle wall of superstitious terror and had pierced through into the unknown South for a distance of nearly two thousand miles; it was not merely that between 1412 and 1460 Europeans passed the limits of the West and of the South, as legend had so long fixed them; not merely that the most difficult part of the African coast, between Bojador and the Gulf of Guinea, had been fairly passed and that the waterway to India was more than half found. This was true enough. When Vasco da Gama was once round the South Cape, he soon found himself not in an unknown and untraversed ocean, but embarked upon one of the great trade routes of the Mahometan world. The main part of the distance between the Prince's farthest and the southern Cape of Good Hope, was passed in two voyages, in four years (1482-6).

But there was more than this. Henry did not only accomplish the first and most difficult steps of his own great central project, the finding of the way round Africa to India; he not only began the conversion of the natives, the civilisation of the coast tribes and the colonisation of certain trading sites; he also founded that school of thought and practice which made all the great discoveries that have so utterly eclipsed his own.

From that school came Columbus, who found a western route to India, starting from the suggestion of Henry's attempt by south and east; Bartholomew Diaz, who reached and rounded the southernmost point of the old-world continent and laid open the Indian Ocean to European sailors; Da Gama, who was the first of those sailors to reap the full advantage of the work of ninety years, the first who sailed from Lisbon to Calicut and back again; Albuquerque, who founded the first colonial empire of Modern Europe, the first great out-settlement of Christendom, the Portuguese trade dominion in the East; Magellan, who finally proved what all the great discoverers were really assuming—the roundness of the world; the nameless adventurers who seem to have touched Australia some time before 1530; the draughtsmen who left us our first true map of the globe. So it is not in the actual things done by the Prince's efforts that we can measure his importance in history. It is because his work was infinitely suggestive, because he laid a right foundation for the onward movement of Europe and Christendom, because he was the leader of a true Renaissance and Reformation, that he is so much more than a figure in the story of Portugal.

COLUMBUS AS S. CHRISTOPHER, CARRYING THE CHRISTIAN
FAITH, IN THE FORM OF THE INFANT JESUS, ACROSS THE
OCEAN.

There are figures which are of national interest: there are others which are
less than that, figures of family or provincial importance; others again
which are always dear to us as human beings, as men who felt the ordinary
wants and passions and lived the ordinary life of men with a brilliancy and
an intense power that was all their own; there are other men who stand out
as those who have changed more or less, but changed vitally and really, the
course of the world's history; without whom the whole of our modern
society, our boasted civilisation, would have been profoundly different.

For after all the modern Christian world of Europe has something to boast
of, though its writers spend much of their time in reviling and decrying it. It
is something that our Western world has conquered or worsted every other
civilisation upon earth; that with the single exception of China, it has made
everyone of the coveted tracts of Asia its own; that it has discovered,
settled, and developed a new continent to be the equal of the old; that it has

won not a complete but a good working knowledge of the whole surface of the globe. We are at home in the world now, we say, and if we would know what that means, we must look at the Europe of the tenth or even the fourteenth century, look at the theoretic maps of the Middle Ages, look at the legends and the pseudo-science of a civilisation which was shut up within itself and condemned for so long to fight in a narrowing circle against incessant attacks from without and the barbarism which this state of things kept alive within. Then perhaps we shall take things a little less for granted, and perhaps also we shall begin to think that if this great advance, the greatest thing in Modern History as we know it, that which is the distinction and glory of the last three hundred years, is at all due to the inspiration and the action of Henry of Portugal, an obscure Prince of the fifteenth century, that obscure Prince may possibly belong to the rank of the great civilisers, the men who have most altered society and advanced it, men like Alexander and Cæsar and the founders of the great world religions.

It may be as well to trace out very shortly the evidence for such a claim as this and to see, how the Prince's work was followed up, first on his own lines to south and east; second, on other lines, which his own suggested, to west and north.

1. King Affonso V., Henry's nephew, though rather more of a hard fighter and tournament king than a man who could fully take up his uncle's plans, had yet caught enough of his inspiration to push on steadily, though slowly, the advance round Africa. He had already done his best to get the great map of Fra Mauro finished: this, which embodied all the achievements of the Navigator and gave the most complete and perfect view of the world that had ever yet appeared, had come out in 1459, just before Henry's death, the last tribute of science to the Prince's work.

Now, in 1461, left alone to deal with the discovery and conquest of Guinea, Affonso repaired Henry's fort in the Bay of Arguin and sent one Pedro de Cintra to survey the coast beyond the Rio Grande, the farthest point of Cadamosto in his first voyage, as generally known. Pedro went six hundred miles into the Bight of Benin, passed a mountain range called Sierra Leone from the lion-like growl of the thunder on its summits, and turned back near the point afterwards known as Fort La Mina (1461). Some time in the next few years, another courtier, one Sueiro da Costa followed Pedro de Cintra to Guinea, but without any new results; when Cadamosto left Portugal (Feb. 1, 1463), he tells us "there were no more voyages to the new-found parts."

The slave-trade nearer home was now, indeed, absorbing all energies and Affonso's main relation with African voyaging is to be found in his regulations for the security of this trade.

But in 1471 there was another move in the line of further discovery. For exploring energy was not dead or worn out, but only waiting a leader. Fernando Po now reached the island in the farthest inlet of the Gulf of Guinea, which is still called after him, finding as he went on that the eastern bend of Africa, which men had followed so confidently since 1445, the year of the rounding of Cape Verde, now ended with a sharp turn to the south. It was a great disappointment. But in spite of this discouragement, at the very same time two of the foremost of the Portuguese pilots, Martin Fernandez and Alvaro Esteeves, passed the whole of the Guinea Coast, the Bights of Benin and of Biafra, and crossed the Equator, into a new Heaven and a new Earth, on the edge of which the caravels of Portugal had long been hovering, as they saw like Cadamosto, stars unknown in the Northern Hemisphere and more and more nearly lost sight of the Northern Pole.

In 1475 Cape St. Catherine, two degrees south of the Line, was reached and then after six more years of languishing exploration and flourishing trade, King John II. succeeded Affonso V. and took up the work, in the spirit of Prince Henry the Navigator.

Now in six short years, exploration carried out the main part of the design of so many years, the southern Cape of Africa was rounded and the way to India laid open. For the time had come, and the man, John, added a new chapter to discovery by the travellers he sent across the Dark Continent and the sailors he despatched to the Arctic Seas to find a north-east passage to China.

He died just as he was fitting up the expedition that was to enter upon the promised land, and the glory of Da Gama's voyage fell to one who had not laboured, but entered upon the fruits of the toil of other men, the palace-king, Emanuel the Fortunate. But at least the names of Diaz, and Diego Cam, and Covilham, the rounding of the Cape of Storms, the first journey (though an overland one), straight from Lisbon to Malabar, belong to the second founder of Portuguese and European discovery, John the Perfect.

VASCO DA GAMA.
FROM THE PORTRAIT IN POSSESSION OF COUNT OF LAVRADIO.

Less than four months after his father's death, John, who as heir apparent, had drawn part of his income from the African trade and its fisheries, sent out Diego de Azambuga with ten caravels to superintend three undertakings: first the construction of a fort at St. George da Mina, to secure the trade of the Guinea Coast; second, the rebuilding of Henry's old fort at Arguin; third, the exploration of the yet unknown coast as far as possible. For this, stones, brick, wood, mortar, and tools for building were sent out with the fleet, and carved pillars were taken to be set up in all fresh discovered lands, instead of the wooden crosses that had previously done duty. Each pillar was fourteen hands high, was carved in front with the royal arms and on the sides with the names of the King and the Discoverer, with the date of discovery in Latin and Portuguese.

Azambuga's fleet sailed on the 11th of December, 1480, made a treaty with the chief Bezeghichi, near Cape Verde, and reached La Mina, on the south coast of Guinea, on January 19, 1482, after a year spent in fort building and treaty making with the natives of north-west Africa. Fort and church at La Mina were finished in twenty days, and Azambuga sent back his ships with a great cargo in slaves and gold, but without any news of fresh discovery. John was not disposed to be content with this. In 1484, Diego Cam was ordered to go as far to the south as he could, and not to "wait anywhere for other matters." He passed Cape St. Catherine, just beyond the Line, which since 1475 had been the limit of knowledge, and continuing south, reached the mighty river Congo, called by the natives Zaire, and now known as the second of African rivers, the true counterpart of that western Nile, which every geographer since Ptolemy had reproduced and which, in the Senegal, the Gambia, and the Niger, the Portuguese had again and again sought to find their explanation.

Cam, by agreement with the natives, took back four hostages to act as interpreters and next year returned to and passed the Congo, and sailed two hundred leagues beyond, to the site of the modern Walvisch Bay (1485).

Here, as the coast seemed to stretch interminably south, though he had now really passed quite nine-tenths of the distance to the southern Cape, Cam turned back to the Congo, where he persuaded the King and people to profess themselves Christians and allies of Portugal. Already, in 1484, a native embassy to King John had brought such an account of an inland prince, one Ogane, a Christian at heart, that all the Court of Lisbon thought he must be the long lost Prester John, and the Portuguese monarch, all on fire with this hope, sent out at once in search of this "great Catholic lord," by sea and land.

Bartholomew Diaz sailed in August, 1486, with two ships, first to search for the Prester, and then to explore as much new land and sea as he could find within his reach. Two envoys, Covilham and Payva, were sent on the same errand, by way of Jerusalem, Arabia, and Egypt; another expedition was sent to ascend the Senegal to its junction with the Nile; a fourth party started to find the way to Cathay by the North-east passage.

Camoëns has sung of the travels of Covilham, who first saw cloves and cinnamon, pepper and ginger, and who pined away in a state of confinement at the Prester's Abyssinian Court, but the voyage of Diaz hardly finds a place in the *Lusiads* and the very name of the discoverer is generally forgotten. Vasco da Gama has robbed him only too successfully.

John Diaz had been the second captain to double Bojador; Diniz Diaz, in 1445, had been the discoverer of Senegal and of Cape Verde; now, forty years later, Bartholomew Diaz achieved the greatest feat of discovery in all history, before Columbus; for the Northmen's finding America was an unknown and transitory good fortune, while the voyage of 1486 changed directly or indirectly the knowledge, the trade, the whole face of the world at once and forever.

Sailing with "two little friggits," each of fifty tons burden, in the belief that ships which sailed down the coast of Guinea might be sure of reaching the end of the continent, by persisting to the south, Diaz, in one voyage of sixteen months, performed the main task which Henry seventy years ago had set before his nation.

Passing Walvisch Bay and the farthest pillar of Diego Cam, he reached a headland where he set up his first new pillar at what is still known as Diaz Point. Still coasting southwards and tacking frequently, he passed the Orange River, the northern limit of the present Cape Colony. Then putting well out to sea Diaz ran thirteen days before the wind due south, hoping by this wide sweep to round the southern point of the continent, which could not now be far off. Finding the cold become almost Arctic and buffeted by tremendous seas, he changed his course to east, and then as no land appeared after five days, to north. The first land seen was a bay where cattle were feeding, now called Flesh Bay, which Diaz named from the cows and cowherds he saw there. After putting ashore two natives, some of those lately carried from Guinea or Congo to Portugal, and sent out again to act as scouts for the European colonies, the ships sailed east, seeking in vain for the land's end, till they found the coast tend gradually but steadily towards the north.

Their last pillar was set up in Algoa Bay, the first land trodden by Christians beyond the Cape. At the Great Fish River, sixty miles farther on and quite five hundred miles beyond the point that Diaz was looking for so anxiously, the crew refused to go any farther and the Admiral turned back, only certain of one thing, that he had missed the Cape, and that all his trouble was in vain. Worn out with the worry of his bitter disappointment and incessant useless labour, he was coasting slowly back, when one day the veil fell from his eyes. For there came in sight that "so many ages unknown promontory" round which lay the way to India, and to find which had been the great ambition of all enterprise since the expansion of Europe had begun afresh in the opening years of that fifteenth century.

AFFONSO D' ALBUQUERQUE.

While Diaz was still tossing in the storms off the Great Cape, Covilham and his friends had started from Lisbon to settle the course of the future sea-route to India by an "observation of all the coasts of the Indian Ocean," to explore what they could of Upper Africa, to find Prester John, and to ally the Portuguese experiment with anything they could find of Christian power in Greater or Middle or Further India.

As King John's Senegal adventurers had been exploring the Niger, the Sahara caravan routes, the city of Timbuctoo and the fancied western Nile, so the Abyssinian travellers surveyed all the ground of Africa and Malabar which the first fleet that could round the Cape of Storms must come to. "Keep southward," Covilham wrote home from Cairo after his first visit to Calicut on one side and to Mozambique on the other, "if you persist, Africa must come to an end. And when ships come to the Eastern Ocean let them ask for Sofala and the island of the Moon (Madagascar), and they will find pilots to take them to Malabar."

Yet another chapter of discoveries was opened by King John's Cathay fleet. He failed to get news of a North-east passage, but beyond the north coast of Asia there was found a frozen island whose name of Novaia Zemlaia or Nova Zembla still keeps the memory of the first Portuguese attempts on the road where so many Dutch and English seamen perished in after years.

The great voyage of Vasco da Gama (1497-9), the empire founded by Albuquerque (1506-15) in the Indian seas, were the other steps in the complete achievement of Prince Henry's ambition. When in the early years of the sixteenth century a direct and permanent traffic was fairly started between Malabar and Portugal, when European settlements and forts controlled the whole eastern and western coasts of Africa from the mouth of the Red Sea to the mouth of the Mediterranean, and the five keys of the Indies—Malacca, Goa, Ormuz, Aden, and Ceylon—were all in Christian hands, when the Moslem trade between east Africa and western India had passed into a possession of the Kings of Lisbon, Don Henry might see of the travail of his soul and be well satisfied.

The supposed discovery of Australia about 1530, or somewhat earlier, and the travels of Ferdinand Mendez Pinto in Japan and the furthest East, the opening of the trade with China in 1517, and the complete exploration of Abyssinia, the Prester's kingdom, in 1520, by Alvarez and the other Catholic missionaries, the millions converted by Francis Xavier and the Jesuit preachers in Malabar, and the union of the old native Christian Church of India with the Roman (1599), were other steps in the same road. All of them, if traced back far enough, bring us to the Court of Sagres, and the same is true of Spanish and French and Dutch and English empires in the southern and eastern world. Henry built for his own nation, but when that nation failed from the exhaustion of its best blood, other peoples entered upon the inheritance of his work.

But though he was not able himself to see the fulfilment of his plans, both the method of a South-east passage, and the men who followed it out to complete success, were his,—his workmanship and his building.

Da Gama, Diego Cam, the Diaz family, and most of the great seamen who followed the path they had traced, were either "brought up from boyhood in the Household of the Infant," as the *Chronicle of the Discovery* tells us of each new figure that comes upon the scene, or looked to him as their master, owed to the School of Sagres their training, and began their practical seamanship under his leave and protection. Even the lines upon which the national expansion and exploration went on were so strictly and exclusively the same as he had followed, that when a different route to the Indies was suggested after his death by Christopher Columbus, the Court of John II. refused to treat it seriously. And this brings us to the other, the indirect side of Henry's influence.

"It was in Portugal," (says Ferdinand Columbus, in his *Life of the Admiral*, his father,) "that the Admiral began to think, that if men could sail so far south, one might also sail west and find lands in that quarter." The second great stream of modern discovery can thus be traced to the "generous Henry" of Camoëns' *Lusiads* no less plainly, though more indirectly, than the first; the Western path was suggested by his success in the Eastern.

But that success had turned the heads of his own people. When Columbus, the son of the Genoese wool-comber, who had been a resident in Lisbon since 1470, submitted to the Court of John II. some time before 1484 a proposal to find Marco Polo's Cipangu by a few weeks' sail west, from the Azores, he was treated as a dreamer. John, as Henry's disciple and successor, was, like other disciples, narrower than his master in the master's own way.

He was ready for any expense and trouble, but no novelty. He would only go on as he had been taught. He had reason to be confident, and his scientific Junto of four, Martin Behaim of Nuremburg among them, to whom Columbus was referred, were too much elated with their new improvements in the astrolabe, and the now assured confidence that the Southern Cape would soon be passed. They could not endure with patience the vehement dogmatism of an unknown theorist.

But as he was too full of his message to be easily shaken off, he was treated with the basest trickery. At the suggestion of the Bishop of Ceuta, Columbus was kept waiting for his answer, and asked to furnish his plans in detail with charts and illustrations. He did so, and while the Council pretended to be poring over these for a final decision, a caravel was sent to the Cape Verde islands to try the route he had suggested,—a trial with the pickings of Italian brains.

The Portuguese sailed westward for several days till the weather became stormy; then, as their heart was not in the venture, they put back to Europe with a fresh stock of the legends Henry had so heartily despised. They had come to an impenetrable mist, which had stopped their progress; apparitions had warned them back; the sea in those parts swarmed with monsters; it became impossible to breathe.

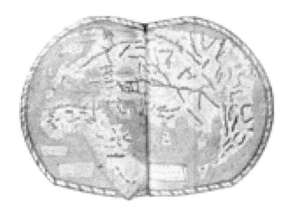

MAP OF 1492.
(SEE LIST OF MAPS)

Columbus learned how he had been used, and his wife's death helped to decide him, in his disgust for place and people. Towards the end of 1484, he left Lisbon. Three years later, when he had become fully as much disgusted with the dilatory sloth and tricks of Spain, he offered himself again to Portugal. King John had repented of his meanness; on March 20, 1488, he wrote in answer to Columbus, eagerly offering on his side to guarantee him against any suits that might be taken against him in Lisbon. But the Court of Castille now became, in its turn, afraid of quite losing what might be infinite advantage; Columbus was kept in the service of Ferdinand and Isabella; and at last in August, 1492, the "Catholic Kings" sent him out from Palos to discover what he could on his own terms.

What followed, the discovery of America, and all the subsequent ventures of the Cabots, of Amerigo Vespucci, of Cortés and Pizarro, De Soto and Raleigh and the Pilgrim Fathers, are not often connected in any way with the slow and painful beginnings of European expansion in the Portugal of the fifteenth century, but it is a true and real connection all the same. The whole onward and outward movement of the great exploring age was set in motion by one man. It might have come to pass without him, but the fact is simply that through him it did, as a matter of history, result. "And let him that did more than this, go before him."

FOOTNOTES:

[1] From a water-colour.

[2] From Major's *Life of Henry the Navigator*.

[3] From the Hakluyt Society's *Select Letters of Columbus*.

[4] From the Hakluyt Society's edition of *Three Voyages of Vasco da Gama*.

[5] From the Hakluyt Society's edition of Albuquerque's *Commentaries*.

[6] [Missing] (Please see the Transcriber's Note.)

[7] Compare Archer and Kingsford, *The Crusades*, in the *Stories of the Nations*.

[8] Rejecting the old idea of an encircling ocean as the girdle or limit of the known world, and replacing it with a new fancy of unbounded continent (on all sides except the north-west)—a fancy which the vast extension of Roman Dominion under the Empire may have fostered.

[9] In using the expressions "Chart," or "Map" of Strabo's description (*c.* A.D. 20), it is not meant to imply that Strabo himself left more than a written description from which a plan was afterwards prepared: "The world according to Strabo." The same applies to Eratosthenes (*c.* B.C. 200) and all pre-Ptolemaic Greek geographers. Ptolemy's Atlas, probably, and the Peutinger Table, more certainly, are maps really drawn by ancient designers; but these are the only ones that have survived from a much larger number.

[10] In which the habitable quarter of the world, situated mainly in the Northern Hemisphere, was just about twice as long as it was broad.

[11] In Columbus' letters to Queen Isabella in 1498, we catch, as it were, the last echo of the Arabic *mélange* of Moses and Greek geography, along with the results of Roger Bacon's corrections of Ptolemy. "The Old Hemisphere," he writes "which has for its centre the isle of Arim, is spherical, but the other (new) Hemisphere has the form of the lower half of a pear. Just one hundred leagues west of the Azores the earth rises at the Equator and the temperature grows keener. The summit is over against the mouth of the Orinoco."

[12] "The Obliquity of the Ecliptic, the Eccentricity of the Sun, the Precession of the Equinoxes."

[13] "With the Sinbad story is connected the historical extension of the Arab settlements in the East African coast through the enterprise of the Emosaid family."

[14] The school of Persian mathematicians who produced the maps of Alestakliry-Ibn-Hankal, the book of latitudes and longitudes, ascribed by Abulfeda to Alfaraby the Turk, was the immediate descendant of Albyrouny.

[15] The world he divided by climates in the Greek manner, taking no account of political divisions, or of those resting on language or religion. Each climate was further subdivided into ten sections. In the shape of Africa he followed Ptolemy.

[16] Yacout "the ruby," originally a Greek slave, who made a brave but fruitless attempt to change his name into Yacoub or Jacob, became one of the greatest of Arab encyclopædists, was checked by the hordes of Genghiz-Khan in his exploration of Central Asia, and died 1229.

[17] By some supposed to be S. Carolina, by others the Canaries.

[18] From St. James of Compostella.

[19] Unless White Man's Land and Great Ireland are the Canaries. See above, p. 63.

[20] Camoëns, *Lusiads*, (Barton's trans.).

[21] And a certain number of Viking sailors seem to have preceded Ohthere on his voyage to the Dwina.

[22] As completed about A.D. 1000-1040.

[23] As in 1071, when they crushed Romans and the Byzantines in the battle of Manzikert.

[24] "*Tartari fecerunt equos nostros trotare.*"

[25]

In Xanadu did Kublai KhanA stately pleasure-dome decree,Where Alph, the sacred river, ran,Through caverns measureless to man,Down to a sacred sea.

COLERIDGE: *Kublai Khan.*

[26] Probably the Andamans.

[27] This new knowledge had been really gained from the gradual spread of the Arab settlements down the south-east coast of Africa, during four centuries, from Guardafui, the Cape of spices, to the Channel of Mozambique.

[28] Cape Non = Fish Cape. But Latini took it as = Not, "from the fact that beyond it there is *no* return possible." And so the rhyme "Who pass Cape Non—Must turn again, *or else begone*" (lit. "*or not,*" *i.e.*, will not be able to return).

[29] *Of* 1306, 1351, 1367, 1375, 1380, 1436, 1448, 1459.

[30] See Note 1, page 137.

[31] W.H. Lecky, *Rationalism.*

[32] See Note 2, page 137.

[33] Except the draughtsmen of the Portolani.

[34] City of "Seven" Hills, as some have derived it.

[35] The attempts of Henry and his family to conquer a land-empire in northern Africa are not to be separated from the maritime and coasting explorations. They were two aspects of one idea, two faces of the same enterprise.

In the same way the new bishopric of Ceuta, now founded, was a first step towards the organised conversion of the Heathen of the South. The Franciscans had founded the See of Fez and Morocco in 1233, but it had not till now been followed up.

[36] In 1418 and 1424-5 Henry purchased and tried to secure certain rights of possession in the Canaries, conceded by De Béthencourt; and these attempts were repeated in 1445 and 1446.

[37] Camoëns' *Lusiads*, iv., 52.

[38] The date of this voyage is brought down as late as 1447 by Santarem, Oliveiro Martins.